Please Help Me with This Family

Using Consultants as Resources in
Family Therapy

Also by Maurizio Andolfi, M.D.

BEHIND THE FAMILY MASK: THERAPEUTIC CHANGE IN RIGID FAMILY SYSTEMS (WITH CLAUDIO ANGELO, PAOLO MENGHI, AND ANNA MARIA NICOLÒ-CORIGLIANO)

THE MYTH OF ATLAS: FAMILIES AND THE THERAPEUTIC STORY (WITH CLAUDIO ANGELO AND MARCELLA DE NICHILO)

Please Help Me with This Family

Using Consultants as Resources in
Family Therapy

EDITED BY

Maurizio Andolfi, M.D.

AND

Russell Haber, Ph.D.

BRUNNER/MAZEL *Publishers* • New York

To protect the confidentiality of clients/patients, all case material is disguised and fictitious names are used.

RC
488.5
.P59
1994

Library of Congress Cataloging-in-Publication Data

Please help me with this family: using consultants as resources in family therapy / edited by Maurizio Andolfi and Russell Haber.
      p.   cm.
   Includes bibliographical references and index.
   ISBN 0-87630-748-9
   1. Family psychotherapy. 2. Psychiatric consultation.
I. Andolfi, Maurizio. II. Haber, Russell.
RC488.5.P59 1994
616.89'156—dc20   94-25864
                                                                  CIP

Published by
BRUNNER/MAZEL, INC.
19 Union Square West
New York, New York 10003

Manufactured in the United States of America
10 9 8 7 6 5 4 3 2 1

This book is dedicated to our dear friend and teacher, Carl Whitaker, whose integrity, creativity, and warmth have influenced our personal and professional lives. This book is an outgrowth of his motto to recruit consultants from the client's and therapist's worlds when therapy is not working.

Contents

Contributors

Maurizio Andolfi, M.D. Director, Accademia di Psicoterapia della Famiglia (Academy of Psychotherapy of the Family) and Associate Professor at the University La Sapienza of Rome, Italy.

Russell Haber, Ph.D., ABPP Coordinator of Training at the Counseling and Human Development Center, University of South Carolina and Director of South Carolina Institute for Systemic/Experiential Therapy, United States of America.

Lars Brok, M.D. Chief Psychiatrist at the Multifunctional Center of Delta Psychiatric Hospital, Rotterdam, Zuid, and the Director of ISSOOH (Institute for Training and Research in the Systemic Approach) Holland.

Marcella de Nichilo, Ph.D. Administrative Director, Faculty Teacher and Supervisor at Accademia di Psicoterapia della Famiglia (Academy of Family Psychotherapy) and Teacher, Department of Psychology, University La Sapienza of Rome, Italy.

Vincenzo DiNicola, M.Phil., M.D., Dip.Psych., F.R.C.P.C. Chairman, Division of Child and Adolescent Psychiatry; Associate Professor of Psychiatry, Psychology, and Paediatrics, Queen's University, Kingston, Ontario, Canada.

Yoel Elizur, Ph.D. Lecturer, Department of Psychology, The Hebrew University of Jerusalem, Mount Scopus, Israel. Director of Maof Institute for Systems-Integrative Therapy and Training.

Audrey E. Ellenwood, Ph.D. Assistant Professor, Department of Special Education, Bowling Green State University, Bowling Green, Ohio, United States of America.

Jim Guinan, Ph.D. President, Professional Systems, Toledo, Ohio, United States of America.

Mary Hotvedt, Ph.D. Private Practice at the El Dorado Psychotherapy Associates, Tucson, Arizona, United States of America.

William Jones, M.A. Private Practice and Episcopal Priest, Toledo, Ohio, United States of America.

Sara B. Jutoran, M.A. Psychologist/Family Therapist/Director at the Instituto de Terapia Sistemica (Institute of Systemic Therapy); Professor at the School of Law, University of Buenos Aires, and Consultant for Family Court, Buenos Aires, Argentina.

David V. Keith, M.D. Director of Family Therapy and Associate Professor of Psychiatry, Family Medicine, and Pediatrics at the State University of New York Health Science Center, Syracuse, New York, United States of America.

Peter D. Liggett, Ph.D. Coordinator of Family Preservation Program at the Columbia Area Mental Health Center, Columbia, South Carolina, United States of America.

Rick A. Pluut, Ph.D. Psychotherapist at St. Willibrord Psychiatric Hospital, Heiloo, and the Director of ISSOOH (Institute for Training and Research in the Systemic Approach, Holland).

Marsha Purvis, Ph.D. Private Practice and Adjunct Faculty, Department of Educational Psychology, University of South Carolina, Columbia, South Carolina, United States of America.

Elizabeth Ridgely, M.S.W., C.S.W. Executive Director of the George Hull Centre for Children and Families and Director of Training of the George Hull Centre Family Therapy Training Program; Adjunct Professor of Social Work and Lecturer in the Department of Psychiatry at the University of Toronto, Canada.

Noga Rubinstein-Nabarro, Ph.D. Initiator and Co-founder and Clinical Director, Israel Institute for Family and Personal Change (Machon Shinui), Herzelia, Israel.

Joseph Simons, M.A. Psychologist, South Carolina Department of Corrections, Greenville, South Carolina, United States of America.

Robert N. Wendt, Ph.D. Professor and Chairperson, Department of Counselor and Human Services Education, The University of Toledo, Ohio, United States of America.

Carl Whitaker, M.D. Emeritus Professor of Psychiatry at the University of Wisconsin Medical School, United States of America.

Foreword

Evolving with the field of family therapy has entailed for me an extraordinarily rich, shaky, unpredictable journey through models, many of which at their inception appeared to challenge the very essence of previous ones, but eventually allowed new synthesis—qualitative enrichments that, in turn, experience evolutionary transformations and new qualitative challenges. This evolution has trained us to constantly shed certainties, to bid farewell to cherished concepts, and to welcome—sometimes with trepidation—new views in a world (and a world of ideas) that proves to be unstable. In exchange, it is delivering to family therapists a rich, complex, highly textured professional field.

Those "newer" paradigms (already some 35 years old) that made family therapy a distinct discipline launched us into a voyage without return beyond the individual: the interpersonal world-in-context became the minimal unit of observation, courtesy of cybernetics and systems theory. Some 20 years later another revolution took place—that of second-order cybernetics. Heinz von Foerster, one of its heralds, provides us with a keen example of the recursivity entailed by cybernetics in the title of one of his series of lectures: "U^2," which denotes "Understanding Squared," which is short for "Understanding Understanding." The word *under-standing* is, by itself, etymologically recursive, as it advises us that in order to grasp our stance we have to place ourselves outside of that locus. Interestingly, the equivalent word in German, *verstehen*, places us *ver* ("in front of"), rather than under *stehen* ("where we are or stand"). And a close etymological and conceptual cousin of *understanding*, the word *epistemology*, locates us *epi* (a Greek prefix that denotes "above," but also "around," "beside," "after," and "upon") and *histanai*, that is, "the place" or "where we stand." *Under, in front of, beside*, or *above*, we are exhorted to place ourselves outside our locus in order to gain perspective about ourselves-in-locus. In turn, as the title "U^2" suggests, in order for us to grasp the process of grasping, we have to stand outside both the "under" and the "standing," a second recursive loop. But outside where? We are part of the process we want to study, regardless of how many steps removed we may want to place ourselves by adding exponents to the "U." In other words, the lack of *terra firmus* from which to generate this observation (including

observations about the therapist or the therapeutic process) is also ob-
server-dependent, challenging any presumption of objectivity. Hence
Maturana's "objectivity in parentheses."

From second-order cybernetics evolved the most recent set of paradigms—constructivism/constructionism, the narrative model, and, ultimately, postmodernism—which threw the preceding models, and the
practices derived from them, through the epistemological looking glass
of recursiveness with its tenet that the observer is part of the observation and of the observed, and hence organizes reality through his/her/
our beliefs. As a reasonable consequence of this notion of the observer-
dependent reality, for a while the focus of interest in our discipline
drifted away from the "family as a system" to make the therapist the
main object/subject of observation. That focus was, in turn, displaced
by an emphasis on the systemic properties of narratives.

This evolution of our guiding assumptions had a shattering effect on
certainty, on directionality, on ways of knowing, on scientific models
and language, and on practices. Objective registrations were replaced
by stories, anecdotes, and accounts. Normative assumptions yielded to
context-dependent, culture-dependent, moment-dependent descriptions. The certainty of the prediction of effects was replaced by a careful avoidance of generalizations. The assumption of a basically stable
reality (the "other things being equal" that prefaced every projection
made by futurologists, akin to the "this intervention is likely to have
that effect" of many family therapists) was replaced by the cautious
assumption that we live in a world of evolving stories of which we
become a part the moment we start to interact with the storytellers that
we (therapists) attempt, at the most, to perturb problem-saturated stories and favor potential transformations, alas, with rather unpredictable effects. The neutral language of academic writings that hid the
authors was replaced by accounts in first person singular. Last, but not
least, the dissolution of a normative paradigmatic guidance about how
things should be (for whom? when?) has brought forth in our field a
renewed emphasis on ethics, a dimension that for decades was considered outside the scientific discourse.

Narrative models; observer-, context-, and culture-dependent realities; unpredictability; case-based and generalizations-shy descriptions;
chaotic processes; ethics; and our daily practices—clinical work, supervision, training, research—in the '90s have been radically affected
by that new understanding of understanding.

*Please Help Me with This Family: Using Consultants as Resources in
Family Therapy* undertakes successfully the formidable challenge of a
'90s revisitation of one of the most cherished of our practices as therapists, that of engaging in a transformative dialogue—be it labeled as

consultation, supervision, advice, or apprenticeship—about our clinical practice with masters, peers, students, agencies, and even patients themselves. The contributors to this book, affected by different lineages of apprenticeship, contextualized by different cultures, and with stances that range from the best of traditional paradigms to the newest postmodern views, provide a rich tapestry of experiences rendered as a collective discourse that is delivered with a harmonious, consonant voice, under the wise guidance of Maurizio Andolfi and Russell Haber, who are esteemed trainers with an impressive track record of written contributions and training experience in family therapy.

The consultant-included systems explored in this book are rich in their variety and extremely enlightening: from the therapist in conversation with his/her split self to complex interactional loci such as the family members' families of origin or multiple agencies involved in a given event; from the free-floating resource of one's own intuition (it's easy for Whitaker to model that; it just takes being a Whitaker!) to structured steps to maximize consultative resources. I found myself reading this book in zigzag, beginning with chapters with titles I found particularly attractive or ones with a clinical example that caught my attention and then filling in the gaps. I ended up reading it all and profiting much from it—not only soothed by occasional reconfirmation of old convictions, but more importantly, frequently shaken by new ideas, new views, and new challenges, thus activating, once again, the never-ending process of learning. For all that, thank you, Maurizio, thank you, Russ, thank you, contributors. And to you, reader, good journey.

Carlos E. Sluzki, M.D.
Director of Psychiatric Services
Santa Barbara Cottage Hospital
Santa Barbara, California

Preface

Families enter therapy in search of a competent resource—the therapist—to help with an identified problem/patient. Frequently, the therapy, itself, reaches an impasse in which additional resources are needed to help the family reach desired goals. The central theme of this book is to examine where and how the therapist and the family can discover new ways to help with the impasse. Two sets of resources will be highlighted: the ones from the family and its social network such as a child, grandparent, friend, or employer and the ones from the therapist's system such as a colleague, referral source, or health care or school professional.

For too long the field of family therapy has been overloaded with theories and practice based on the principles of efficiency and behavioral modification; the main strategy has been oriented to fix symptoms and to control "social disorders." Less understanding has been given to the emergence of problem/pathology as a critical moment in the evolution of a family that seems incapable of using its own resources at a particular stage of its development. If we look at symptoms from a developmental perspective, instead of trying to control the patient's irrational or destructive behavior, then we might start by accepting and joining the "problem." This initial material, presented as negative, wrong, or undesirable by the family or referral source, must be respected by the therapist. The problem has special significance because it is at the crossroads of several generations and because it represents the first linkage between the family and the therapist. Similarly, the systems that contain symptoms must also be accepted, respected, and acknowledged as having underdeveloped resources. Therefore, we bring in familial and social network consultants because we believe that their inherent resources and transformation can facilitate the continuing development of the family.

Consultation has been the professional gym to enter into the delicate balance between belonging and separating: a way to intervene in a therapeutic impasse without "taking sides" with the clients' system or the therapeutic entourage. Entering in a position of relative freedom from either side allows consultants to creatively search for help in both territories, without the risk of locking competence or pathology inside one or the other system. Thus, the consultant has become the translator of different languages—the language of generational, gender, social, and institutional structures and the "culture of pain."

Please Help Me with This Family is a search for many different "hands" to embrace health and family crises with strength and care. Historical, transgenerational, gender and cultural diversity, and multiprofessional collaboration are among the "hands" we asked for help, which we received. *Please Help Me with This Family* is more than an edited book; although it closely resembles one author's writing, it speaks with the personal and professional voices of more than twenty therapists-authors who took the courage to disclose their ideas and clinical cases on specific topics about consultation. This book is the result of a very special transcultural experience among the authors in that they live and work in different parts of the world and for several years they have met (with additional colleagues) on a regular basis to share their personal/professional experiences and to discuss common dilemmas with families, marriages, cultural diversities, etc. The characteristics and singularities of the participants, the limitations of each person's social bonds have been stretched and challenged by the universality of suffering and the capacity of renewal and hope present in every human system.

A special merit for the realization of this book, above all, goes to Russell Haber. Without his dedication, patience, and extreme competence in eliciting, reviewing, and shaping material written in different languages with different structures from Europe, North and South America, and the Middle East, this book would not exist.

Finally, a special thanks to the 150+ participants in the Rome Summer Practicums during the last 15 years. Their personal motivation to go beyond techniques to reach their full personhood and the constant dialogue among so many different cultures have strongly inspired my work and the realization of this volume.

Maurizio Andolfi, M.D.

Acknowledgments

The editorial process of this book, similar to our consultations, has relied on many professionals and nonprofessionals who have helped us. We appreciate the assistance of the following people who have helped us through the editing process: Shirley Kirby; Joseph Simons; Marsha Purvis; Elizabeth Ridgely; Alma Mitchell; Peter Liggett; Annette Alber; and the fine editors of Brunner/Mazel, especially Natalie Gilman, Bernie Mazel, and Patricia Wolf. Thanks also to Roger Bowersock, Debra Scott, and Carolyn Sutton of the Counseling and Human Development Center, University of South Carolina, for their support.

I (R.H.) acknowledge also the members of my family—Karen, Nathan, Darelyn, Chris, Beverly, Raymond, Jonathan, and Irwin—who have been inspirational, emotional, intellectual, and loving resources.

Special thanks to Marcella and Diego whose consultation inspires and motivates me (M.A.) in the many facets of my life.

Finally, thanks to the authors, our friends, for contributing their creativity, wisdom, and enthusiasm to this project.

PART I

AN OVERVIEW OF CONSULTATION WITH FAMILY THERAPY SYSTEMS

1

Introduction: Consultative Resources in Family Therapy

Russell Haber

Many of us have seen brilliant consultations by the "Masters" in Family Therapy. The consultations, similar to a professional theatrical performance, include a cast of characters (the family), set designer and casting director (therapist), seasoned star (the consultant), producer (the conference organizer), and of course, an expectant audience (professionals attending the seminar).

The courage demonstrated by this theatrical event is noteworthy: the therapist brings forth a treatment problem and bears the responsibility of suggesting the necessity of the consultation, the family exposes their pain and the intractable nature of their problems in a public forum (frequently with video camera), the consultant bares his/her clinical skill in overcoming a difficult therapeutic impasse with strangers, the organizer agonizes over the unpredictability of the live encounter between all of the protagonists, and the audience relishes the improvisational anxiety of this encounter and expectantly hopes that the consultant will remedy the family and therapeutic dysfunction.

The power and anxiety created by the live consultation frequently help the newly formed consultative system (consultant, therapist, and family) to venture into novel and more productive relatedness. The applause at the end of the interview salutes the willingness of all members of this theatrical consultation to expand personal/professional options in the face of their anxiety.

What happens to the therapist and family system after the consultant, organizer, and audience smugly go home after a successful perfor-

3

mance? Do they apply the lessons of the consultation, do they miss the consultant and the audience, do they go back to their old relational patterns, or do they have the courage, knowledge, and fortitude to continue on the new path toward more differentiated and healthier relatedness? Is the theatrical consultation more attuned to a successful demonstration of the theory and skills of the master presenter (Harari & Bloch, 1991) or to the future empowerment of the therapist and of the therapeutic and family systems? Minuchin (1986) contemplated this issue:

> The families, the therapists, and I were satisfied with the consultations...But when I did a follow-up a few years later, I learned that in a significant number of my consultations, I had failed to understand the context of therapist and family. In effect, I had constructed and then proceeded to consult an ideal family in therapy with an ideal therapist, divorced from the social context....I now try to include a feedback procedure in my consultation; never again can I be that blissfully ignorant. (p. xii)

This book similarly expanded its focus. Initially, it was intended to explore Maurizio Andolfi's crosscultural consultations with his consultees/trainees. The clinical assumptions and theoretical concepts behind these consultations would have provided a framework for demonstrating and discussing his interesting and skillful approach to psychotherapy and consultation. Focusing solely on Andolfi's clinical ideas and consultations, however, would have limited the range of consultative resources to a particular master consultant. Therefore, the focus of this book was expanded to explore consultations with diverse professional and nonprofessional resources. This expansion uncovers consultative resources from all walks of community life rather than just the limited arena of organizers, stars, and audiences. The goal of this book is to weave consultation into the context of therapy rather than present it as an exclusive, adjunct intervention with "master" therapists.

Employing ecosystemic, discontinuous resources follows the schema of family systems therapy (Auerswald, 1968; Schwartzman, 1985). Essentially, family therapy assesses and involves the interpersonal relationships of the family to ameliorate and resolve symptomatology. Individual therapists resisted involving "outsiders" because they saw this as an intrusion into the privacy needed to resolve transferences in the therapeutic relationship. Family therapists found, however, that family and social network members facilitated therapeutic progress by reporting, illustrating, and augmenting the interaction of relevant systems. Co-transference in family therapy is mitigated (although, not eliminated) because interpersonal needs can be addressed within the family and social network. Rather than fostering dependence in the therapeutic relationship, family therapy inherently encourages more developmentally appropriate dependence in the clients' social world.

Similarly, consultative resources in family therapy offer support for the family and the therapeutic relationship. Even the discussion about bringing in a consultant induces the therapeutic system to view its process through the eyes of an outsider (Foerster, 1981). This reflexive act punctuates and defines the therapeutic process, creates discontinuity, and opens the possibility for redefinition and change. This volume will explore the different consultative capabilities of a master therapist, professional colleague, and social network member with families in therapy. The wide range of consultative resources addressed in this volume will stimulate responses to the questions of whether, when, and why to invite a consultative resource, as well as whom to invite.

ROOTS OF CONSULTATION

The act of getting a second opinion for a medical problem has been practiced for centuries. The Hippocratic oath encouraged physicians to get help for problems that were beyond their expertise or that were not progressing as expected. In 1847, the American Medical Association adopted this practice in their Code of Ethics: "Consultations should be promoted in difficult or protracted cases, as they give rise to confidence, energy, and more enlarged views in practice" (Rothstein, 1972, p. 83). The medical-consultative model focused upon the relief of the patient's illness as the primary goal, whereas education and growth of the consultee were indirect by-products.

Caplan's (1963,1970) classic work on mental health consultation extended the medical model by considering the development of the therapist as a priority. The limited mental health resources in Israel prompted him to develop a consultative model that would also develop and train staff. The "problem became the means for educative interventions in which the consultee is taught rather than the patient 'cured' " (p. 32). Therefore, the focus of the problem or the unit to be changed was expanded to include either the consultee (therapist) or the client. In addition, Caplan's psychoanalytic orientation enabled him to discern the negative effects of the consultee's emotions in the therapeutic impasse.

The organizational-development model (Schein & Bennis, 1965) complemented mental health consultation by viewing the process of the consultee, client, and problem in the workplace. Their approach paralleled the scientific method by designating the problem or goal for consultation; observing the interpersonal process and gathering information; generating hypotheses; planning and implementing interventions; evaluating the results; and planning or terminating the consultation contract. This process approach to consultation combined a problem-solving model with the mediation of interpersonal difficulties.

Wynne, McDaniel, and Weber (1986) developed an innovative and influential model of systems consultation that emerged from ideas about mental health consultation, organization development, and general systems theory (Bertalanffy, 1968). They defined consultation as a "process in which a *consultee* seeks assistance from a *consultant* in order to identify or clarify a *concern* or problem and to consider the options available for problem resolution" (their italics, p. 8). This is similar to Gallesich's (1982) components of consultation, "The consultant (a specialized professional) assists consultees (agency employees who are also professionals) with work-related concerns (the third component)" (p. 6).

These definitions imply a hierarchical, problem-focused view of consultation. This is similar to Caplan's formulation of mental health consultation except that Caplan also dealt with the personal issues of the (consultee) therapist. Wynne et al. (1986), however, expanded the unit of consultation to include the systemic relationships between and among the consultant, consultee, and client. "We have found it more helpful if the consultee and client (and the 'concerns' or 'problem') are viewed as inextricably functioning within the same system" (p. 7). "A distinctive feature of *systems* consultation is that the consultant explicitly attempts to consider the multiple contexts or systems of the presenting problem" (p. 9).

This volume's premise, that consultative resources are a natural extension of family therapy, is both similar to and different from the concept of consultation as described by Wynne et al. (1986). Both approaches agree that many family therapists have a reductionistic view of the family as the system rather than as a subsystem (Haber, 1987, 1990a,b). If one perceives the family as a subsystem, then the inclusion of other ecosystemic members is as logical as inviting "extraneous" family members to a therapy meeting. Similarly, both approaches view the therapist-in-context as a subsystem. The therapist's employment, relationship with other relevant professionals, and personal issues greatly influence the therapeutic system. Therefore, relational issues operate in multiple contexts. Both approaches recognize the usefulness of the consultant being "meta" (observer) to the therapeutic system while acknowledging that the observer is part of the consultative system, the therapeutic system, and the consultant. Both approaches see the consultant as a collaborative, discontinuous, time-limited resource.

Two differences in our theoretical approach compared to that of Wynne et al. (1986, 1987) are: 1) our primary emphasis is on the wide range of ways in which consultative resources can be used within the process of ongoing family therapy, while systems consultation is a more generalized approach applicable not only with families before and during family therapy but also with other systems; and 2) our approach is more experiential and developmental while the approach described by Wynne et al. (1986) is the more problem centered. They describe systems consultation as providing "a strategic and appropriate framework for identifying problems and considering options for action" (p. 6). Although they conceptualized systems consultation and therapy as overlapping along a continuum, with a minimal distinction between consultation and brief, problem-centered therapy, they also clearly perceived systems consultation as a broader means of avoiding the constraints of therapy. "While the role relationship of 'therapist' and 'patient' implies that the problem involves a disorder or illness that needs to be cured, the concept of a consultation system leaves open for exploration whether a significant problem can be identified, and who is able and willing to take responsibility for further action (if any)" (1986, p. 9).

Although we agree with their formulation that therapy implies a model based on illness, whereas consultation is a nonpathology-based resource intervention; we are dedicated to integrating systemic therapy and consultation. Therefore, the consultant's goal is to help the therapy function more adequately. It may be necessary to dismantle the therapy relationship, change its focus and direction, recruit additional resources, render advice, support the therapist, intervene in the family or therapeutic impasse, or help resolve symptomatic problems.

CONSULTATION VERSUS OTHER THERAPEUTIC MODALITIES

Family therapy is based on a triadic model (Hoffman, 1981). A dyad is limited by the necessity for both individuals to be involved in direct communication. When a triad is formed, there is the potential for one person to observe two people in direct communication. This vantage point of meta-position enables the observer to comment on the interaction between the dyad. Furthermore, cybernetic theorists (Foerster, 1981; Keeney, 1983) maintain that the observer intrinsically influences the observed dyadic system.

Consultation, similarly, is inherently based on a triadic model. The family system and therapist form a dyadic therapeutic system. The consultant adds a third pole, a reference point for the family-therapist dyad (Andolfi & Angelo, 1988). Thus, the therapeutic system can experience through the eyes of an observer their relationship, repetitive patterns, and progress toward explicit and implicit goals. The third pole (consultant), then, becomes a reference point or a reflective mirror for each individual in the therapeutic system. This reference point can live in the minds of the members of the therapeutic system long after the consultation.

Similarly, other triadic relationships such as supervision, co-therapy, and team interventions construct a third pole to view the therapy relationship. Each of these positions can introduce novelty and flexibility into therapeutic systems experiencing a paucity of resources. The contract and consequent range of intervention functions in each of these professional relationships contain some distinct differences.

Supervision (Column a, Figure 1) fosters a hierarchical or generational relationship between the supervisor and the therapist and between the therapist and client family (Montalvo, 1973; Haley, 1976). The supervisor has two agendas with the therapist: 1) to enhance the skills of the therapist, and 2) to insure quality service with the client family. The supervisor's usual point of entry to meet these goals is through the therapist. This could be performed in direct ("live") or indirect (video or case discussion) supervision.

The supervisor typically has an ongoing relationship with the therapist and is ultimately responsible for the case. The therapist has the vantage point of being in the room, and is consequently much closer to the emotional experience of the interview. The supervisor, on the other

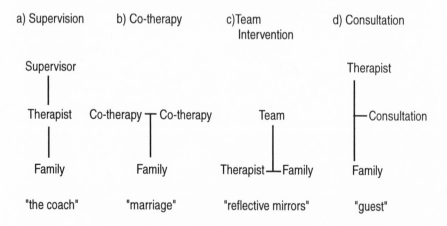

Figure 1

hand, has much more emotional distance behind the one-way mirror or video monitor and is, therefore, more able to discern the patterns and process of the therapeutic system. In this sense, the supervisor is like a coach who can sit on the sidelines and see the entire field. The therapist, on the other hand, could be seen as the team captain with the dual role of being a leader and one of the players. By instructive interventions, the supervisor can coach the therapist to be a more effective and self-assured captain with the family.

Co-therapy (Column b, Figure 1) is an egalitarian relationship between two therapists who work conjointly with the family. Keith and Whitaker (1983) have compared co-therapy to a professional marriage with the parental task of raising the family members to be developmentally intimate and autonomous. Thus, co-therapy consists of a professional relationship treating a familial relationship. The interactive nature of both systems allows more opportunities for modeling, mirroring, and forming alliances than do the other professional roles.

The relationship between the therapists can also become the third pole between the family and the therapeutic system. The inner experience of the co-therapy marriage—tumultuous, hierarchical, confused, or desperate—can provide a fulcrum to understand and/or challenge the rigid complementary sequences involving the therapists. In addition, a co-therapist can take psychological distance in an interview while the session is being facilitated by the partner. In this way, the "We" capabilities of the co-therapy team nurture the freedom to experience a clearer perspective of the "I" position. Thus, co-therapy models a symbolic relationship that promotes greater intimacy and differentiation.

Team interventions (Column c, Figure 1) can readily illuminate multiple "reflective mirrors" of the different realities and patterns in the family and therapeutic systems. Seminal writings about teams include Papp's (1980) portrayal of the Greek Chorus; Selvini-Palazzoli, Cecchin, Boscolo, and Prata's (1978) description of the Milan team; and Andersen's (1987, 1991) representation of the reflective team. Papp (1980) described several strategies in working with the variations within the team such as highlighting the differences between the male and female team members or between the team and the therapist. Portraying dialectic positions such as one co-therapist who is an advocate for transformation while the other respects the status quo could also be done in a co-therapy relationship (Haber & Cooper-Haber, 1987), but the invisibility of the team makes it more difficult to disqualify the position that it endorses.

Whereas co-therapy and supervision involve a professional alliance, team approaches place the professionals and the family in the observed system. This is vividly illustrated by Andersen's (1987, 1991) procedure of the reflective team that discusses the therapeutic system's "conversation" while the therapist and the family sit together and observe the team's commentary. This process intervention amplifies the importance, involvement, and mutuality of the therapeutic system while conveying the team's reflections of different perspectives and realities.

Consultation (Column d, Figure 1) has the triadic qualities of the other positions (a, b, c), but also has distinct differences. Previously, the supervisor has been described as the coach, co-therapists as marital partners, and team members as reflective mirrors. The consultant could be metaphorically described as an invited guest. Like the team, the guest is not an ongoing member of the therapeutic household and, unlike the coach or partner, is not responsible for the continuity and outcome of the household. However, the guest is invited into the interior of the house, perhaps into some of the bedrooms.

The extent and duration of the invitation depend upon the trust level and the needs/desires of the hosts. If a room needs repair and the guest has the inclination and skills to remedy this problem, then the household may want to show the guest this room. The guest can then determine if he/she has the skill, desire, and time to work with the problem. The guest does not have the authority of the coach, the intimacy of the partner, nor the anonymity of the mirror, but has the freedom to join and contribute to the household and then leave.

This inherently differentiated position enables the guest to show how a stranger experiences the household and, conversely, how the household reacts to the impact of the guest. The relationship and social role of the guest (adolescent friend or international dignitary) will greatly influence the visit. Nonetheless, this mutual exchange can live long after the physical departure of the guest.

SYSTEMIC/EXPERIENTIAL CONSULTATION

Systemic/experiential consultation encompasses a temporary intervention by a professional colleague or a kin/social network member to deepen the process and the competence of the therapeutic system. This model (Andolfi, 1979; Andolfi, Angelo, Menghi, & Nicolo-Corigliano, 1983; Andolfi, Angelo, & de Nichilo, 1989; Haber 1990b) evokes family and therapeutic resources that are embedded in the historical, future, or present ecosystems. The goal of this developmental model is to advance differentiated relationships (Bowen, 1978) that can tolerate more intimacy and separation.

Process of Change

The family, therapeutic, and the consultative systems are linked in their desire to move through rigidity and chaos into a new paradigm that embraces increased options for the self and family/social relationships (Dodson, 1991). Similar to Maslow's (1968) assertion that there is a self-actualizing tendency in each individual, a system of collected members inherently desires developmentally appropriate, differentiated (self-actualized) relationships. This evolutionary world would sequentially include the ebb and flow of intimacy and separateness.

Relationships, like rivers, are never the same. However, members of the system may get lost in the river and feel that they are stuck in the same spot or merely going in circles. Although there is comfort with the coherence (Dell, 1982) of the river's familiar surroundings, there is an intermittent pressure to explore novel situations further down the stream. The systemic response to that pressure—chaotic, rigid, enmeshed, disengaged (Olson, Sprenkle, & Russell, 1979)—will determine how it copes with the process of change. The therapist's objective is to challenge the rigid responses of the family system while supporting family members in their past, present, and future journey.

The opposite of a differentiated therapeutic system is one that is locked in a therapeutic impasse, an "unhappy bilateral symmetrical dance" (Whitaker, 1982), in which members of the therapeutic system become rigidly defined in relation to one another. The therapist and the family members, particularly the identified patient, become trapped in a pattern where they feel overly responsible for both cohesion and change in the system. The therapist could become "overbounded or underbounded" (Connell, Whitaker, Garfield, & Connell, 1990), the therapist either is an introjected member of the family or is kept outside the system.

The process of being too "in" or "out" is disconcerting for both the therapist and the family. If left unchecked, an existential conflict arises where the therapist cannot sequentially "belong" and "be" in the therapeutic system. If the therapist is experiencing this existential dilemma, he or she frequently develops a rigid, defensive approach to avoid facing frustration, aloneness, or failure.

Consultation allows the family and the therapist to expose their vulnerability and rigidity, thus inducing a search for new roles in the therapy relationship. Whitaker (1986) succinctly stated, "...if the therapist does dare to be vulnerable by inviting the consultant in, he or she models for the family...that they too can be vulnerable without being destroyed" (p. 81).

The Therapeutic Encounter

Figures 2 and 3 will illustrate the developmental phases of the therapeutic and the consultative processes.

When the family initiates the therapy process (phase 1), the identified patient is frequently at the nexus of most of the stressful triangles in the family. Most of the tensions in the family are absorbed by the symptomatic process while other developmental problems are put on the back burner. The therapist enters the system when family/social network members or other referral sources feel that they lack the resources to resolve the problem or tolerate the pain and anxiety in the family. The therapist finds the family almost exclusively defined by the angst of the problem.

In the second phase, the therapist joins the family through the powerful, central position of the identified patient. The therapist "marries" (see Andolfi, Chapter 5 and Ridgely, Chapter 3) the identified problem through questioning, respecting, and appreciating the logic and considerable amount of voluntary energy needed to maintain the symptomatic cycle. If the family and the patient allow the therapist to work with the developmental and existential dilemmas of the family members, then the therapist can assume the central role previously occupied by the patient. From this position inside the family, the therapist can work with the problematic past, present, and future triangles in the family. The patient, by allowing other issues to be discussed, implicitly agrees that he/she and the family trust the therapist to help the family system manage the anxiety necessary to continue its journey.

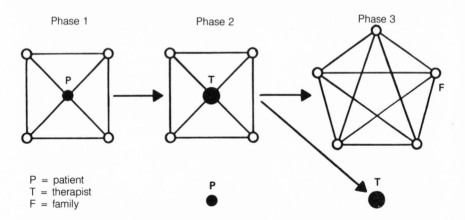

P = patient
T = therapist
F = family

Figure 2. Progression of the Therapeutic Process *(Reprinted with permission from Andolfi, Angelo, & de Nichilo, 1989, p. 144)*

The third and last phase occurs when the therapist separates from the family. Therapy is considered successful when:

1. The identified patient's behavior appears profoundly modified, and the symptoms for which therapy was requested have disappeared or, at least, have decreased in intensity;
2. the family has reset its developmental tempo and the identified patient no longer has the function of stopping it by placing himself in the center of family conflicts. Anyone can speak openly about other relationships and important unresolved problems between different parts of the family...(Andolfi et al., 1989, p. 143)

In the third phase, the physical presence of the therapist is unnecessary for the family to confront and resolve problems. In the ideal scenario, therapy has taught the family to incorporate the change process. The images developed in the therapy process may be catalytic reminders of the inherent resources in the kin/social network and the family members. Termination of the therapy can be a gradual process consisting of longer intervals between sessions.

The Consultative Encounter

There are significant parallels between the therapeutic encounter and the consultative encounter. There is great similarity between the therapist and identified patient in the therapeutic process and the consultant and therapist in the consultative process. In either a familial or therapeutic impasse, the lines of communication and roles in the system become rigidly stereotyped. In a protracted impasse, the members of the system feel hopeless about their capacity to make any substantive changes. By encountering a therapist or a consultant, both systems are brave enough to expose their pain, vulnerability, and failure to an outsider. They hope that the professional can help them uncover/recover/discover a new perspective, renewed hope, greater intimacy and separateness, and other tools necessary to help them meet their personal and relational goals.

The first phase has been divided into two common therapeutic impasses referred to earlier as "underbounded" or "overbounded." In Phase 1-A (see Figure 3), the underbounded predicament, the therapist is too far outside the family to make an impact. The identified patient or problem is unchanged and relentlessly remains as the transactional linkage and focus. Family problems are blamed on the identified patient or problem to the exclusion of reflecting on or addressing other

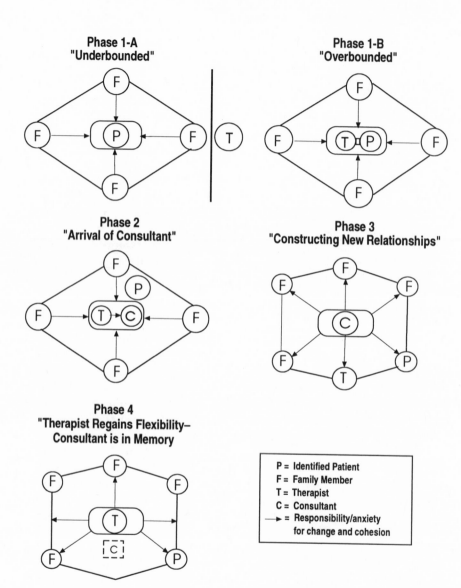

Figure 3. Progression of the Consultative Process

stressful dilemmas. The therapist loosely belongs to the therapeutic system (as noted by the line dividing the family and therapist).

Phase 1-B, the overbounded quandary, finds the therapist stuck in a role inside the family. The therapeutic process becomes repetitious as the therapist's rigid, role-defined position allows limited maneuverability within the family system. The therapist is frozen in the dialectic of *belonging* to rather than *being* in the system. This happens when the therapist forms a stable alliance with one family member, regularly acts as a social control agent, repeatedly responds in an overly responsible way, or engages in other stereotypically complementary or symmetrical behaviors. Rather than facilitating change and growth in the family, the therapist becomes the stable intermediary between the problem and the family. In this sense, the therapist assumes the same position that the patient occupied in Figure 2, Phase 1.

Phase 2, the arrival of the consultant, creates triangles between the consultant, therapist, and family members. The consultant's position in the triangle allows the therapist to talk about his/her internal experience and external position in the therapeutic system while the family observes the dialogue. Similarly, the consultant questions the family about their perceptions of the family and the therapeutic system while the therapist observes someone else work with his/her clients.

The clients have a unique opportunity to hear their therapist talk about them to the consultant in the third person. This provides a process intervention, much like the reflecting team. Similarly, the therapist observes the consultant's interactions with the family without the responsibility of conducting the interview. The triadic relationship in the newly formed consultative system stimulates a system that can be more reflexive, thus provoking an augmented perception and experience. Newly formed internal perceptions and external behaviors in the therapist, family member, subsystem, or ecosystem can transform the therapeutic system.

In Phase 3, constructing new relationships, the consultant addresses other tensions in the therapeutic system. Since the consultant is not invested in the stability and continuity of the system, he/she can conduct the interview without replicating the previous role of the therapist. As the consultant engages the impasse (see Chapter 5 on the identified patient as the consultant), the fused anxiety that results from the dichotomous desire for change and predictability becomes manifest. The heightened anxiety produced by the therapist's failure to resolve the impasse becomes the lubricant for searching for new resolutions. The added energy and attention of the consultant encourages members of the therapeutic system to take greater risks.

Phase 4 represents the more flexible therapeutic system after the consultation. Optimally, the therapist assumes a more flexible and focused position in the therapeutic system after the consultation. Thus, he/she works from this newly assumed position to unbalance and restructure the triadic, rigid complementarity rather than feeling overly responsible for the stability and growth of the family. The therapist aligns with the intrinsic anxiety arising from the family's developmental impasse as a means to help them resolve their identified and existential problems. After the consultation, the family members could more clearly discriminate the responsibilities of the family and those of the therapeutic systems. Having seen their therapist request help, family members could become more determined to help resolve the anxiety in the family system. When family members or the therapist revert to rigid roles and patterns, each can refer to the "voice" or position of the consultant, who is now in the historical memory of the therapeutic system. The consultation provides a reference point for the therapeutic system and can be recalled to mark progress or deterioration.

Figure 3 is drawn from the perspective of a collegial consultant for the therapist. However, a member of the kin/social network could also be a consultant. The type of relationship, generational position, and gender greatly affects the focus of the consultation.

Figure 4 demonstrates how an ally to one family member skews the direction of the interview. The therapist not only observes the dyadic relationship of the alliance, but can also perceive how each family member responds to that dyad. Do other family members respect, embrace, or reject the dyad? The therapist can likewise note how the friendship relates to other family members.

The therapist needs to form an alliance with the "lay" (social network member as opposed to a professional) consultant in the service of helping the family. This alliance is crucial since the lay consultant is being invited to help the therapy, not take sides within the family or the therapeutic system. The consultative position of the social network member usually promotes concern for the welfare of the family. Like the collegial consultation, new relationships are formed and the therapist has new ways to see the family members. The presence of the lay consultant remains vivid in the memory of the therapeutic system and, unlike the collegial consultant, that consultant maintains an active relationship to family members outside the therapy context.

As illustrated, Systemic Experiential Consultation may employ resources from the kin/social network or the professional system. The choice of consultative resource needed to empower the therapeutic system depends upon the idiosyncratic circumstances in the family,

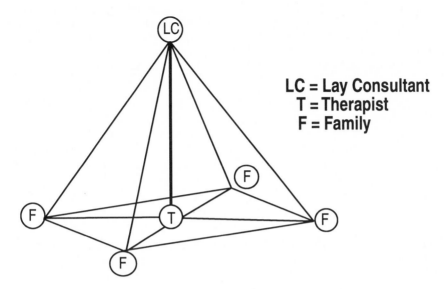

**LC = Lay Consultant
T = Therapist
F = Family**

Figure 4. Consult by a Social Network Member

therapeutic, and ecological systems. The following two sections will explore the nature of some of these resources.

KIN/SOCIAL NETWORK CONSULTANTS

Sluzki (1985) postulated "the family" to be no more than a social construct. He noted that the etymology of the word "family" is rooted in Middle English and was originally used as a reference for household servants. "We see and treat the nuclear family... because we are specialists in seeing it, not because it is out there as a clearly delineated shape. We treat the family because we see the family and we see the family because we evoke the family with our models and our inquiry" (p. 1).

Thus, the form into which the family has evolved today is a recent invention. Even so, recent dramatic changes of the structure and roles within families are testaments to the evolutionary nature of the human system that we call the family. Dammann and Berger (1983) contemplated the distinction of whom to include in the household and family units. They found that many households include non-family members and many other families have members living outside the household. Therefore, they and other therapists have flexibly adjusted the definition of who constitute the relevant "family." Guinan (1990) expanded the relevant treatment unit to include three family systems: the home family, social family, and school/vocational family. Network therapists (Speck and Attneave, 1973; Attneave, 1969; 1990) also include the "tribe of relevant relationships" rather than limiting the resources to just the family. Friends and selected lay consultants (Haber 1987; 1990b) have proven to be resources helpful to the therapy system and to clients in their interactions outside the therapy hour.

Consultation, as proposed in this book, philosophically and pragmatically includes relevant subsystems in the healing process of therapy. Publicly affirming the family's goal to expand its vitality and development can be a part of the healing process (Kiev, 1968; Rueveni, 1979). Social network involvement counters the isolation of the nuclear family that is prevalent in our culture (Brofenbrenner, 1979). The goal of family and social network consultations is to support the health of the community rather than assuming that the therapist is the main resource for the family. The following are some nonprofessional resources that can enhance the family's efforts to develop greater intimacy and autonomy.

Family of Origin

Besides present interactions and relationships, the family of origin locates the family's development over time (Keith, Chapter 6). When grandparents talk about their parents and grandparents, therapy develops a five-generational framework. Grandparents can provide opportunities for grandchildren to see their parents as children. Thus, the motivation behind their parents' behavior can become more evident. At least, children can empathize with the "children" inside their parents.

Similarly, other extended family members can present different views of the family of origin, its members, and the struggles that were faced back in childhood. These consultants can help therapists understand problems, coping mechanisms, and relationships over time. Besides reflecting on the "there and then," they can be invaluable resources in the "here and now."

Friends

Friends bring a unique, generational viewpoint to the therapy and an affirmative relationship with at least one member of the family (Haber, Chapter 7; Haber, 1987). When there is a generational or developmental impasse, friends have shown an ability to bridge polemic views of both generations. As consultants, they can use their own life-cycle experience to understand the family's dilemma. Since they are not directly involved in the presented problem, their position can be more clearly differentiated than that of family members. Thus, their consultative feedback engenders less defensiveness than feedback from a family member or a member of a different, more remote generation (including an adult therapist to a child or teenager).

Social Network Members (Lay Consultants)

The choice of who can be a consultative resource depends on the meaningful social network of the family members (Guinan & Jones, Chapter 8; Attneave 1990; Attneave & Verhulst, 1986; Haber, 1990b). Some family members may not have friends, but know people from other contexts such as religious settings, school, work, self-help groups, or teams. These individuals can help the therapist have greater understanding, empathy, and knowledge of the social resources of family members. This information can help the therapist treat the family differently and help family members gain a different perspective of one another.

Operationally, there are several advantages to the premise that selected social network members from clients' ecosystems can, at times, contribute more significantly than the professional skill of a therapist. First, such a position encourages the therapist to share the role of expert and predominant resource. The therapist's declaration of "impotence" (Whitaker, 1976) induces clients to search for their own resources since the therapist apparently is not able to meet their needs.

Second, activating social network members helps elicit resources that may be unfamiliar or unknown to the therapist. The therapist, then, could more fully understand and appreciate the values, history, and social-cultural-religious influences that affect the client system.

Third, social network members are generally concerned and promotive of clients' well-being when they are invited in as consultants. It is essentially more facilitative for the therapist to assume that the clients' social networks can be a help rather than a hindrance. If some members of the network take a negative view of the therapy, then requesting their help may diminish their distrust and resistance and increase the possibility of their support. This is particularly true of persons who are very close to family members, such as extended family or friends.

Fourth, lay consultants could extend the therapy goals and process into the community.

Fifth, lay consultants could share, if appropriate, their experiences about how they handled similar types of problems. The proliferation of self-help groups suggests that nonprofessional sharing can be instrumental in helping people gain support, provide hands-on help, feel accepted as part of a group, and frequently offer some homespun wisdom and advice. Broderick (1988) concisely cautioned clinicians to consider the social network: "The point is that virtually every therapeutic encounter is also an encounter with a network. Rarely can that reality be ignored to the benefit of clients" (p. 229).

PROFESSIONAL/COLLEGIAL CONSULTANTS

The therapist could request a consultation from a colleague, supervisor, referral source, or other professional expert as another way to expand the therapeutic system. Whitaker (1989) cautioned therapists to be aware of the seductiveness for both the family and the therapist to act "as if" the therapist is socially and biologically in the clients' world. A professional consultant realigns the therapist as part of the professional team hired to do a job.

The professional consultant enhances the content and process within the therapeutic system by providing: 1) a second opinion or additional information and clinical perspectives about the family's problems, 2) a forum to understand more fully how the therapist is personally involved and perceived in the therapeutic system, and 3) a context for the therapist and clients to reflect on the process and goals of the therapeutic interface.

The range and focus of the consultation can vary depending on *who* is the consultant and the consultee, *what* is the relationship between the consultant, consultee, and the therapeutic system, *why* the consultation is requested, and at what point in the therapeutic relationship (*when*) the consultation is requested. The following are examples that reflect the range of different professionals who can enrich the therapeutic process by their attention to and knowledge of the family, therapist, or therapist-family interface.

Past Therapist or Referring Professional

Most often, families or family members have seen other professionals before entering our office. The information that these professionals have about the family and their rationale for the referral could speed up the therapeutic process and avoid potential pitfalls. Typically, a frank discussion of the history, role, and experience of the professional's previous involvement and present concerns is best accomplished with the family present and with minimal jargon. The new therapeutic system can then build on what has already occurred. Additionally, the referring professional could remain instrumental throughout the therapeutic process (Brok, Chapter 9).

School/Agency Personnel

Clients are always involved in systems outside the family. The perspective of professionals from these systems could shed light on how the family members operate outside the family context. The information could point to additional resources or acknowledgment that the problem is replicated in systems other than the family. These professionals could extend the goals of the therapy in these other contexts (Wendt & Ellenwood, Chapter 13).

Specialty Consultants

Since systemic therapists are usually generalists, it is often useful to acquire additional information or a linkage to the culture of families that are difficult or foreign to the therapist. Recruiting resources from these families can facilitate compassion, understanding, cooperation, and the relevance of therapy. In addition, a specialty consultant could underscore the "reality" problems that affect the family. The range of specialty consultants is limited only by the issues confronting the family. The following have been found useful: medical (Elizur, Chapter 10), ethnic (DiNicola, Chapter 2 and Jutoran, Chapter 11), gender (de Nichilo, Chapter 17; Goodrich, Rampage, Ellman & Halstead, 1988), and religious consultants.

Auxiliary Professionals

Often there is a need to involve other mental health professions in a case. There may be a need for a psychiatrist (Griffith, Griffith, Meydrech, Grantham, & Bearden, 1991), psychiatric institution (Brok, Chapter 9), individual therapist (Feldman, 1992; Wachtel, 1986), group or multiple family therapist, or addiction specialists (Guinan & Jones, Chapter 8). Telephone discussions and conjoint meetings with these professionals promote cooperation, coordination, and understanding of complementary services. Thus, the group of professionals works together rather than competitively or contrarily.

Colleague

Collegial consultation is a cost-effective, time-efficient procedure for getting a second opinion on difficult cases. The collegial consultant, by definition, has a dual role—consultant and colleague. The consultative role has a responsibility to assist the therapeutic effort, while the collegial role hopefully involves a relationship based on honesty, respect, and trust. The collegial consultant needs to integrate the commitment of these roles and respect the best interests of the therapeutic system (Rubinstein-Nabarro, Chapter 12).

Whitaker (1986) and his colleagues at the Atlanta Psychiatric Clinic were the first group to regularly schedule consultations during the second family interview. "Bringing the consultant in early means that the consultant will be present in the mind of the family and on call for either the family or the therapist when things begin to become ineffective or too uncomfortable" (p. 85). Psychological Services in Toledo, Ohio, arranged for "instant supervision (consultation)," where colleagues entered therapy sessions at crucial moments (Guinan & Doane, 1983). These arrangements provide and model creativity, trust, intimacy, and resourcefulness for the family, therapist, and collegial system.

Collegial consultations provide a sounding board and perhaps assistance or protection with legal and ethical dilemmas. In addition, a colleague may support and help a therapist deal with personal issues that resonate with a client family (Penn & Sheinberg, 1986). Limited exploration and disclosures of the inner world of the therapist could help the therapist see the client family with clearer eyes. Furthermore, the therapist's personal reactions are often the keys needed to enter and understand the analogic and relational processes in the family system. Collegial consultation supports the therapist personally and professionally and is a powerful antidote to the deadly triad of professional isolation, overresponsibility, and consequent burnout.

Supervisor

A supervisory consultation is similar to a collegial consultation except that a supervisor has authority for the case. Rather than indirectly supervising a case, the supervisor enters the therapy room and becomes directly involved with the case. Thus, the supervisee/consultee can observe how a more seasoned therapist would work with the family. The supervisory consultant can choose to return administrative control to the therapist, maintain an active role as an ongoing consultant or supervisor, or make administrative recommendations that would change the responsibility or structure of the therapy. Thus, supervisory consultation could become an effective technique for case evaluation, training, and supervision of supervisees (Whitaker & Garfield, 1987; see also Liggett & Purvis, Chapter 15).

The different consultants from the family's and therapist's system each provide "news of a difference" (Bateson, 1972). The multiple descriptions allow a more complete picture of the family and of the therapist system. Seeing more of the gestalt of the system encourages less projection and more appreciation of the consultative resources.

Elizur and Minuchin's (1989) summary of consultation, written from the lens of a master consultant, equally applies to the professional and nonprofessional consultants enumerated above.

> From a systemic perspective, consultation is a process of increasing the complexity of the therapeutic process in such a way that it opens new alternatives. To achieve this goal, the consultation interrupts the established patterns in the therapeutic system, creating discontinuity that is often followed by a reconceptualization of problems and an exploration of new pathways for change. When this step is successful, it is followed by a mobilization of resources. The consultant and therapist team join in coauthoring an alternative way of constructing the bits of the family story, one that allows family members to find different ways of positioning themselves with respect to each other and to the significant social system. (p. 244)

RESEARCH

Despite the influence of consultation as a training modality for family/system therapists, there has been minimal research on the outcome and process of family therapy consultation. Perhaps the financial benefits for more efficient treatment procedures will influence the National Institute for Mental Health, insurance companies, and other researchers to study how consultation, as the medical "second opinion," increases the quality of care while reducing costs and unwarranted treatment.

Although there have been no reviews and few empirical studies specifically on the specialty of family therapy consultation, reviews for general mental health consultation (Horton & Brown 1990; Mannino & Shore, 1972; Meade, Hamilton & Yuen, 1983) conclude that consultation improves therapeutic effectiveness, facilitates the relationship between the consultee and client, and needs greater clarification and research. This section will review two recent studies that investigated the impact of a professional and a nonprofessional consultation. Green & Hegret (1989a; 1989b; 1991) researched a professional team consultation, whereas Bray, Williamson & Malone (1986) studied clients who participated in a family of origin consultation.

Green & Hegret (1989a) randomly assigned to 11 therapists two cases matched for the severity of presenting problems. One case received a "Milan-informed," five-part team consultation, whereas the other case received therapy and constituted the control group. Results one month after the consultations concluded that the consultation team clients' therapeutic progress was significantly ($p<.05$) greater than the 11 non-team clients. Furthermore, improvements on goal attainment were maintained at significantly higher levels at the end of a 3-year follow-up. Upon further analysis of the data, Green & Hegret (1991) found that ratings of the therapist's relationship skills (warmth and active structuring) significantly predicted client improvement at 1-month and 3-year follow-ups. Green and Hegret (1989b) distinguished their systemic/strategic team consultation approach as "down-to-earth, warm, personally accessible, sometimes challenging, sometimes playful, which is in contrast to the Milan team's (Selvini-Palazzoli et al., 1978) more formal stance" (p. 421).

Green & Hegret saw the impasse as "...a well-rehearsed play. The characters are comfortable in their established roles and, when necessary, improvise lines consistent with these roles" (p. 431). They felt that the team offered "novel ideas to the therapeutic system without jeopardizing the strength and continuance of the treatment alliance" (p. 432). They concluded, "The introduction of new members—who are not yet bound into the previous constructions of therapeutic reality or established relationship definitions—disrupts the therapy's status quo. Thus, ...we strongly encourage expanding or contracting the treatment system's membership (at least temporarily) when faced with an impasse" (p. 431).

The major limitations of this study were the small sample size (22 for the 1-month and 16 for the 3-year follow-ups), subjective sample selection, lack of a treatment control group, and reliance on one measure (goal attainment). Therefore, one must be cautious in generalizing these results to other populations or consultation modalities. Clearly, there is a pressing need for research with larger sample sizes, different treatment populations, and other consultative modalities. For example, a single consultant (versus a team) could be studied, especially since a single consultant is much more logistically manageable and less expensive than a team of professionals.

Bray, Williamson & Malone (1986) studied the impact of recruiting parents as intergenerational consultants in systems oriented psychotherapy. Williamson (1981, 1982, 1992) conceptualized a new stage in the life cycle, Personal Authority in the Family System, and a methodology to help adults to become peers with their parents. "The goal is...to move to a position from which it is possible to know directly the persons behind the parental roles.... Knowing the parents in this reciprocal sense demystifies and humanizes them. It is the prime experience that creates peerhood between the generations and dissolves intergenerational intimidation" (Bray et al., 1986, p. 426). Williamson believes that personal authority within the family of origin encourages adults to take responsibility for their lives rather than feel trapped and intimidated by the past.

The study included 70 individuals who were currently participating in the Intergeneration Family Therapy Group (IFTG) and 24 former clients, who had completed a systemically oriented psychotherapy, in a Control Group (CG). The results indicated that those who participated in the intergenerational consultation reported significantly less intergenerational triangulation and intimidation and more personal authority than the CG. Additionally, the IFTG subjects reported significantly more satisfaction with peer relationships.

These results indicate that the goals of personal authority and diminished intergenerational intimidation can be better realized when one's parents are involved in the therapeutic process. The combined power of the intergenerational consult, the preparatory work for the consultation, and the post-consultation integration can restructure relationships in the family of origin. Bowen (1978) stated that one's differentiation from the family of origin will eventually affect other family members. In this light, it would be interesting to investigate the impact of intergenerational consultation on parents and their view of the relationship with their adult child.

In tandem, these studies begin to support Whitaker's notion that it is useful to add a consultant from either the therapist's side or from the clients' side. The who (types of consultants), what (focus), when (the point in the therapeutic relationship), how (the process) and why (reason for the consult) will determine the nature of the consultation. The given is that expanding the therapeutic system inherently changes the system.

More research is needed to determine who can make the most efficient changes, for what problems, at what point (when) in the therapeutic relationship, how the consultation should be accomplished, and why the consult affects the therapeutic system. The answers to these issues will help us make more informed decisions.

CONSULTATIVE PROBLEMS AND CONSIDERATIONS

Despite cost-effectiveness, efficiency, and modeling by the masters, consultation is less widely employed than co-therapy, supervision, and team interventions. Possible reasons for this neglect include the following: A) Consultation is not regularly taught in academic programs because it is considered an advanced skill. B) Masters' consultations intimidate the average clinician because they seem too magical and extraordinary. C) The consultative role requires juxtaposing a dual relationship with the consultee, consultant, and colleague. D) Consultations intrude on the privacy and the continuity of the therapy relationship. E) The request for a consultation necessitates that therapists be willing to reveal their vulnerabilities. F) Consultation means temporarily giving up control of the therapy, which could create fear of the unexpected.

Although the reasons for resisting consultations become ameliorated with increased trust and practice, there are other unique difficulties and problems in consultative relationships. This section will examine some problems and offer suggestions to circumvent obstacles.

1) Consultant has a different theoretical view than the family or therapist. Consultation provides a binocular view of the problem, the family system, and the therapeutic system. If the consultant's view is too similar to the therapist's perception, then the consultation will not provide a significantly different picture. Thus, there is no depth perception. However, if the views are too dissimilar, the therapeutic system would be unable to converge the two incongruent perspectives. Therefore, the consultant needs to calibrate his/her interventions and suggestions to the theoretical orientation, skill level, and work context of the therapist and to the resources of the family. When the consultant (for example, analytic psychiatrist, lawyer, or adolescent friend) has basic differences from the therapist, it is their mutual responsibility to respect and decipher each other's viewpoint. Nonetheless, the authority to incorporate or dismiss the suggestions and inferences from the consultant usually remains with the consultee.

2) Isomorphic problems in the consultative and therapeutic systems. The relationships in the newly formed consultative system (therapist and consultant, consultant and family member(s), or other alliances and triangles involving the consultant) may recreate complementary and symmetrical patterns that are evident in the family and therapeutic systems. Consultants need to consider the implicit and explicit roles assigned to them, their external position in the system (whether focused on the therapist, identified patient, or other family member), and the internal experience of that position (Haber, 1990c). If consultants can maintain a differentiated "I" position, then they will usually not engage in rigid sequences. Since the consultant is a temporary and hierarchical figure, it is important to discern generational, gender, power, and intimacy relationships that involve the consultant.

3) The therapist's position is undermined in the therapeutic system after the consultation. Since the consultant's role is temporary, it is crucial that the consultant respect the therapist's authority for the case. The consultant should defer to the therapist in the beginning and at the end of the interview. That is, the therapist should present information about the therapeutic system and reason for the consult in the beginning of the interview and retain administrative control at the conclusion of the consultation. The consultant could overtly respect the collegial relationship with the therapist by affirming the work accomplished, commitment and relationship to the family, and willingness to expose a therapeutic impasse.

During the consultation, the therapist joins the family as the consultee, the unit of observation and intervention. Optimally, the therapist assumes a nondefensive, growth-oriented posture in the consultation system. This may include the revelation of professional shortcomings and personal reactions to the family. The consultant may explore the therapist's countertransferential reactions in the family system, but the emphasis of the consultation is to empower the therapeutic system—increase intimacy, honesty, creative energy, and dedication to personal growth.

The therapist should be prepared to face changes in the post-consultation therapeutic relationship. The consultation could alter the dependence between the therapist and the family member(s). Additionally, family member(s) could be intimidated by the prospect of change by the therapist or a family member. The family could attempt to nullify the anxiety produced by the consultation through a familial crisis or the termination of therapy. The therapist needs to consider the process/outcome of the consultation and the ramifications of his/her response.

4) Consultant does not join the therapeutic system. The consultant, as previously described, is truly a guest in the bedroom (sometimes the bathroom) of the therapeutic system. Although the consultant may have been presented as an "expert," the family may resist the intrusion of the consultant. The consultant needs to join with the family before inspecting the inner chambers of the system. Self-disclosure, humor, attention, interest, play, stories, respect, and other joining strategies are necessary to facilitate a "bedside manner." This will promote greater cooperation, trust, and hope in the consultation process.

Sometimes, the therapist may overprotect the client family by sharing only their strengths. In such cases, it would be unwise for the consultant to force his/her way into the bedroom and it might be wise to linger in the hallway or retreat to the foyer. It is important for the consultant to recognize that the responsibility for the success of the therapy is between the therapist and family.

5) The therapeutic system repeats similar patterns after the consultation. Usually, consultations are one-shot interventions. Although much can be accomplished, it may be overly optimistic to anticipate that a brief, consultative encounter will forever liberate a rigid family from their emotional tyranny. The therapist may use the experience of the consultation as an internal reminder to approach the system differently, to reiterate the message of the consultation, or to reconstruct the presence of the consultant.

Sometimes, the therapy benefits by a follow-up session with the consultant. The second consultation discerns the outcome of the consultant's interventions and suggestions, explores new territory, rekindles the juices of transformation, or provides another punctuation in the therapeutic process and family development. Additionally, the second consult can explore errors and oversights of the consultant. For instance, the consultant may have viewed the problem too narrowly by not considering non-familial influences in the therapeutic system.

6) Outcome of the post-consultation with a member of the social network. The social network member, by definition, maintains a nonprofessional relationship with one or more family member(s). Therefore, it is necessary to determine whether there are any deleterious effects from the consultative experience (Haber, 1990b).

The benefits of consultation far outweigh the risks. Consultations invite systems to examine and change aspects that are problematic and dysfunctional. The process of change involves chaos and reorganization. The therapist should anticipate this and support the family's ability to develop.

CONCLUSION

Good psychotherapy empowers the client system to become more fully evolved. Similarly, consultation can enhance the development of the consultee system (the family and therapist). Effective consultation and psychotherapy teach creative approaches for handling dilemmas so that the system can solve problems without the need for an outsider's interventions. The brief and intense nature of consultation is efficiently well-suited for challenging the status quo without promoting a dependent relationship.

The efficacy of consultation is supported by its diverse applications in many fields including medicine, education, and business. Additionally, consultation has been practiced by therapists of numerous orientations. Its wide utilization comes from two simple assumptions: 1) nobody has all of the answers to life's puzzles, and 2) it's easier to be an expert with other people's puzzles than with our own. Consultation interrupts the old way of dealing with the puzzle by engaging in a new process that redefines and augments the puzzle. This chapter has provided an overview of the diverse resources for solving puzzling situations in family therapy. The keys to unlocking the family therapy puzzle may be stimulated by a master problem solver, another member of the professional audience, or somebody from the family's neighborhood.

REFERENCES

Andersen, T. (1987). The reflecting team: Dialogue and meta-dialogue in clinical work. *Family Process*, 26, 415–428.

Andersen, T. (Ed.) (1991). *The Reflecting Team: Dialogues and Dialogues About the Dialogues.* New York: W.W. Norton & Company.

Andolfi, M. (1979). *Family Therapy: An Interactional Approach.* New York: Plenum Press.

Andolfi, M. & Angelo, C. (1988). Toward constructing the therapeutic system. *Journal of Marital and Family Therapy*, 14, 237–247.

Andolfi, M., Angelo, C., & de Nichilo, M. (1989). *The Myth of Atlas: Families and the Therapeutic Story.* New York: Brunner/Mazel.

Andolfi, M., Angelo, C. Menghi, P., & Nicolo-Corigliano, A. M. (1983). *Behind the Family Mask: Therapeutic Change in Rigid Family Systems.* New York: Brunner/Mazel.

Attneave, C. L. (1969). Therapy in tribal settings and urban network intervention. *Family Process*, 8, 192–210.

Attneave, C. L. (1990). Core network intervention: An emerging paradigm. *Journal of Strategic and Systemic Therapies*, 9, 3–10.

Attneave, C. L. & Verhulst, J. (1986). Teaching mental health professionals to see family strengths: Core network intervention in a hospital setting. In M. Karpel (Ed.), *Family Resources: The Hidden Partner in Family Therapy.* New York: Guilford Press.

Auerswald, E. H. (1968). Interdisciplinary versus ecological approach. *Family Process*, 7, 202–215.

Bateson, G. (1972). *Steps to an Ecology of Mind.* New York: Ballantine.

Bertalanffy, L. Von. (1968). *General Systems Theory.* New York: Braziller.

Bowen, M. (1978). *Family Therapy in Clinical Practice.* New York: Jason Aronson.

Bray, J. H., Williamson, D. S., & Malone, P. E. (1986). An evaluation of an intergenerational consultation process to increase personal authority in the family system. *Family Process*, 25, 423–436.

Broderick, C. B. (1988). Healing members and relationships in the intimate network. In R. M. Milardo (Ed.), *Families and Social Networks*. Newbury Park, CA: Sage Publications.

Brofenbrenner, U. (1979). *The Ecology of Human Development by Nature and Design*. Cambridge, MA: Harvard University Press.

Caplan, G. (1963). Types of mental health consultation. *American Journal of Orthopsychiatry*, 33, 470–481.

Caplan, G. (1970). *The Theory and Practice of Mental Health Consultation*. New York: Basic Books.

Connell, G. M., Whitaker, C. A., Garfield, R. & Connell, L. (1990). The process of in-therapy consultation: A Symbolic-Experiential perspective. *Journal of Strategic and Systemic Therapies*, 9, 32–38.

Dammann, C. & Berger, M. (1983). Household and family: creating a workable treatment unit. *Journal of Strategic and Systemic Therapies*, 9, 32–38.

Dell, P. (1982). Beyond homeostasis: Toward a concept of coherence. *Family Process*, 21, 21–41.

Dodson, L. (1991). Virginia Satir's process of change. *Journal of Couples Therapy*, 6, 119–142.

Elizur, J. & Minuchin, S. (1989). *Institutionalizing Madness*. New York: Basic Books.

Feldman, L. (1992). *Integrating Individual and Family Therapy*. New York: Brunner/Mazel.

Foerster, H. von. (1981). *Observing Systems*. Seaside CA: Intersystems Publications.

Gallessich, J. (1982). *The Profession and Practice of Consultation*. San Francisco: Jossey-Bass.

Goodrich, T. J., Rampage, C., Ellman, B., & Halstead, K. (1988). *Feminist Family Therapy: A Casebook*. New York: W. W. Norton & Company.

Green. R. J. & Hegret, M. (1989a). Outcomes of Systemic/Strategic team consultation: I. Overview and one-month results. *Family Process*, 28, 37–58.

Green. R. J. & Hegret, M. (1989b). Outcomes of Systemic/Strategic team consultation: II. Three-year follow-up and a theory of "emergent design." *Family Process*, 28, 419–437.

Green. R. J. & Hegret, M. (1991). Outcomes of Systemic/Strategic team consultation: III. The importance of therapist warmth and active structuring. *Family Process*, 30, 321–336.

Griffith, J. L., Griffith, M. E., Meydrech, E., Grantham, D., & Bearden, S. (1991). A model for psychiatric consultation in systemic therapy. *Journal of Marital and Family Therapy*, 17, 291–294.

Guinan, J. (1990). Extending the system for the treatment of chemical dependencies. *Journal of Strategic and Systemic Therapies*, 9, 11–20.

Guinan, J. & Doane, D. (1983). Instant supervision. *Voices*, 19, 71–76.

Haber, R. (1987). Friends in family therapy: Use of a neglected resource. *Family Process*, 26, 269–281.

Haber, R. (Guest Editor). (1990a). Inside and outside the family: Eliciting resources from different contexts. *Journal of Strategic and Systemic Therapies*, 9, 1–2.

Haber, R. (1990b). Family and social network members as lay consultants. *Journal of Strategic and Systemic Therapies*, 9, 21–31.

Haber, R. (1990c). From handicap to handy capable: Training systemic therapists in use of self. *Family Process*, 29, 375–384.

Haber, R. & Cooper-Haber, K. (1987) Paradox and orthodox: a co-therapy approach. *Journal of Strategic and Systemic Therapies*, 6, 41–50.

Haley, J. (1976). *Problem Solving Therapy*. San Francisco: Jossey-Bass.

Harari, E. & Bloch, S. (1991). Potential perils of the demonstration-consultation interview in family therapy: A case study of contextual confusion. *Family Process*, 30, 363–371.

Hoffman, L. (1981). *Foundations in Family Therapy*. New York: Basic Books.

Horton, G. E. & Brown, D. (1990). The importance of interpersonal skills in consultee-centered consultation: A Review. *Journal of Counseling and Development*, 68, 423–426.

Karpel, M. (Ed.) (1986). *Family Resources: The Hidden Partner in Family Therapy*. New York: Guilford.

Keeney, B. (1983). *Aesthetics of Change*. New York: Guilford Press.

Keith, D. V. & Whitaker, C. A. (1983). Co-therapy with families. In B.B. Wolman and G.S. Stricker (Eds.), *Handbook of Family and Marital Therapy*. New York: Plenum Publishing.

Kiev, A. (1968) *Curranderismo: Mexican American Folk Psychiatry*. New York: Free Press.

Kingston, P. & Smith, D. (1983). Preparation for live consultation and live supervision when working without a one-way screen. *Journal of Family Therapy*, 5, 219–233.

Mannino, F. V. & Shore, M. F. (1972). Research in mental health consultation. In E. Golann & C. Eisdorfer (Eds.), *Handbook of Community Mental Health*. New York: Appleton-Century-Crofts.

Maslow, A. (1968). *Toward a Psychology of Being*. New York: D. Van Nostrand.

Meade, C. J., Hamilton, M. K., & Yuen, R. K. (1982). Consultation research: The time has come the walrus said. *Counseling Psychologist*, 10(4), 39–51.

Minuchin, S. (1986). Foreword. In L. C. Wynne, S. H. McDaniel, & T. T. Weber (Eds.), *Systems Consultation: A New Perspective for Family Therapy*. New York: Guilford.

Montalvo, B. (1973). Aspects of live supervision. *Family Process*, 12, 343–359.

Olson, D. H., Sprenkle, D. H., & Russell, C. S. (1979). Circumplex model of marital and family systems I: Cohesion and adaptability dimensions, family types, and clinical applications. *Family Process*, 18, 3–28.

Papp, P. (1980). The Greek Chorus and other techniques of family therapy. *Family Process*, 19, 45–58.

Penn, P. & Sheinberg, M. (1986). Is there therapy after consultation?: A systemic map for family therapy consultation. In L. C. Wynne, S. H. McDaniel, & T. T. Weber (Eds.), *Systems Consultation: A New Perspective for Family Therapy*. New York: Guilford.

Rothstein, W. G. (1972). *American Physicians in the 19th Century.* Baltimore: John Hopkins University Press.

Rueveni, U. (1979). *Networking Families in Crisis.* New York: Human Sciences Press.

Schein, E. H. & Bennis, W. G. (1965). *Personal and Organizational Change Through Group Methods.* New York: Wiley & Sons.

Schwartzman, J. (1985). Macrosystemic approaches: An overview. In J. Schwartzman (Ed.), *Families and Other Systems: The Macrosystemic Context of Family Therapy.* New York: Guilford Press.

Selvini-Palazzoli, M., Boscolo, L., Cecchin, G., & Prata, G. (1978). *Paradox and Counterparadox: A New Model in the Therapy of the Family in Schizophrenic Transaction* (translator, E.V. Burt). New York: Jason Aronson.

Sluzki, C. (1985). Families, networks, and other strange shapes. *AFTA Newsletter,* 19, 1–2.

Smith, D. & Kingston, P. (1980). Live supervision without a one-way screen. *Journal of Family Therapy,* 2, 379–387.

Speck, R. V. & Attneave, C. L. (1973). *Family Networks.* New York: Pantheon.

Wachtel, E. (1985). *Family Dynamics in Individual Psychotherapy: A Guide to Clinical Strategies.* New York: W.W. Norton & Company.

Whitaker, C. W. (1976). The Hindrance of theory in clinical work. In P. J. Guerin (Ed.), *Family Therapy: Theory and Practice.* New York: Gardner Press.

Whitaker, C.A. (1982). Guest editorial: The impasse. In J. R. Neill & D. P. Kniskern (Eds.), *From Psyche to System: The Evolving Therapy of Carl Whitaker.* New York: Guilford Press.

Whitaker, C. W. (1986). Family Therapy Consultation as Invasion. In L. C. Wynne, S. H. McDaniel, & T. T. Weber (Eds.), *Systems Consultation: A New Perspective for Family Therapy.* New York: Guilford.

Whitaker, C.A. (1989). *Midnight Musings of a Family Therapist.* New York: W.W. Norton & Company.

Whitaker, C.A. & Garfield, R. (1987). On teaching psychotherapy via consultation and co-therapy. *Contemporary Family Therapy,* 9, 106–114.

Williamson, D.S. (1981). Personal authority via termination of the intergenerational hierarchical boundary: A "new" stage in the family life cycle. *Journal of Marital and Family Therapy,* 7, 441–452.

Williamson, D.S. (1982). Personal authority via termination of the intergenerational hierarchical boundary: The consultation process and the therapeutic method. *Journal of Marital and Family Therapy,* 8, 23–37.

Williamson, D.S. (1992). *The Intimacy Paradox: Personal Authority in the Family System.* New York: Guilford Press.

Wynne, L. C., McDaniel, S. H., & Weber, T. T. (1987) Professional politics and the concepts of family therapy, family consultation, and systems consultation. *Family Process,* 26, 153–166.

Wynne, L. C., McDaniel, S. H., & Weber, T. T. (Eds.) (1986). *Systems Consultation: A New Perspective for Family Therapy.* New York: Guilford.

2

The Strange and the Familiar: Cross-Cultural Encounters Among Families, Therapists, and Consultants

Vincenzo DiNicola

In this chapter, I hope to illuminate the consultation experience by exploring translation not just as a practical problem or technical task in family therapy, but as a fundamental metaphor of human communication. I do this by offering both literature and therapeutic experiences as examples of narratives. Family therapy has recently added to the older notion of "punctuation" (Simon, Stierlin & Wynne, 1985, pp. 284–285) the metaphor of family life as a "narrative." The family narrative or tale, originally written and edited by the family, may be rewritten and edited with therapists and consultants.

In other areas of social science and the humanities, the narrative metaphor has been made concrete (what Gregory Bateson called, "a metaphor that is meant") by reference to lived experience as a "text." Applied across cultures, translation is another dimension of this textual reading of family life. Cultural translation is necessary for the text of the family narrative to be understood in cultural context. Without this dimension of cultural translation, the cross-cultural consultation experience remains alien, fragmentary and incomplete.

FROM FAMILY SAYINGS TO FAMILY MYTHS

There are five of us children. We live in different cities now, some of us abroad, and we do not write to one another much. When we meet we can be indifferent and aloof. But one word, one phrase is enough, one of those ancient phrases, heard and repeated an infinite number of times in our childhood ... would make us recognize each other in the darkness of a cave or among a million people. These phrases are our Latin, the vocabulary of our days gone by, our Egyptian hieroglyphics or Babylonian symbols. They are the evidence of a vital nucleus which has ceased to exist, but which survives in its texts salvaged from the fury of the waters and the corrosion of time. These phrases are the foundation of our family unity which will persist as long as we are in this world and which is recreated in the most diverse places on earth ... (Ginzburg, 1989, pp. 23–24).

We all begin with the private language of the family, what Natalia Ginzburg calls the *lessico familiare*. The translation of this phrase as "family sayings" misses her *double entendre* or pun on *familiare*. Her meaning might be better translated by the pairing, "familial/familiar," emphasizing both the biological and social connectedness of family members. This shared early experience is the basis of the family myth (Ferreira, 1967).

We move from family sayings to family myths—an organization of our experiences and our worlds. Like young children moving out from a secure home base to progressively wider and unknown places, we move from the familiar to the strange, seeking to familiarize even the most foreign experience. As our world expands, we develop another layer of sayings and myths: We move to community and to culture. And we develop a cultural identity and the cultural costume that accompanies it. Cultural costume is made up of the sayings and the mythology from the larger community in which the family lives that defines its experience (Friedman, 1982).

This growth can also make familiar parts of ourselves and our worlds foreign. Every door we open is both an entrance and an exit. To move beyond the familiar and the established self is to enter a dance of polarities: The dance between self and other is a pivot between the strange and the familiar, between personal and social being, and a fluid switch of perspectives between insiders and outsiders.

For people who live in stable communities, all these elements of identity may appear to form a seamless whole. From the familiar to the strange, each individual in each family constructs a composite identity of personal and social being (Harré, 1979, 1984). But in a world of immigrants, shifting boundaries, refugees, and rapid cultural change, the different elements can create a veritable Babel of confusion (Berry, 1992; DiNicola, 1985b, 1985c, 1992, 1993). Let me give an example from therapy.

CASE STUDY: "THE FROZEN SEA WITHIN US"

Montreal in the early 1980s. A Russian/Jewish family in therapy. The identified patient is a 12-year-old boy, Nikolai, who is brilliant, quirky, and troubled. He carries disturbing, violent imagery in his head. The father, a Russian Jew, is an electronics engineer from Moscow. The mother, a non-Jewish Russian, is a costume and set designer who has worked in theatre and cinema. They are very cultured, literate people whose rich understanding of the world outside their apartment contrasts starkly with their relative lack of insight into their own lives.

For this reason, I tried to give meaning to Nikolai's violent ideation by referring to Franz Kafka, a writer whose life was marked by ambivalence and lack of individuation from his parents. The situation of Kafka's life led to ambivalence: He was a Czech Jew living in Prague, writing in German. Critics have said that his disturbing writing prefigures Nazism and the Holocaust (Pawel, 1984). In a letter to his friend Oskar Pollak in 1904, Kafka wrote that what were needed were "books that grieve us deeply, like the death of someone we loved more than ourselves, like being banished into forests far from everyone, like a suicide. A book must be the axe for the frozen sea within us." Using a literary reference that this family could appreciate, I presented Nikolai's troubling mental imagery as a response to the frozen sea of his family.

Perhaps the family sea had been frozen over by ambivalence and neglect. The parents had never resolved their ethnic and religious differences, so that they are torn as to which community and which religion to join. In the official atheism, classlessness, and denial of ethnicity of the former Soviet Union, these had not been pressing issues for them. In stepping out of that orbit, however, all these issues came out of hibernation. They had considered emigration to Israel, but the mother was not Jewish and she and Nikolai would have to convert. Having settled in Montreal, Nikolai experiences painful alienation at the French public school that all immigrants must attend in Quebec. After some family deliberations, which restage their dilemmas, the boy is enrolled in a

Jewish private school where the other children are from observant Jewish families. Instruction is in English, French, and Hebrew. Again, the boy encounters problems: He is not considered Jewish (which is a matrilineal religion) and, in any case, he comes home from school with enthusiasm for religious observances that are neither understood nor followed at home. This sets off the ancient conflicts between the two sides of his family.

How can this child absorb a religion that is not truly his own within a family that has not resolved its core religious and ethnic identities? The city they live in plays out their own private divisions in a battle over the language of instruction for immigrant children. It must be French, but some families opt out by sending their children to private schools where both English and French are taught. (For historical and cultural background on this situation in Quebec, see Richler, 1992.) The family's confusion is potentially amplified by their encounter with a therapist who is also an immigrant to this city and has one foot in Christianity by upbringing and another in Judaism by adoption. Lastly, the therapist is committed to working with the family while his supervisor/consultant, a psychoanalyst and a Coptic Christian, works within an individual perspective.

These shared experiences encoded in language and in family and cultural myths shape both personal and social being. When new experiences are encountered in the form of new words, people, and places, there is the experience of strangeness. Nikolai came from a family that had not resolved important differences in their families of origin. One suspected that they left the Soviet Union partly to escape these unresolved differences. If so, their new encounters only enhanced Nikolai's confusion and mistrust.

My supervisor/consultant formulated Nikolai as a child developing the characteristics of a "borderline personality," with a profoundly disoriented core identity. I agreed that he was much like Kafka, torn between alliances and lacking in age-appropriate separation-individuation from his parents. In Kafka's case, this literally followed him to his grave: He is entombed at the Strasnice Cemetery in Prague with both his parents where the tombstone bears all three names (Pawel, 1984). If my consultant's developmental hypothesis is correct, did Nikolai's identity confusion generate his other, interpersonal conflicts? Or did his confusion have its origin in confounding experiences within his family? If the latter is correct, then those confounding experiences may continue to be generated and played out within the family, amplifying Nikolai's confusion and alienation.

THE FAMILY THERAPIST: A STRANGER IN THE FAMILY

When strangeness comes in the form of an encounter with a family therapist, several levels of strangeness may be discerned. One or more family members are behaving strangely; they may have become estranged from themselves or from other family members. The family turns to outsiders or strangers with an experience of strangeness within the familiar. In Nikolai's family, for example, his parents recognized that within their familiar experiences with each other, something different and strange was occurring. Nikolai was increasingly "estranged" from them. The family turned with this puzzle to a real stranger outside the family—a family therapist. There came, in turn, other strange aspects of their encounter with a therapist: negotiating new and difficult tasks through a newly acquired language in a cultural context that was alien and sometimes hostile to them.

A family therapist joins these strangers in search of the familiar and the reassuring. My definition of the task of family therapy is to give structure and meaning to a family's predicament. In Pirandello's play *Six Characters in Search of an Author* (1952), the characters are members of a family who come in search of the playwright (who they fear has abandoned them) to complete their story so they can find the meaning of their existence. Nikolai's story is a troubling one for me. When it was time for me to move on to another rotation in my psychiatric training, my supervisor did not agree to transfer the case to another institution. So this story (like many others) has no ending for me. At times, this family visits me in the middle of my work with other families to ask me about my commitment to what I am doing and to finish the task I started with them.

The therapist may or may not be successful in alleviating their suffering or in giving meaning to their story, but families inevitably suture the story of therapy and of the therapist into the narrative of their lives. Even the most reluctant families have stories to tell about previous encounters with therapists: the personality, the quirks, the beliefs, the perceived successes or failures of their encounter with the therapist all become part of the history and mythology of the family.

I listen to stories about other therapists with great interest, looking for clues about how my own encounter with the family may be understood. It is also worth noting because families are sometimes successful in casting a previously negative therapeutic experience in different, more positive terms. I find this exhilarating because this often demands a whole new vocabulary—"New experiences call for new descriptions" (DiNicola, 1993, p. 49). I wonder what story Nikolai's family would tell about our unfinished therapy?

THE CONSULTANT: ANOTHER STRANGER

Into this complex story, the consultant is brought in as one more stranger, creating yet another level of strangeness. What the consultant can do is open the system up for the introduction of novelty. If the family is open to new experiences, this will be incorporated into their history and their repertoire of skills in a helpful and positive way. If not, this new stranger will be dealt with in their usual way: perhaps to keep rigid boundaries, to confirm survivorhood, to legitimize and validate their pain and their reasons to prize it and retain it.

Of course, the therapist may have his or her own reasons for not changing and for experiencing the consultant as an unwelcome stranger. In fact, the consultant can be approached by the therapist for all the same reasons that families come into therapy. A common reason for a consultation is for validation for the therapy to continue. "Am I doing the right thing?" the therapist asks the consultant, meaning, "Please help me with this family!"

In order to understand this, we need an overview of what interventions family therapists have available to them. In my reading of the field (DiNicola, 1990), family therapy interventions are ways of feeding back, transmitting, or transforming the information obtained from the family and the therapeutic systems. With all their interventions, family therapists do three simple things: (1) enhance uncertainty, (2) introduce novelty, and (3) encourage diversity.

If we understand the consultant as a stranger visiting the therapeutic system (family plus therapist), an obvious role for the consultant is to *introduce novelty*. The consultant imports information from the outside. This is an active, sometimes directive role of the consultant who uses himself or herself as a source of information for this family. In the encounter with families across cultures, the consultant may be culturally different from the family, the therapist, or both. When the consultant is culturally different from the family, this gives him or her great freedom to make radical redefinitions, to bring almost anything from outside the system.

When the consultant is culturally similar to the family, the therapist, or both, but the family is situated in a new society, this gives the opportunity to *enhance uncertainty*, information already in the family or therapeutic system can be released. Past and present information is reflected back to the family, releasing it as "news." The news allows the family to experience the problem differently, making them uncertain of their solutions.

Any combination of differences or similarities among the family, therapist and consultant can be used to *encourage diversity*. Old information is perceived as new (i.e., transformed) or new information is received into the system by its members. This is beyond introducing novelty from the outside: The family members try out new definitions, roles, and behaviors for themselves. This is especially helpful for families who see new situations as threats rather than opportunities.

THE ARRIVAL OF THE CONSULTANT AT THE CASTLE OF CROSSED DESTINIES

One of the guests drew the scattered cards to himself, leaving a larger part of the table clear; but he did not gather them into a pack nor did he shuffle them; he took one card and placed it in front of himself. We all noticed the resemblance between his face and the face on the card, and we thought we understood that, with the card, he wanted to say "I" and that he was preparing to tell his story (Calvino, 1977, p. 6).

A consultant arrives at a family meeting much as the knight in Calvino's tale arrives at a castle. He/She finds people whom he/she does not know (the family) assembled by a host (the therapist). The castle (the treatment context) is to some greater or lesser extent unknown to him/her, as are the circumstances that have brought these people together (the histories of the family and of the therapeutic systems). The knight (the consultant) does not know why he/she is really there or what may emerge.

The knight must rely on language and other shared symbols to communicate and understand the stories of the host and the other guests. The possibilities would appear to be endless, but the opportunities, the time and the tools may be limited. Furthermore, the knight finds that he/she cannot speak (the consultant may not speak the same language as the family members or the therapist).

Using the analogy of the arrival of the knight at the castle with the consultant's work in a therapeutic system, three sorts of questions come to mind: (1) Where do you start? (2) How do you stay on track? (3) How can you tell where you are going (if you have not been there before)?

1. Where Do You Start?

Can the seemingly endless variety of human stories be told with a limited number of symbols or cards? If the consultant is a stranger to the world of the family, the therapist, or even the society in which the therapeutic system has been constructed, is there some set of family stories for the consultant to fall back on for guidance? Although the consultant meeting a new family across cultures may feel as though he/she is in a labyrinth of endless blind alleys or a territory without a map, he/she has personal resources to fall back on. No one starts with nothing. The consultant cannot be a blank screen, without a personal, family, and cultural history. Furthermore, there is no value-free social science, medicine or therapy. The goal is not to be neutral or unbiased, but culture-fair.

Three strategies can help to make the consultant more culture-responsive. First, by acknowledging these starting points, the consultant can proceed by the method of differences: Is this the same as or different from what I have encountered before? Second, the consultant can take the attitude of asking the family and therapeutic systems to instruct him/her on these differences and enter a cultural encounter. Third, and above all, the consultant needs to have a sense of irony about his/her own starting points and about the systems he/she is about to enter. Without irony, the consultant risks the arrogance of imperialism (my culture is dominant and superior), the naiveté of common sense which assumes universalism (everybody does supposedly basic things in more or less the same way), or the circular and impotence-inducing stance of extreme cultural relativism (every cultural group is distinct and must be understood on its terms, even by its own people).

2. How Do You Stay on Track?

If the consultant is to enter a cultural encounter, can it be only a one-way street? If one is foreign to the environment one visits, can one truly understand others without revealing something of oneself? It is actually very difficult in the face of cultural differences not to tell something of one's own story. Even at scientific meetings dealing with empirical research on ethnocultural factors in psychiatry and therapy, presenters directly discuss their own involvement in their work or at least reveal it indirectly by their choices of terms, methods, and how they evaluate their results.

My assumption is that one cannot conduct therapy as a one-way street, with the flow of information from family to therapist or consultant. One strategy is to employ the perspectives of insiders and outsiders (DiNicola, 1986). These perspectives offer a useful way to map the relationship between the therapist and the family. In turn, one can map the relationship of the family and the therapeutic system to the society at large and to the consultant. For example, an immigrant or refugee family may see themselves as outsiders to the society. However, their goals may be to integrate into their new society or to hold themselves apart. This may have implications for how they see therapists and consultants. Immigrants and refugees with an integrationist view are more likely to be accepting of authority figures and health care providers in their new society (Berry, 1992).

The therapist and the consultant can learn to use different personal qualities and identifications to adopt a role that will meet the family's needs. In different situations, we all occupy both insider and outsider roles; neither is superior, both can be useful. As an insider, the therapist or consultant takes a position of shared common experiences with the family. The advantage is that one can acknowledge what is shared and act accordingly. There is an atmosphere of working together, especially when the family and the therapist or consultant are different from the host society. This occurs for me when I am treating an Italian family or any family when we define ourselves as immigrants in Canada and discuss our reactions to Canada and other Canadians.

As outsiders, the therapist and consultant can be explicit about their differences or inequalities in relation to the family. The advantage with this perspective is that one can take either the posture of an expert or a one-down position by acting as cultural outsider. For example, while acknowledging individual experiences, one can discuss common reactions that immigrants or refugees have in coming to a new country. Alternatively, one can emphasize the uniqueness of their experience and invite family members to be experts on their own culture and their own journey of change.

Of course, taking these different perspectives enhances the experience of irony in both the individuals and the systems. By experimenting with multiple identifications, the consultant can help the therapist to expand his/her repertoire of therapeutic resources. By observing this process, the family can model the growth of the therapist by expanding their views of themselves as individuals and as a family. Over the course of therapy, by seeing many possible insider and outsider perspectives, a family may also start to play with such definitions, seeing them as more fluid and open to change.

This parallels the model of the therapist's role in the family articulated by Andolfi and his colleagues (1989). First, the identified patient is detriangulated by being taken out of the center of all interactions. This allows the therapist to occupy that role for a time. Later, as the family has new experiences through therapy, the family can give up their need to have anyone (including outsiders) play such a role.

The most intriguing example of this is Andolfi's use of the identified patient as a co-therapist. Sometimes, Andolfi works through the identified patient on a telephone or intercom while he observes the family behind a one-way mirror. This more directly challenges the distinction between being inside (healthy, part of, same as) and outside (unhealthy, separate from, different than) the family. (See Chapters 3 and 5 in this volume.)

3. How Can You Tell Where You Are Going (If You Have Not Been There Before)?

Does each of us hold enough of the cards to tell one's own story or to see it played out in the hand of another player? If you do not have a great deal of experience, how can you recognize the patterns and connect them to each other and to yourself?

I open my mouth, I try to articulate words, I grunt, this would be the moment for me to tell my tale, it is obvious that the cards of these other two are also the cards of my story, the story that has brought me here, a series of nasty encounters that is perhaps only a series of missed encounters (Calvino, 1977, p. 99).

Consultants not only hear the tales of other people, but also do their work because they have forgotten their tales, confused them in the telling, or wish to be freed of them. In other words, consultants cannot put aside their lives while working, and indeed may be consulting during a time of personal crisis and change. This may be used creatively and therapeutically for the family and the therapist. As another stranger, the consultant occupies a liminal position, at the border, on the boundary, ready to redefine himself/herself (or opt for congruence), to enter a new experience (or define himself/herself by renouncing it). This is the so-called madness of psychiatrists and the craziness of doing therapy: to explore one's own madness by immersing oneself in the madness of others, to redefine oneself by repetition and reexposure, to learn new words by attending to the lost meanings of old ones, and to find one's place by leaving it for the experience of new places.

FAMILY THERAPY AS CULTURAL TRANSLATION

My understanding of empathy and of how to conduct cross-cultural therapy is similar. We locate the other person's experience within our own. However, keeping in mind Korzybski's (1933) statement that "the map is not the territory," our resonance or empathy with another person is not the same thing as his or her own experience.

You cannot empathize with experiences totally outside your own experience. What you can do is to enlarge your repertoire so that you get better at making bridges between what is genuinely your own and other, new experiences. Andolfi does this explicitly by creating a therapeutic space wherein the therapist can reveal him/herself. In guiding the family to share its vulnerability, the therapist reveals some of his/her own vulnerability to the family (for a review of these ideas from Andolfi's earlier work, see DiNicola, 1985a).

If you do not understand another language, you must rely on translation, constantly referring to a starting point, your mother tongue. Translation across languages is notoriously difficult, hence the adage from Latin—*traduttore, traditore*: translator, traitor. There is always the danger of mistranslating or reducing the other's person words into something closer, less alien to your own language and experience. But this is a counterfeit; cultural encounters are about the alien and the strange, not glosses on the familiar. Anthropologist Mary Douglas (1975) suggests that if we do not examine what we find obvious or "self-evident," "our only recourse ... is to translate from other cultures into our own" (p. 277). The more familiar the translation is made to seem, the more we impose our provincial point of view on other cultures. "So the consequence of good translation," Douglas concludes, "is to prevent any confrontation between alien thought systems" (p. 277).

Here I will present an encounter with a family in therapy across cultures and across languages. It took place at the Institute of Family Therapy in Rome with Maurizio Andolfi in June 1987 during a Practicum in Family Therapy for an international group of family therapists. In this case, the meaning was not conveyed entirely *with* words, but perhaps *through* the words, even in spite of them. We might say that the meaning of this encounter was lost across cultures but found in translation. During the practicum in Rome when the visiting trainees became concerned that they could not understand all the interactions of the Italian families, Andolfi would say: "Forget the words, pay attention to the process."

CASE STUDY: "THE BERLIN WALL"

I am a consultant to an Italian family therapist working with a family from Rome. Both parents and the identified patient, a young woman, are in the session, accompanied by an older sister. I am presented as a Canadian of Italian origin with some knowledge of Italian, but more comfortable in English. For this reason (and for the other practicum trainees behind the mirror), we use a translator. Imagine my experience: Everything that is said has to be translated. Although I can follow both languages, I have to wait for each message to be translated before I can respond in English. The session is effectively duplicated or *double-coded*.

At first, I find the process of translation frustrating because it slows down the pace of the session. However, double-coding gives me the opportunity to process the session through two languages and two cultures. Sometimes, I do not agree with the translator's choice of words or images to convey the meaning. I find myself looking for my own versions of what I am hearing.

After a while, I take advantage of my own experience to connect with what the family is presenting to me. Although it is not immediately evident in any bizarre behavior or words from the identified patient (IP), there are many tortuous, verbally indirect interactions. I feel a split between words and feeling in this family. I understand the words but not the feelings. The overall impact is confounding, as though we were in a fog. This is a family with a schizophrenic member and it is probably not accidental that misunderstandings between words and emotions arise among them. I begin to experience a connection with the identified patient. The double-coding that is going on for me in the session with Italian and English, my need to wait and react to the translation, and at the same time my doubts about the accuracy of the translation are clues to the IP's verbal confusion and the family atmosphere of fog.

I begin to feel that she is also experiencing confusion and fog. I begin to hear her words as attempts to capture two different, perhaps incompatible worlds. Then it hits me: She is also double-coding. Her slowness, her tortuous delivery, her odd way of phrasing and rephrasing expressions are her attempts to articulate divergent experiences (inside herself or within the family). This also explains my own language discomfort. At first, I doubted my fluency in Italian because of her unusual expressions; then I doubted the translator's accuracy. However, the translator's real mistake is in trying to convey something "sensible" in English rather than allowing the patient's idiosyncracies to come through from the Italian. All of this is amplified by the fact that the other family members have also adopted a somewhat indirect and evasive manner of communicating (which was also glossed over by the translation). As Joseph Brodsky (1986), a Nobel laureate in literature who translates his own poetry from Russian into English, has stated, "Translation is the search for an equivalent, not for a substitute" (p. 140).

As to the content of the session, at the beginning there is discussion of the missing male members of the family and what this means. Since the Italian therapist is a woman, I decide to use my presence as a man to side with the baffled and ineffectual father. I want to know why he is alone with all these women and why the other men in the family (his sons) are not there with him. I consciously choose to work with splits in this family. So far, I have noticed two: the split between words and feeling (which was the original definition of schizophrenia, which in Greek means "split mind") and the split between the women and the men. And of course, all the people present have been going through a third: the split between Italian and English.

To capture these splits, I chose a concrete metaphor for this family and my experience with them—"the Berlin Wall" (this was before the fall of the Berlin Wall in 1989). The wall is an image of divisions in the family between women and men, sickness and health. As often happens in families with a schizophrenic member, there is a pseudoprotective attitude toward the schizophrenic member. Madanes (1980) calls such attitudes "protection rackets." While there is protection going on, it is aimed at the rest of the family, especially the siblings, not at the IP. This is probably why the other siblings are absent. Parents of schizophrenic patients are afraid of the unaffected siblings becoming "contaminated" by the "sick" one. Towards the end of the session, I ask, "Is the wall there to keep somebody in or to keep people out?"

Practical Guidelines for the Use of Translators (see DiNicola, 1986)

1. When using professional translators, you need to be clear about the therapeutic process and who is guiding it. The therapist or consultant should not allow the translator to take over.
2. Therapist and family members should face and speak directly to each other; the translator should sit to the side between therapist and family. There should not be direct exchanges between the family and the professional translator.
3. Firmly insist that all exchanges between therapist and the family are translated fully, without editorial comment from the professional translator.

4. When using family members as translators, you cannot keep them out of the family process. The therapist or consultant should be aware of their involvement in the process. You may or may not decide to make them part of the therapeutic process as a co-therapist, but this should be a conscious therapeutic choice, not left entirely in their hands or unknown to you.

5. When using members from the family's own community or culture, keeping them out of both the family and the therapeutic processes is very important. They are tempted to act as "interpreters" of their culture and of the family process. "Interpreting" is the role of the therapist or consultant (as in "interpreting experience"), while "translating" is a more technical linguistic task (as in "translating the words"). This may be an artificial distinction, but it is one worth keeping in mind when one is conducting therapy.

Deeper Implications of Translation in Therapy

1. The translator's experience instructs us that in the attempt to translate across cultures, many insights may be garnered. The attempt to chart a one-to-one mapping of experience between cultures reveals some features common to both worlds, but more importantly the distinct features that make a particular family's world unique. This is just as true for ethnography, where a comparative encounter between cultures teaches us something about each culture, as it is for cultural family therapy, where we meet each different family as the bearer of a unique set of personal, family, and cultural myths.

2. Translation is a metaphor for communication and for relationships. When astute observers from the social sciences and the humanities pay attention to culture, they not only deal with translation but conclude that it is fundamental to all human communication. In his seminal work on language and translation, George Steiner (1975) states:

> A human being performs an act of translation, in the full sense of the word, when receiving a speech-message from any other human being. In short: *inside or between languages, human communication equals translation* (p. 47, italics in original).

Translation is so fundamental that it has become the major metaphor for all my clinical work. Meeting strangers, whether across cultures or other differences, always involves a process of double-coding, of making comparisons, of translating. For these reasons, I concluded in my discussion of cultural family therapy (DiNicola, 1986) that:

All therapy is a form of translation—of language, of culture, and of family process (p. 189).

THE TRANSLATOR'S TURN: "I ALSO TRY TO TELL MY TALE"

In Calvino's (1977) novel, there is a chapter called, "I Also Try To Tell My Tale." Calvino the story-teller also needs to tell his story. And I believe that the tale of the therapist or the consultant is in all the stories of their families in treatment and in their selection of stories they choose to immerse themselves in. The professional handicap of the therapist or consultant is the story of their therapeutic impasses, the stories that they repeat and revisit in their efforts to master them.

As for my own tale, the key metaphor for my life and my work as a therapist is translation. For many years, my professional experience has been to translate others' experiences. Sometimes, this is quite literal, as my encounter in Rome demonstrates. But even when working in one language understood by all present, I will turn to a co-therapist or a family member and ask him/her to "translate" what someone has just said. Or, if I feel that something I have said is obscure or misunderstood, I will ask if someone is willing to translate my thoughts into different words. When a co-therapist is present, this is a useful way to expand the possibilities in a given message (enhancing uncertainty or encouraging diversity) by having my co-therapist interpret and add his or her own thoughts. Often, a family member will come to my rescue when I request an interpreter. I am especially intrigued by how well young children and other unexpected translators (such as "mute" siblings and other "uncooperative" family members) can perform this task.

This is a form of reflection within the session that I had used long before I read Anderson's (1990) interesting work with reflecting teams. I have called these reflections "translations" (in the film "Being There," a simple gardener is turned into a political phenomenon when the Washington power brokers translate his simple phrases into spin-doctored political prescriptions) or I have used terms from theater and cinema such as "asides" (when one character speaks but other characters do not hear, common in Shakespeare's plays) and "breaking roles" (when an actor turns to speak to the audience, memorably in the movie "Alfie"). Through these translations, asides, and role changes in the course of a session (which can be understood as the introduction of novelty, the enhancement of uncertainty, and the encouragement of diversity), one can also discern peering between the art and the artifice of language and therapy, the translator's turn.

CASE STUDY: "TWO OLD MEN"

A consultation from Beirut. Ottawa, early 1990s. An Arabic immigrant family from the Middle East were referred by both the court and the child welfare systems to me as a cultural consultant. Samya, a 13-year-old girl, had made inconsistent allegations about physical and sexual abuse at home and in her community. No one had been able to get at the "truth," although all the officials acknowledged cultural differences in the construction of appropriate personal and family boundaries and in the perceptions of abuse.

My contract with the referring agencies and with the family was not to discover the truth, but to help the family heal whatever trauma had occurred and the suffering they were undergoing. The family was extremely angry with the Canadian authorities over the allegations, the removal of their daughter, and her alleged promiscuity and rape while she was kept in a group home. By the time I met them, they had great difficulties accepting the good will of anyone involved in their case.

The nodal point in my work with this family occurred at the very beginning. The problem was how to begin family therapy with people who were both hurt and angry. How does one enter a family system characterized by "familism" (a family-centered way of being) enhanced by its encounter with an individualistic culture, and made rigid by accusations of child abuse?

My approach was to "go with the culture." I asked the parents what their view of the problem was and what solutions would be acceptable to them. The key question was: If a family problem occurred in Lebanon, to whom would you turn for help? Their answer was clear: to the elders of the family. Following their own preferred solution, I invited them to bring one of the child's grandparents to a session. After some discussion, we established that Samya's maternal grandfather was visiting the family in Ottawa from Beirut. I referred to this person as "the head of the family" and their "moral leader." They felt obliged to comply with my request because this view of the grandfather as a moral leader was culturally sanctioned.

I then reframed their predicament not as a psychiatric problem or a protection issue, but as a "cultural question" which the father qualified as a "human question." This is an instructive reframing because for the father, his culture is universal and therefore "human" rather than Arabic or Islamic. This is a characteristic of many traditional societies. Even after living in Canada for decades, my grandmother who is from the small mountain towns of central Italy, refers to people as *cristiani*; for her being Christian and being human is synonymous.

When the grandfather arrived at the next session, I received him with great ceremony as the head of the family. As he spoke only Arabic, we communicated through a family member, although we faced each other directly the whole time. My message was simple: He was the old man (leader) of the family and I was assigned by the courts as the old man (expert) for therapy. As one old man to another, I wanted to consult with him about how to help his children, Samya's parents. He nodded with understanding. He had a clear-headed view of the problem: "The girl's father," he said, "is trying to raise his family in Canada the way we do in Beirut." Although he was visiting Canada for the first time and had never been outside of Lebanon before, he stated with authority that "Canada was a different place with different rules."

This created a therapeutic opening for me. Surely few "Canadian" therapists would have had the knowledge or authority to make such a statement or have it accepted by the family. The old man of the family gave me the authority to help his children and grandchildren live in Canada by a new set of rules. This also offered a bridge for the intergenerational tensions felt by Samya and her siblings in trying to be dutiful traditional Arabic children at home while living in the pluralistic Canadian society. What followed was a year of family therapy. Many difficult issues were encountered, but the family was able to develop trust in the treatment team. The girl eventually returned home. By their own respective measures of child development and family life, the outcome was very successful and gratifying for both the family and the treatment team.

My own diverse experiences constantly bring me back to a common thread, to my point of origin, even as I draw farther away from it in time, in distance and in the nature of my activities. After many attempts at redefinition, many detailed investigations and attempted solutions, I recognize my own story more clearly in the stories of my families in therapy. The experiences brought to me resemble more and more a series of tarot cards, or perhaps my favorite books and films, with their familiar faces and well-known tales. "I have seen this face before, I know this story," I say to myself, only to recognize, some time later, that the family was a mirror held up to my own face.

And so Nikolai's story, "The Frozen Sea Within Us," is part of my story, about living in different, sometimes incompatible worlds. His presence in my life is a reminder of all the tasks I have left unattended and incomplete and, more painfully, of the cherished people I leave behind each time I move. It is also a personal reminder of the limits of the therapist's power and influence, a lesson reinforced by Elizur and Minuchin (1989) in their self-critical review of the real social context of family therapy.

"The Berlin Wall" case is also part of my story, representing the rigid boundaries between incompatible systems (that may collapse for a time). This case illustrates my notion of family therapy as cultural translation. "Two Old Men" is my most successful attempt to integrate two cultures in therapy and to harness the authority that a traditional society invests in the elderly to solve complex family problems in a pluralistic society. Furthermore, I was able to move beyond translation into actually being a co-editor of the family story. It represents my construction of therapy in postmodern society (see DiNicola, 1993). This means constructing a framework that allows people to live more comfortably with social contradictions and cultural diversity while respecting the private values that give meaning to their lives.

I have spent a good deal of time translating words, preoccupied with conveying experiences from one culture in the language of another. Like Calvino's silent knight communicating with tarot cards, I have been forced to expand my therapeutic resources through consultations with others. And the only available vehicle for all of this is language, which confounds and divides us like the Tower of Babel (that toppled because people could no longer understand each other's tongues) and reaches across differences as the Rosetta Stone did (that was the key to the translation of the hieroglyphics and the whole civilization of ancient Egypt). The Tower of Babel and the Rosetta Stone are two contrasting images of human communication. One is the image of the problem; the other the image of the solution. Through language, in the translation and editing of family stories, I feel that I can arrive at some provisional peace with my cross-cultural and other liminal experiences at the borders of human interactions:

> Thus I have set everything to rights. On the page, at least. Inside me, all remains as before (Calvino, 1977, p. 111).

ACKNOWLEDGMENTS

I wish to thank Maurizio Andolfi, M.D., for numerous opportunities to train and work with him over the years in several cultural contexts. I am grateful to Ellen Corin, Ph.D., an anthropologist at McGill University, for her invitation to present my family work in an anthropological perspective on which this chapter is partly based (DiNicola, 1988). Another alumnus of the Practicum with Andolfi in 1987 has been enormously helpful: John Theis, Ph.D., Chair of Psychology at the University of St. Jerome's College, who acted as a consultant throughout the therapy of the Arabic family presented here during his sabbatical at the University of Ottawa. Finally, thanks to Mumta Gautam, M.D., who was my co-therapist with the Arabic family during her Fellowship in Child Psychiatry.

REFERENCES

Anderson, T. 1990. *The Reflecting Team: Dialogues and Dialogues about the Dialogues*. Broadstairs, U.K.: Borgmann.

Andolfi, M., Angelo, C. & de Nichilo, M. 1989. *The Myth of Atlas: Families and the Therapeutic Story* (Ed. and translated by V. F. DiNicola). New York: Brunner/Mazel.

Berry, J. W. 1992. Acculturation and adaptation in a new society. *International Migration, 30*: 69–85.

Brodsky, J. 1986. The child of civilization. In *Less than One: Selected Essays*. New York: Farrar, Straus & Giroux, pp. 123–144.

Calvino, I. 1977. *The Castle of Crossed Destinies* (Translated by W. Weaver). New York: Harcourt Brace Jovanovich.

DiNicola, V. F. 1985a. The acoustic mask: A review of "Behind the Family Mask," family therapy workshop with Maurizio Andolfi, M.D., Montreal, Quebec, April 12–13, 1984. *Journal of Strategic & Systemic Therapies, 4(1)*: 74–80.

DiNicola, V. F. 1985b. Family therapy and transcultural psychiatry: An emerging synthesis. I. The conceptual basis. *Transcultural Psychiatric Research Review, 22(2)*: 81–113.

DiNicola, V. F. 1985c. Family therapy and transcultural psychiatry: An emerging synthesis. II. Portability and culture change. *Transcultural Psychiatric Research Review, 22(3)*: 151–180.

DiNicola, V. F. 1986. Beyond Babel: Family therapy as cultural translation. *International Journal of Family Psychiatry, 7(2)*: 179–191.

DiNicola, V. F. 1988. Invited lecture—Lost across cultures, found in translation: Family therapy in cultural context. *The Anthropological Perspective in Psychiatry Residency Training*, McGill University, Montreal, Quebec, February 26.

DiNicola, V. F. 1990. Family therapy: A context for child psychiatry. In J.G. Simeon and H.B. Ferguson (Eds.), *Treatment Strategies in Child and Adolescent Psychiatry.* New York: Plenum Press, pp. 199–219.

DiNicola, V. F. 1992. De l'enfant sauvage à l'enfant fou: A prospectus for transcultural child psychiatry. In N. Grizenko, L. Sayegh & P. Migneault (Eds.), *Transcultural Issues in Child Psychiatry.* Montréal: Éditions Douglas, pp. 7–53.

DiNicola, V. F. 1993. The postmodern language of therapy: At the nexus of culture and family. *Journal of Systemic Therapies, 12(1)*: 27–41.

Douglas, M. 1975. Self-evidence. In *Implicit Meanings: Essays in Anthropology.* London: Routledge & Kegan Paul, pp. 276–318.

Elizur, J. & Minuchin, S. 1989. *Institutionalizing Madness: Families, Therapy, and Society.* New York: Basic Books.

Ferreira, A. J. 1967. Psychosis and family myth. *American Journal of Psychotherapy, 21*: 186–197.

Friedman, E. H. 1982. The myth of the Shiksa. In M. McGoldrick, J. K. Pearce & J. Giordano (Eds.), *Ethnicity and Family Therapy.* New York: Guilford Press, pp. 499–526.

Ginzburg, N. 1989. *Family Sayings* (Revised from the original translation by D. M. Low). New York: Arcade/Little, Brown & Co.

Harré, R. 1979. *Social Being: A Theory for Social Psychology.* Oxford: Basil Blackwell.

Harré, R. 1984. *Personal Being: A Theory for Individual Psychology.* Cambridge, MA: Harvard University Press.

Korzybski, A. 1933. *Science and Sanity.* Chicago: International Non-Aristotelian Library.

Madanes, C. 1980. The prevention of rehospitalization of adolescents and young adults. *Family Process, 19*: 179–191.

Pawel, E. 1984. *The Nightmare of Reason: A Life of Franz Kafka.* New York: Farrar, Straus & Giroux.

Pirandello, L. 1952. Six Characters in Search of an Author. In *Naked Masks: Five Plays by Luigi Pirandello* (Ed. by E. Bentley, translated by E. Storer). New York: E.P. Dutton, pp. 211–276.

Richler, M. 1992. *Oh Canada! Oh Quebec: Requiem for a Divided Country.* Penguin: Toronto.

Simon, F. B., Stierlin, H. & Wynne, L. C. 1985. *The Language of Family Therapy: A Systemic Vocabulary and Sourcebook.* New York: Family Process Press.

Steiner, G. 1975. *After Babel: Aspects of Language and Translation.* London: Oxford University Press.

3

The Self of the Consultant: "In" or "Out"?

Elizabeth Ridgely

The use of self of the consultant varies from consultation to consultation. How the consultant chooses to participate with the professional system and the family system is the skill and art of consultation. Just as there can be no formula for therapy, there is no formula for consultation. There are, instead, ideas to be carefully placed according to the consultant's intuition and sense of the problem presented. Such ideas are at times placed in the professional system, and at other times placed in the family system. The consultant usually expands the request of the referring therapist just as the therapist expands the definition and treatment of the presenting problem. Consultations are unpredictable, startling and thereby useful to challenge therapeutic impasses. The consultant must have a new idea, a different idea and the ability to plant the idea for growth to occur.

The consultation in this chapter shows Dr. Maurizio Andolfi "marrying the symptom," which is death through starvation. To marry the symptom, one must enter the system through the identified patient, stay with the identified patient at the exclusion of others, and, in collaboration, follow the path of the symptom to other sources. The identified patient becomes the co-therapist to the consultant. While amplifying the symptom to expand it, he expands the idea of death to include other deaths. Death is redistributed from the self, to the father, to the family, to hope.

In this instance, the identified patient willingly joins the consultant in the marriage of the symptom. Together, they redirect the search for hope and resources *from* the professional system *to* within the family.

How does the consultant decide to find life from within the family rather than life from within the professionals? At what point does the consultant enlist the identified patient, bypassing the therapist? From the beginning of this consultation, Dr. Andolfi declined the invitation of the professional system to be physically included inside the consultation room. Instead, he required the family to issue the invitation for his entrance into the room by becoming more honest about their feelings and more committed to the power of the family to make substantive changes. He worked through the identified patient for the invitation.

NITA'S ANOREXIA AND THE MANY INSTITUTIONAL HANDS

The Morgan family consisted of the father, an engineer, age 53, and his wife, a homemaker, age 40, both from Bangladesh. The couple had been married for 18 years and their marriage, following the tradition and custom of their country, had been an arranged marriage. They had two children: Nita, 18 at the time of the consultation, and Lila, age 14.

The family was referred to the George Hull Centre for Children & Families in Toronto by a local hospital where Nita had been an anorexic patient for three months. She had been hospitalized because her weight had dropped to a critical level. During her stay, she was force-fed, participated in group therapy, and met individually with a psychiatrist twice weekly.

The onset of the anorexia symptoms had first been noticed when Nita was 14 and entering high school. The parents spoke about their daughter's decrease in appetite, her refusal to participate in family meals, and her reluctance to leave the home. When an increase in personal autonomy might have been expected, the opposite had occurred. At the same time, the maternal grandmother in Bangladesh became very ill. The mother and both daughters made two trips to Bangladesh to be with her.

Prior to the consultation with Dr. Andolfi, the therapist from the George Hull Centre worked with this family every other week for 15 months. After nine months, the therapist decided to see the couple alone because of the pronounced physical and emotional distance in the marriage. The father worked long hours away from home while the mother had no life of her own outside of the house. The mother complained that she could not communicate her emotions to her husband and he agreed that he was very distant from his feelings. He seemed more available and accessible to his daughters. Consequently, there was a sense that the couple would continue to live together but remain distant. Three years previously, the couple had stopped sharing the same bed and at the time of the consultation they had been in separate bedrooms for three months.

The therapist's impression was that Nita was very sensitive to this distance in her parent's marriage and to the sadness in each of her parents. He felt that Nita's worries about her parents interfered with her desire to fully participate in her own life. The anorexia slowed her development and resulted in mutual protectiveness between Nita's symptoms and parental concern about their own problems. In the work with the couple, the therapist hoped to help them improve their relationship, thus giving both daughters the message that they need not worry about their parents.

The work with the couple was difficult. The wife seemed to agree with the direction of therapy but was reluctant to challenge her husband. The husband did not seem accessible to his wife or to the therapist. At the same time, the individual therapist was also discouraged by the lack of change in the girl and the recurrence of her symptom. Therefore, in the context of this therapeutic impasse and the persistence of the anorexic symptoms in Nita, Dr. Andolfi was requested to provide a consultation.

THE CONSULTATION: WHERE TO SEEK THERAPEUTIC RESOURCES

The family therapist and Nita's individual therapist felt stuck and thought it would be useful to have the different professionals who were involved around the question of re-hospitalization of Nita come together to reach some consensus about the therapeutic direction. The family members readily accepted the idea of a consultation, as did the family doctor, the referring psychiatrist and the team from the hospital. This was to be a systemic consultation given the number of different institutional hands that at different points had tried to intervene to help Nita's family.

To our dismay, Dr. Andolfi's first question was, "Why should I see this family? To be defeated like all the other professionals? This family has no hope for change. The professionals have no hope for change. So why should I have hope for change when there is no hope?"

Dr. Andolfi's first question addressed the function of consultation where all other experts had seemingly failed. The risk was apparent of looking for hope from the outside, through new attempts by the helping system which would continue to place the burden of change on the outside system.

Thus, the consultation began with a discussion about hope for change in the face of no change. The impasse was redefined as one of loss of hope, both within the family system and within the larger therapeutic system. Dr. Andolfi's view was that the consultation would have value only if the family could provide some "evidence" of hope, which meant that the family needed to become a protagonist and not a client waiting for new institutional propositions. Otherwise, the consultation would only bring about a new impasse that would include the consultant.

Rather than entering the therapeutic system with the expectation of magic or failure, the consultant went behind the one-way mirror while the two therapists brought the following message to the family.

Therapist: Since Bangladesh has failed and since Toronto has failed in terms of being helpful to you as a family with problems, Dr. Andolfi wonders how Rome, how Italy, could possibly be helpful this morning?

Mother: (*with fearful recognition*) What do you mean failed?

Therapist: Failed in the sense that nothing has changed.

Mother: It is not failure yet.

Therapist: Not failed, I think, in the sense that nothing has changed. Nita, you were in the hospital, your weight was way down, you weren't eating, and the family was concerned about that.

Individual Therapist: As a team, we also feel a sense of failing. And this is why we suggested, when we knew Dr. Andolfi was coming, that you might meet him.

Father: (*very detached*) After being in hospital, and out of hospital, everything has changed, except she is not eating as much as she is supposed to do.

Therapist: Isn't that why you came?

The beginning of the session, with the consultant behind the mirror, was crucial to setting the stage for the consultation. From the start, the consultant put sufficient distance between himself and the "failure" so that there was an opportunity for new possibilities to arise. Had he been working directly with the failed family system and the failed therapeutic system, he would have been working in omnipotent isolation. With the distance established and with a few colleagues in the observation room, the consultant was not isolated and was free to be interested in the impasse.

The effect of putting sufficient distance between the consultant and the failure allowed the consultant to freely observe the emotional reactions and the relational connections between the failures of Bangladesh and those of Toronto. It provided an opportunity for vigilance on the part of the consultant in recognizing any sign of life that could appear as a result of this first therapeutic provocation.

Having challenged the family for the first time (has Bangladesh failed?), Dr. Andolfi began a more delicate operation: the construction of a therapeutic alliance with the identified patient; at first indirectly, and then, more and more explicitly.

Andolfi: (*to the therapist by telephone from the observation room, firmly and warmly*) Go close to the girl and say, "You know what Dr. Andolfi means, with no hope in Bangladesh and Toronto." No explanation and then you sit.

Therapist: (*standing in front of Nita*) Nita, that was Dr. Andolfi, and he wanted me to convey the message that you know what he means when he says there has been no hope in Bangladesh and no hope in Toronto either.

The mother's response was that she felt there was hope. After both therapists reiterated that there was no hope, Dr. Andolfi suggested that neither therapist should speak for five minutes.

During the awkward silence from the therapists, the identified patient began to speak to her father.

Nita: (*Nita acknowledges the consultant's position*) I don't care and I don't listen to anybody else whoever they are. I just do what I want to do. So he is probably right in saying that nothing will change.

Father: Well, how do you expect to have a normal health, do you want to have a normal health?

As the father protests with the daughter about her "health," the consultant intervenes again, saying to the therapist:

Andolfi: Just say to the father, your talking is the biggest sign of no hope. Can you try to keep three minutes in silence and to feel the "death" in this family? Then you go and sit and say nothing.

THE SEARCH FOR A CO-THERAPIST IN THE FAMILY

The silence was deafening. It had a strength and a dignity that belonged to the family. It was seen as the first "Bangladesh" sign in the session. The anxiety seemed to belong to the observers. The fact that the silence was respected, even by the father, was a positive sign. If the family were connected with aspects of death, perhaps they would be able to rediscover some resources of life, to discover the impasse between life and death. From the beginning, the symptom of anorexia became the symbol of lack of hope, while containing the hope that the girl, by dying, would push the "dead" family to life.

It was the silence, laden with meaning for the family, that helped the consultant to break away from normal professional alliances and to nominate Nita for the function and role of co-therapist. By telephone, the consultant talked directly to Nita from the observation room.

Andolfi: Do you think Daddy is able to feel the death of the family now?
Nita: (*cooperatively*) I don't know.
Andolfi: (*with caring and softness*) Can you try to check, because if Daddy can experience the death of the family, probably there is some hope, but if he cannot do that, I think it doesn't make any sense that I join you. Can you try to check with him if he is experiencing the death and the failure of this family.

This contact through the telephone, through sound but not sight, became a very powerful co-therapy relationship over the next hour. Nita increasingly leaned against the wall, smiling, while talking to Dr. Andolfi—the unseen but gently voiced Dr. Andolfi.

Eventually, Nita elicited a long response from her father in which he denied his feelings and spoke of anorexia. His comments did not make contact with self or others. The consultant called again.

Andolfi: (*softly and reassuringly*) Nita, can you try to help me. Can you just look at your father in the eyes and ask him this question: Did you die first as a husband or as a father? Try to do it in a way to show you really would like an answer from the heart, not an answer from the head, and you know about the difference between heart and head very well. Can you try to ask him just facing him, did you die first as a husband or as a father? And then just wait for the answer, facing him. Good luck.
Nita: (*after a long internal struggle*) Daddy, do you feel that you died first as a husband or as a father?
Father: Say that again.

The father listened intently, putting on his glasses as if to read accurately a painful and important question. For the first time in the session, the father seemed to be more personally involved.

Nita: Did you die first as a husband or as a father?
Father: I've never died.
Nita: You mean the only way you would feel a sense of loss is if there was a death.
Father: Yes, you are certainly right.

At this point the co-therapy has become so strong that the identified patient now asks her own questions. Dr. Andolfi called again.

Andolfi: Hello, Nita, you did very well. Do you think you reached his heart or not?
Nita: It is very hard to do.
Andolfi: It is very hard to reach his heart? Or it is very difficult for you?
Nita: For anybody.

The consultant asked Nita to pose the same question to her mother. She did not get much response from her mother and he asked her to move the parents together and to ask them about the meaning of death in their lives.

Andolfi: Can you ask Mommy the same question to see if Mommy may be more available to open the heart? As soon as you feel that there is some hope in your family, call me and I will come in, but don't call me if you feel there is no hope. Do you understand me? There is some hope if your parents can experience some death that is not your dying day after day, but some previous death or some person that was very important in this family or some death in the marriage, some other death than you, because right now you are the only death in the family and I think that this is fake. So try to help me to look for other graves, okay? And call me only if you feel there is hope in their hearts. Good luck.

Dr. Andolfi had responded to Nita by moving to expand the problem from the father to include the mother, treating the "patient" by training the "co-therapist."

Nita: (*to both parents*) What has been the most important death in your life? Before I became caught up in this anorexia?
Father: I know in my case, my parents.

With the establishing of these other losses, Andolfi moves to the meanings of the losses and how the losses affect the impasse.

Andolfi: Ask what he lost, not just the number of graves. I need to know what he lost most because his heart is still locked and your anorexia holds the key to his heart. You know that, so use the key on both of them. If you don't open their hearts there is no hope for therapy. So try to get to the feelings of what they lost. Okay? You know about dying more than anybody else in this family, so try hard.

Nita: What is it you lost, due to the death of your parents? You lost your parents, but what inside you did you lose?

Father: Well I lost that belonging, the relationship between parents and son. The loving, the care they used to give me, and the closeness I had with them.

Nita: And then it died when they did. So you're saying you don't feel close to your parents anymore, even though they are dead. Because they are dead, you can't feel close to them anymore.

Nita: (*to mother*) And you?

Mother: No, I didn't feel that way.

Nita: What is it? Your mother died recently.

Mother: (*very moved, starts crying*) But because I didn't see her, I didn't feel she was dead, you know.

At the time of her grandmother's death, Nita had been hospitalized because of suicidal thoughts, and her mother had remained in Toronto with her instead of returning to Bangladesh to see her dead mother.

Nita: She is still close to you.

Mother: Yes.

Nita: She is dead.

Nita has successfully included other deaths in the family to produce a more complex impasse. With her mother in tears, Nita continued with questions about her own death.

Nita: So if I died, you would feel the same way?

Father: I don't know. It's a different situation. It would be hard. I don't know the situation.

Following Nita's touching death directly, the consultant called her to decide whether or not there was enough hope. They planned together an intervention to discover more about the impasse and its connection to Bangladesh.

Andolfi: Can you help me more? This is now the most difficult part of the story. Is anybody from Bangladesh in town who can unlock

Daddy's and Mommy's hearts, some people who are more grown up than you? Now I have an idea. If you think it might be useful, okay, otherwise we won't do it. The idea is that we meet after lunch again, and this time I come in, but your parents have to bring in someone from Bangladesh who knew their life over there.

I think you are too much the Bangladesh connection for them. You know, you create too many roles. Sometimes when you talk, you talk like you are 73 years old, you talk like a grandparent. You act, you feel, like a grandparent, and I think this is nice but totally wrong. So, probably we need more people from Bangladesh, more grown up, and people your parents trust very well, maybe just one for each.

The diversion, by the symptomatic child, of the parents from the deaths of their parents places her into a grandmotherly role in which she is older, and wiser and acts to protect her adult children. With this in mind, the symptom takes on new meaning and the session ends with the added expansion of the significance of the symptom.

Andolfi: Now, at the same time, when you have lunch, I would like you to try to eat thinking that you are 18.

Nita: (*with laughter*) Not as a grandparent or anything.

Andolfi: Not as a grandparent, you know, grandparents have problems with their teeth, with digestion, you know, grandparents sometimes don't even eat. Because they don't need much, they are wise, they don't need much food to grow, they are already grown up okay. So eat as an 18-year-old Bangladesh-Canadian girl. Okay?

Nita: Okay.

Andolfi: And try to think that your sister is your sister, because I am not sure that you think there is a sister in this room. (*The sister had been sitting quietly but expressed anger about being left out. Initially, she didn't want to return to the afternoon meeting.*)

Nita: What do you think I treat her as?

Andolfi: You treat her like a little pet. Or like she is your child.

Nita: (*laughing with pleasure*) Exactly.

Andolfi: Exactly. All the time. But you know, if she is your child, then, of course, you don't need to have your own children, later on in your life.

Andolfi: So, try to say most of the things we are discussing now to your parents, and see if they want to do something and come back at 2:30. If you feel that they resist too much, just forget it, but try your best. Because you have a lot of tricks.

Nita presented the afternoon session clearly and firmly to her parents. Together with her mother, both the father and the sister are convinced to return in the afternoon with two friends of the family. The parents came alive as they used the telephone to invite their friends, speaking in Bengali. There was much hugging and kissing and vitality as they prepared to leave for lunch. The father telephoned to the observation room to "confirm" with Dr. Andolfi that they will return at 2:30.

BANGLADESH ALIVE

The family came back after lunch with two friends, a husband and wife from Bangladesh, who were also godparents to Nita. Dr. Andolfi joined the session. The busy atmosphere in which the morning had ended continued into the afternoon and the session became a very interesting meeting about memories, Bangladesh customs, and the difficult integration into North American life. But the climate was a climate of happiness and life. Nita participated but was replaced by the visiting couple as "consultant to the consultant" in relation to the family.

The friends talked about the culture of the family, about differences and similarities between the two families: the arranged marriages, the difference between the men in showing their feelings, the difference between the women in asking for help from the children, expressions of affect among family members and the deaths in each family. Throughout the session, both girls participated in the history-taking and punctuation of significant events.

"More Bangladesh" not only lightened Nita in her central role as designated patient, but also changed the equilibrium in the family. Up to that moment, just like Nita, the many professionals had substituted themselves for Bangladesh, as if the story and the transcultural evolution of the family did not have weight or value in the present, blurred so much by the North American anorexia of Nita.

In the presence of their friends, the conversation focused on migrating from one country to another, what you leave behind, what you gain. The family's perception of itself changed from being a family with losses to one with life in a new country.

The afternoon gave the opportunity to explore, beyond the anorexia, other aspects on which the family could reflect. The meeting, furthermore, gave the husband and the wife a new curiosity with regard to their marriage; in other words, whether this marriage needed to remain an arranged marriage or could they now choose each other.

The role of the mother in the family became more evident. She feared getting sick and the whole family disintegrating. This redistribution of health and sickness in the system was crucial. Through many avenues, the relationship of the parents with their friends and their common experiences in North America were examined. The youngest girl was benevolently depicted as a mischievous daughter, a little bit delinquent, thereby redistributing symptoms and health in the younger generation.

The naval career of the father was explored, which helped to explain his rigidity and difficulties in being in touch with his feelings of sadness and loss. Growth and more contact between the two families was encouraged as this would help to keep Bangladesh alive as a resource, even in Canada. At the end of the afternoon, the family came to see itself not as a family of an anorexic, but as a family with many interesting relationships, more complex than before and with an ability to laugh. Above all, they rediscovered themselves as a family alive and full of resources.

The family was reluctant to leave. All the members congregated around the cafeteria in the Centre, engaging the therapists in light conversation. It was decided then to invite them for the rest of the discussion with the team and participants of the seminar. The friends went away but the family remained for more than an hour until the end of the seminar. They seemed relaxed, the father more active and free in answering questions around his "naval syndrome," his rigidity, thereby showing through action his capacity to risk. The mother experienced the respect and concern of the group in relation to her recent mourning, which she had up to then kept buried so as not to worsen Nita's health or add to her own sadness.

A YEAR LATER

The family was followed up a year later by the family therapist and the individual therapist. During the intervening months, the family members had reassured the team at the George Hull Centre that things had improved and that they did not need to continue in therapy. They agreed to meet with the therapist and with Dr. Andolfi, but more to satisfy the professionals' curiosity and their need to follow up on the effects of the consultation than for any other reason.

Nita, by then, had finished high school and was enrolled at a university. The anorexia had disappeared. The mother worked outside of the home with a great deal of satisfaction. Both husband and wife considered the marriage to have improved. The father still exhibited some form of the "naval syndrome," but was less of an "admiral" and more of a person. The younger daughter was doing much better in school and was actively involved in sports.

The most dramatic effect of the consultation was that it had ended the therapy. There are a number of ways to interpret this result. One is that during the period of therapy the family had learned many things concerning themselves and that, as a cumulative effect over time, they could now experiment by themselves without outside help.

The consultant's redefinition of the problem, "the family needs to find more Bangladesh," represented a catalyst to break away and separate from the therapeutic system. It helped to open up possibilities for more activity by the family in the community, while renewing their interest in their own story (memories, relatives, friends, and losses).

Therefore, the situation shifted from a psychiatric problem to a developmental cultural crisis in the family. When Dr. Andolfi suggested to Nita that she eat like a Bangladesh-Canadian girl of 18, he was not attempting to give her a prescription regarding food nor to look for a diagnostic clue regarding her body. He used the metaphor of the food to give her back her double cultural membership and her capacity to live as an 18-year-old, previously lost in her efforts to control or guard over the happiness/sadness of the family. It appeared from Nita's smiles during the follow up that she was able to understand the message.

THREE YEARS LATER

Three years later and on the occasion of another workshop at the George Hull Centre, Dr. Andolfi telephoned the Morgan family. He spoke briefly to everyone. It seemed to him as if he were resuming a conversation interrupted two weeks ago.

Nita was engaged to a Japanese fellow student and still at the university. The father's good sense of humor was more available to the family. Lila was continuing to do well at high school. The mother was pleased to be remembered by Dr. Andolfi and invited him to a "Bangladesh" dinner during his next visit to Toronto. For the consultant, the invitation to dinner was tangible proof that the family had moved on, that the process of change had begun where therapy ended. The family did not need a therapist to stay on as a witness to change.

CONCLUSION

The consultation was particularly useful because it supported the family in its natural infrastructure as opposed to keeping it within the professional system. The definition of the problem as "not enough Bangladesh" paradoxically opened the door to all sorts of "Canadian" activity. In essence, the involvement with Bangladesh freed the family for Canadian involvement.

Through the combined eyes of the consultant and the identified patient, it became possible to follow other directions to understand the impasse better. The consultant shared the "homeostatic chair" with the identified patient (Andolfi, Angelo, Menghi & Nicolo-Corigliano, 1983). Through her participation, the identified patient, who had been trying for so long to treat the family while helping the family to stay the same, became the co-therapist and the guide for the therapist to other areas in other generations. In this family, Nita had become the grandmother, representing all the losses left behind in Bangladesh.

By following the symbolism of the symptom, it was possible to explore other areas of sadness in the family. The father's loss of his parents and his subsequent loss of a "feeling of belonging" could be examined, as well as the mother's losses, especially of her mother two months previously—a fresh grave that had remained unexplored.

The invitation of Nita becoming a co-therapist was followed by the invitation to the friends, who shared the same culture and heritage, to become consultants to the consultant. This was an invitation to consult on issues of the past and issues of transformation from Bangladesh to Bangladesh-Canada. The effect of the second consultation from the friends was rich and informing for the Italian consultant and the Canadian therapist as it described the ritual of arranged marriages, the culture's definition of masculinity and femininity, gender roles, and the adaptability of this particular family to a new culture. Thus, the consultations evolved from marrying the symptom and entering the family to a curiosity about and a validation of the existing resources of the family through the exploration of cultural issues.

As in the consultation, while Dr. Andolfi was "out" (behind the mirror), he was "in" the family through Nita. And when he was "in" (in the room), he was "out" as the friends became more important than the professionals. More Bangladesh brought him "in" and simultaneously kept him, and subsequently all of us, "out."

ACKNOWLEDGMENTS

Acknowledgment to Paul Regan, M.S.W., and Martha Howard, M.S.W., of the George Hull Centre, Toronto, for their input.

REFERENCE

Andolfi, M., Angelo, C., Menghi, P. & Nicolo-Corigliano, A. M. (1983). *Behind the Family Mask*. New York: Brunner/Mazel.

4

The Inner Life of the Consultant

Carl Whitaker and Joseph Simons

I feel that to be invited, as a consultant, into the relationship that exists between the therapist and the family is a high compliment and distinct honor. It is an experience for me like being invited to review an autobiography—to be asked to look at the most personal parts of a therapist and his or her relationship with the client family. The intimacy of the situation, of being made a part, at least temporarily, of this very special relationship, leads me to feel that I am like a father who comes home after a day at work and is invited by the mother (the therapist) to talk in front of the children (the clients) about the problems that have occurred during the day.

As the process of consultation begins to unfold, I am always filled with a sense of excitement as I become aware of the needs and expectations of the therapeutic family: the needs of the "mother" (for support or to find a way out of a confusing therapeutic morass), and the expectations of the "children," who may be looking to the consultant as the outsider, the expert, the "father," to bring about something magical.

I am also deeply aware of the need to search for those fragments of the therapist's and clients' past experiences that have not yet been revealed or assimilated into the therapy. As these experiences are brought into the light of our awareness, they cast their shadows upon what is being said and felt in the therapy. These shadows, which are a part of the unacknowledged cultural and family-history context, lend depth and meaning to the therapy—as though we change a photograph into a hologram, making what was only a representation of perspective into a truly three-dimensional experience. And, of course, I bring my own "context-shadows" of past experience to the therapy so that the consultation becomes, for me, an opportunity to discover new parts of myself.

I feel that it is important to understand that when I do a consultation I am a consultant to the relationship between the therapist and the family, rather than simply a consultant to either the therapist or the clients alone. When this is the case, what happens in actual practice is that the consultant treats the entire therapeutic family, which includes both the therapist and the clients. This may not be clear to either the therapist or the clients—and it doesn't really need to be. It may seem to everyone present that the consultant is working on one thing, when in fact something quite different is occurring.

For example, I was once asked to do a consultation for a resident of mine who was working with a schizophrenic and family. Very quickly it was clear to me that the father of the family was a very powerful and dictatorial figure who was completely taking over the therapy, telling the therapist how to operate. So I spent the entire hour talking to the father about his mother and father, and brother and sister, and grandmother and grandfather, in such a way that by the end of the session he was completely impotent—or at least was demoted from "father" of the therapist to "child" of the therapist. This also changed his position with his wife and children from a kind of head-of-the-family-bully to just another family member who could no longer dominate and dictate either the course of the therapy or the family process. It may have seemed that I was working with the father, but in reality I was treating the therapeutic relationship, changing the perspectives and positions of everyone there.

The other part of all this change has to do with the way the talk of the father's family of origin brought in the "context-shadows" I mentioned above. I expect that after this consultation the father was more real to everyone in his family. He was no longer just a representation—an authority figure—but much more of a three-dimensional person.

At the beginning of a consultation, after hearing what the therapist has to say, I usually ask the family members to describe their experience of the therapist and the therapy. Meanwhile, internally, I am asking myself a number of questions about the family, about the therapist, and about myself.

About the family, I may be wondering whether it is operating as a whole or as fragments; whether it is truly invested in making an effort to change, or if the family members are waiting for the therapist (or the consultant) to perform some liberating magic for them. I try to assess the level of stress the family is under and whether we (the therapist and I) can safely raise that level.

In regard to the therapist, I am interested in who he or she is as a colleague, and how I can interact with him or her in the midst of this dance with the family. Furthermore, I want to find out how much control the therapist has over the family and what kind of "mother" he or she is. Is the therapist's parenting style overprotective, judgmental, or rather like a foster or adoptive mother? The questions I ask the therapist in the presence of the clients are often intended to make him or her into a patient of sorts. I may ask, "Do you have any idea whether the way you talk about this father is connected with your life?" or "Can you tell me what this family means to you after hours? Have you dreamt about them? Do you think about their next appointment? Or do you leave them where they belong, in the office?" In certain situations I may escalate my questions a little bit and ask, "What do you think you're leaving out in order to protect this family from me?" I want the therapist to be a patient in the sense that he or she must assess his or her degree of personal commitment to the therapy; must become aware—and make me aware—of his or her distance from the family.

The questions I ask myself are crucial to my success as a consultant. ("How invested am I in this process? What is my level of tension? Am I free enough from what is happening here and within myself to be authentic? What are the effects of the 'shadows' of my past that I bring to this experience?"). The essential quality I am striving for with these internal questions, with the kinds of questions I ask out loud, and with the movements I make with the therapeutic family is to increase the level of creativity in the therapeutic system. And I feel that in order to be truly creative I must concentrate my efforts on being as spontaneous and free-associative as possible.

The most essential quality of the consultations I do is embodied in the condition that I have an unusual amount of freedom to be more of myself than is possible in any other place—either presenting to an audience or actually being the therapist. A therapist must wear multiple hats: administrator, process organizer, reempowerer of the client family, watchdog of the self (being suspicious of and vigilant about his or her role in the therapeutic process), and many other roles as well. As the consultant, on the other hand, I have the freedom and willingness to be less suspicious of myself and more and more open to simply "going with the flow" of things. I think I have become more ready to assume a kind of a stance similar to that of an artist with a blank canvas, and have become more willing to take hold of a fragment of the process and go where it seems to want to go—and to let the therapist carry all the roles that create borders around the therapeutic experience. It is this attitude or approach to consultation that can allow the consultant to have greater access to his or her own authenticity.

However, to the extent that the consultant assumes this very creative, free-associative approach to the process, it becomes very difficult—if not impossible—to assume any kind of objective or "meta" position. Simply because the process is so creative, it's often below the level of awareness. Generally speaking, the more spontaneous I become, the less likely I am to be aware of the whole of the process—the less likely it is that I can be able to be outside looking in on the process. Under those circumstances I am just inside operating, unaware of the larger picture. On the other hand, there is a simultaneous sharpening of my *self*-awareness. As a result of this I am frequently—and wonderfully—surprised by the pieces of me that I discover during the process of the consultation.

In fact, it is the discovery, or rediscovery, of myself in the consultation process that often has the most powerful effect on the therapeutic family. What I am doing at times in consultations is using my personal life and experiences to bring reality into the consultation and into what is happening between the patient family and the therapist. I am enacting the part that the family members represent in *my* family, presenting the *me* that is the family's father or grandfather or mother or teenager— or whoever. I am enacting, in effect, my own internalization of each of these roles so that I begin the process of bringing healing reality into the consultation.

For example, I once did a consultation with a therapist who was working with a Peruvian couple. The couple was trying to decide whether they should stay married or get a divorce. The wife was complaining about her husband's lack of accessibility. I began by asking the husband about himself and his father, and from there I started to get in touch with my own experiences of depression and suicidal feelings— the feelings of worthlessness and impotence that I had had in my life. This became a catalyst for the father to begin to experience and talk about his feelings of worthlessness.

The father and I, by speaking about ourselves, were speaking to each other—through the vehicles of ourselves. It was the realness of my self and my passionate feelings about my experiences that brought reality into the consultation for the father. My focus at such times is not on caring about the family members, but on caring about myself, in their presence. What makes the experience real for them is that I am talking about my life. If I am talking to clients about their life (as a family or as individuals) then I am just manipulating them.

Another way in which this focusing away from the family can work is illustrated by a consultation I did for a woman therapist in Italy who had been working with a family and felt she needed help. During the consultation, she talked to me about the family and what they were dealing with, and I talked to her about what she was talking about—then she talked to me, and so on. And that is all we did for the entire hour of the consultation. We talked about our lives as therapists and consultants, about her struggles with being useful to the family, and about my perceptions of how she could be more valuable to them. Neither of us spoke or looked at the family. We never got out of the meta-role and never dipped into their lives at all. And afterward, I felt that had been one of the most useful consultations I had ever done.

In summary then, the consultation experience is an exciting and creative process that provides the consultant with an opportunity to be more of him or herself than is possible for a therapist (who is working to be the "responsible foster parent"). The consultant comes into the therapeutic family as a visitor—a guest who arrives and will stay for only a short time, and who knows that by being aware of who he or she is while visiting, and that by talking creatively about the house and everyone's place in it (without actually moving any furniture or rearranging any of the pictures on the walls) that changes will be set in motion, and that the therapist is likely as a result to have greater therapeutic leverage than before the visit began.

PART II

ELICITING RESOURCES
FROM THE CLIENTS'
SYSTEM

5

The Child as Consultant

Maurizio Andolfi

PREMISE

The therapist, as enabler, facilitator, and curious anthropologist, needs to be creative, metaphorical, flexible, and playful in working within a multigenerational framework. This chapter explores the utilization of the child as the consultant to the family. This method enhances information gathering, creativity, flexibility, and playfulness, with the ultimate goal of aiding families in their search for competence and health. The therapist's position in the trigenerational family, as the child's "colleague," creates systemic ripples. By recruiting the child as consultant, the therapist joins forces with the evolutionary desire for health in the younger generation.

The ideological position of embracing the symptomatic child as the channel to reach the existential and developmental dilemmas of the family is a reformulation of our previous work (see Andolfi, Angelo, Menghi, & Nicolo-Corigliano, 1985; Andolfi, Angelo, & de Nichilo, 1989). We described the importance of considering the child as the *point of entry* into the family system. Then we hypothesized that the child could be the *regulator of the entire therapeutic process*: a kind of Ariadne thread to help the therapist enter the family labyrinth while being connected to the family, but also equipped with a way out of the family. We have always worked with the identified patient as the key to enter the family, but, through many years of clinical work, we have reformulated our philosophical position. The following will explain this reformulation as three phases in the development of our work with the identified patient: Signal Phase, Functional Phase, and Evolutionary Phase.

The Signal Phase

The research for relational significance of inexplicable problems has characterized the first period of our clinical work with families (Andolfi, 1979). We hypothesized that the child "is not the problem," but rather the alarm signal of a deep uneasiness in each member of the family that has increased over time. The child's symptoms lessens the tensions of the family members by refocusing concern on the problematic child versus an unhappy marriage, dissatisfaction with a career, or identity problem developed in the family of origin. So we asked ourselves: "what does the child signal in this situation and to whom does the child send the message?"

The first effect of this idea of signaling was to shift the significance of the symptoms, as perceived by my colleagues and myself. This initial effect was not experienced by the child or family, but it influenced our way of thinking. At this point, we had to search for other relevance beside the most obvious, which is: problem = patient. This research led us to interesting hypotheses that were not always well accepted by the family, who often felt threatened by this reframing of the problem. This research was even less accepted by psychiatric institutions, where the child was treated as a patient (at significant costs).

Beyond the predictable difficulties mentioned above, what are the major limitations of this thought about signaling? First of all, the child's symptom was not fully considered in terms of its specificity. There was very little difference ascribed to various symptoms, whether a child displayed a phobia, enuresis, eating disorder, or violent behavior. We focused on the intensity of the signal more than its intrinsic qualities, considering that the signal intensity was sufficient to explain its urgency rather than looking at the type of suffering and persistence of certain symptoms.

All the symptoms seemed to be part of the same unspecified problem, leaving something ambiguous to search for. Often families resisted the therapist's hypotheses because they felt attacked and seemed to ask themselves: "What is the therapist looking for? We came because of the child and instead he/she turns the problem around, looking for something else to cure our child." The more these families resisted the therapists' ideas, the more we explained our ideas and asked their cooperation so that our hypotheses became something absolute. I remember times when we would ask the family: "What if the child's problem would not exist?" And they would answer: "There is no other problem." Since we saw problems as signals, we tried to make them admit that there were other problems. Anyhow, I think that this "problem hunt" proved to be a limitation in those days. Even worse, when the child felt that the harmony in the family was attacked, he/she developed a very healthy strategy by intensifying the symptom. Thus, the patient would successfully absorb the attention while we attempted to enlarge the view and reframe the problem as belonging to the whole family.

The Functional Phase

The second phase was characterized by the study of the child's symptoms in terms of functionalism. Considering each member's *function* as the special point where the individual and the system connect, we began to pay greater attention to the intricate interaction between the tasks and the role that the family system assigns to its members. I spent several years with my group researching family typologies based on the network of functional performances of family members. Departing from Minuchin's theory of differences between enmeshed and disengaged families, we distinguished families according to temporal aspects, based on the persistence of symptoms over time. We distinguished between FAMILY AT RISK and FAMILY DESIGNATED RIGID along the dimensions of more or less flexibility of family functions and change. In the book, *Behind the Family Mask* (1983), we mentioned, for example, that one way for the family to react to the possibility of change, which seems to be traumatic to the whole system, is for one of its members, especially the child, to assimilate stress by expressing symptomatology.

The symptomatic behavior of the chosen member serves to distract the attention away from the group at a risky moment for the stability of the whole group. The designated patient has the temporary function of maintaining the equilibrium of the system, as well as fulfilling other functions such as the decision maker, the nurture provider, the wise parent, the switchboard of family communications, etc. However, if this reversible and temporary mechanism of designation does not successfully secure the family stability, it runs the risk of becoming a rigid mechanism, whereby the designated patient's and the family members' identity become progressively replaced by repetitive functions, mostly predictable and automatic. The rigidity of functions (the one who is sick, healthy, detached, overinvolved, etc.) confirms the family in its unchangeable solution.

The Third Phase: Back to Evolution

My stance as a therapist has undergone profound changes since I adopted an evolutionary theory. This approach follows a humanistic-experiential methodology similar to the one described by Whitaker & Keith (1981). The central idea is to offer families in therapy a space where they can circumscribe their creative world and a chance to rejuvenate processes of choice, which seem to have stopped with the disease of one of its members. Let me explain how our way of thinking has further developed by using a clinical image.

John, a 10-year-old child, has been presenting encopretic behavior for the past year. The parents bring their child to therapy and describe his difficulties. Initially, the child displays disinterest in the therapeutic endeavor because the whole thing makes him uneasy, and he prefers to think that the search for solutions concerns the adults and not him. What does it mean if we assume that the family did not bring the child to therapy, but the child brought the family to us? Is this only a change of strategy to involve the family in therapy or a shift in ideology?

We prefer the second thesis, because it is a workable construction of the therapeutic encounter. If the child brings the family, it's the child that gives us indications and guides us into the intricacies of his family world. Undoubtedly, the first reaction we noticed was surprise and curiosity by the child: "How is it possible that I brought the family? Me, who did not want to come, who felt forced and ashamed, who came only to make them happy." The parents themselves similarly expressed disbelief: "How is it possible that a child who 'craps' in his pants at age 10 brings us, when we brought the child after consulting with our pediatrician?" But, these questions pose an intense dilemma regarding expectations and motivations for the therapy.

If John brings the family to therapy, perhaps it can be an occasion for all of them to grow, rather than being only a "fixing up symptoms" operation. The therapy can be an occasion to review emotional positions and basic assumptions rooted in the family, and it's not the place to feel blamed for the child's symptoms. Instead of facing the symptoms with a sense of guilt and reciprocal accusations, they became an evolutionary incident that can have potential for enormous vitality, not only for the child, but through the child to the whole family.

I believe that this belief system embraces and transmits strong moral convictions, being able to oppose the most technical and contingent idea that our work only concerns pathology. The child becomes a fundamental passageway in the evolutionary pathway from pathology to health. Thus, the therapeutic system is formed by a professional therapist and a therapist of the family, who share the difficulties of the therapy.

So we have to look for developmental clues in order to give a relational meaning to John's crap. In this case, John's crapping in his pants was the first link between family and therapist. Therefore, we have to thank the crap for creating the opportunity to meet. If John's poop was a very big gift for his parents when he was a small child, maybe it is another gift at a different developmental stage. Perhaps it is now the "glue" that holds together a marriage that would otherwise fall apart. If the therapist is able to play with the images of the poop-glue, he/she could help the parents reconnect without John being pushed in the middle of their differences. Thus, even a strange, regressive behavior can become an opportunity for new considerations around issues of intimacy and separation.

If a therapist can explore ways that John's parents, too, have tried to "fix parental problems" at age 10, we could reenact the emotional bond of three generations and give back to them the responsibility for constructing their future. If the family is not considered the main stumbling block, the family itself becomes its major resource.

My orientation in therapy took an important turn when, instead of trying to control or fix the child's irrational or pathological behaviors, I "married" them. Or, in other words, I experienced them as something rich, intense, and symbolic only when I began to accept and play with the symptomatic process. I speak about "marriage" in the best sense: the vitality, harmony, sense of solidarity, and unspoken understanding that marriage can offer. If the therapist "embraces" the destructive behavior of the child, the family feels safe and understood, and can risk exploring personal contradictions and fears that have been transmitted over several generations.

THE CHILD AS CONSULTANT

When there is an actual child in the therapy session, the therapist can form a co-therapy or consultative alliance with the child by requesting his/her assistance in working together to help the parents. The child, thus, functions as a conduit for messages to his/her parents. This communicates a message of hope to everyone, as well as a message of competence to the child. Complimenting and employing the competence of the child indirectly compliments the parents who have raised a competent child. Through the child, it is possible to access the memories and lives of other generations, touching the parents at other developmental stages. For example, you can ask a son about his ideas and fantasies regarding what the relationship looked like between his father and grandfather, when his father was his age.

Placing the child "in the middle" raises him/her to the level of a competent adult. It is useful to ascertain from the child if he/she trusts you enough to relinquish to you the job of looking after the parents. The child consultant can remain in the therapy through devising a system where he/she can telephone or send a letter if the child is concerned that the parents are deteriorating. This serves the dual purpose of reassuring the child as well as sending a message to the parents to stop including their child in their marital discord.

Often, families in therapy are overinvolved with one side of the family of origin while underinvolved with the other side. The children internalize the distortion out of their sense of duty and loyalty. Children's involvement in the evaluation stage can be useful if you request that they help you invite the underinvolved side to a therapy session or make some contact with them. The child's reaction is diagnostic. If the child displays curiosity, then there is hope. If he/she has an immediate and steadfast negative response, this signals significant rigidity and, therefore, much less hope.

Adolescents are often less accessible than younger children in the role of consultant. They will test the therapist's capacity to engage in a relationship with them by resisting and rebelling against the function of a therapeutic relationship. However, if the therapist is able to join with them through their denial and disgust, and work on their ambivalence, they are potentially competent, resourceful consultants.

For example, Laura is a very pretty 16-year-old girl who has been invited to a session with her younger sister in order to help the therapist. Her parents separated once a few years ago and at this point their marriage is again at risk. Laura accepted the invitation to join the therapy, but protested very loudly in the session because of "losing my time on something that is totally irrelevant to me. Maybe my younger sister can help because she still needs them."

Her disinterested attitude, expressed through words, sharply contrasted with the intensity of her denial that was so visible in her eyes. So the therapist highlighted her ambivalence by asking her which part of her to believe: her mouth with her big NO or her sensitive eyes. Thereafter, Laura began to be more accepting of the therapeutic process. The therapist felt comfortable in establishing an alliance with her eyes, using them as a competent guide to explore family issues. The following questions created the context for building up a complicity with Laura. "How were the eyes of your mother when she was still in love with your father? Did they first change because she lost him as a companion or as a support in the house? Are your eyes sad because they cannot overcome this new crisis or because you would like to be nurtured as a little girl and nobody is available anymore for you? How were the eyes of your mother when she was 16. Was she as concerned as you about the marriage of her parents?"

It is amazing to see how much adolescents become available and competent if adults are able to play with their arrogant, distancing facade, without challenging it directly. It is also very important to learn how much they care for family harmony, if they are not forced to admit it in the open.

THE PROBLEM-CHILD AS CONSULTANT

If the symptoms are regarded as being a mental disorder originating within the child, then the parents will want to understand "what is wrong with his/her brain." The child in difficulty becomes an object of observation, and his sick behavior will be analyzed. Psychologists, psychiatrists, and social workers, "experts of the mind," will suggest therapy: medications, educational consultation, individual psychotherapy, or, in more severe cases, hospitalization. In every case the logic is the same: "The experts know how to change things," while the children and parents experiencing difficulties don't possess this knowledge.

It is more of a challenge and more effective to engage the child who is the identified patient as the consultant. The child must first be convinced that, despite the label of "problematic" or "incompetent," he/she is really the most competent. In order for the identified patient to shift into the consultative role, he/she (as well as the family) must shift from a problematic to a healthy perspective. Very often children choose symptoms according to what they want to profoundly touch.

For example, Sanders, a huge, angry boy with a puppy dog face, was brought to therapy by his fearful parents because of his violent behavior at home and in school. The boy shifted from arrogance and aggression toward his parents and the therapist to collaboration when the therapist stated that, "Sanders has been drinking milk and anger for too many years." The therapist elicited the boy's expertise by intruding into his body and exploring which parts belong to him and which to his angry mother. The therapist suggested that if Sanders stopped drinking mother's sugar, he would start losing weight and bad behavior. Later, he elicited the boy's resources in understanding how his father, an early orphan and neglected child, expressed his anger when he was Sanders' age. As a further way to help their therapist, Sanders was asked to arrange a special family session, inviting the mythical grandma—father's mother—whom everybody described as a "monster" and who dominated the parents' marriage and the entire life of the family. Everybody in the family has been very angry at her for a long time.

In a few sessions, Sanders changed from being the "troublemaker" to becoming a real consultant. Through the issue of his violence, three generations were compelled to reconsider their life cycle, which had been overloaded by mutual fears of rejection and equal desire to be appreciated and loved. The three generations began to look for alternative directions in their relationships with the help of therapy. The intergenerational impasse had been managed by the transmission of anger, intensively absorbed in the younger generation and carried in Sanders' body. His body and behavior began to relax when the violence was no longer his "specialty," but was developmentally resolved by the parent and grandparent generation.

We must ask ourselves how the family is able to accept such a risky plan. We noticed that if we give back to the family the confidence and competence in their resources, the family does not oppose the hypotheses of the therapist. If the parents feel that the child is the expert, they implicitly realize that they are experts through the child. If the problematic child is the expert, then the symptoms are regarded with respect, with delicacy. Very often we think that in order to make a good diagnosis we have to concentrate on the severity of psychiatric symptoms and antisocial behaviors of the child. Less often, we think of symptoms as having creative and symbolic significance.

Surely there is a pathology and suffering, but this does not mean that these observations have to guide our diagnostic operations. To respect the suffering can be helpful; however, being respectful does not require that we become a pain-stricken member of the family. Instead, we must know how to create a position of distance from the situation of suffering, thus allowing us to appreciate and understand the pain in its complexity. I believe that we show respect by our capacity to remain whole, with one part of us remaining outside and another one eventually invading the complex, emotional family world. Here the child is an incredible security valve; the child's function as a consultant allows us to maintain an adequate distance.

The child represents the most recent evolution of the trigenerational family. Children have been immersed in systems even before they have become aware of it. So why should we not use their systemic competence? Minuchin coined the term "parental child" to define children who assume parental functions. In addition, Selvini-Palazzoli has elegantly described the process of children's parentification as a sign of severe family disturbance.

We have added one more step to this generational configuration: the "grandparental child." Thus, we like to think that the child takes not only the father's or mother's place as a parent, but also the grandparent's role as a parent for his/her parents. At this point, the dilemma shifts between the child and the grandparents, not the parents. The child consultant no longer remains just the pathology carrier, but becomes the pathway to historical and unconscious meanings, which go beyond his/her knowledge.

USING AN UNBORN, MYTHICAL CHILD IN COUPLES THERAPY

The therapist can introduce the child as consultant to marital and child-parent relationship issues even if a couple is childless, operating from the realm of an "as if" reality. When this representation is concretized through the asking of questions such as the name, age, gender, physical description, personality traits, loyalties, alliances, position in the family, sense of hopefulness/hopelessness, and ideas to help the therapist intervene with this couple, the "child" becomes a resource. With the aid of the mythical child consultant, the therapist creates space for the couple to become more reasonable, less defensive. This indirect line of questioning by the therapist, asked through the thoughts and feelings of the couple's internalized child is devoid of the judgmental, critical tone often ascribed to adults, whether they be spouses, grandparents, or members of the adult therapeutic system.

The use of an unborn child when one is working with a marital dyad serves a number of purposes. First, the conceptualization of a child in the adults' fantasy adds complexity to the system, transforming the dyad into a therapeutic triad. This, in turn, allows the therapist increased flexibility in terms of his/her position within the therapeutic system. The therapist can either act as this child or use the image of the child to withdraw from the newly formed triad in order to gain a different, more distant perspective of the family.

The difference in the therapist's questions as a result of the presence of an unborn child can be dramatic. For example, a therapist may ask a member of the couple in a direct manner, "What attracted you to this relationship?" Framing the question as though a child were involved ("What would you tell your child about the beginning of your relationship?") encourages a shift from a dialogue with the therapist to a family discussion observed in a therapeutic context.

When one is attempting to add complexity to the family system, it is helpful to think in terms of the number and types of triangles available to the family members. Triads available to a couple without children are restricted to themselves and their families of origin—a two-generational model with a variety of configurations. Adding a generation consisting of the couple's child enables the formation of a separate two generational model, transforming the couple from children (of their parents) to adults with a parental role. In addition, it allows for a trigenerational configuration of grandparents, parents, and child. Thus, by simply adding the idea of a child into the couple's therapy, there is a multiplication of the number of triadic combinations available to the therapeutic system. Again, this addition builds complexity that causes the couple to think about relationships ("Would your baby be a boy or a girl? What name would you choose? Who would get up at night to change the baby's diaper? Whom would the child look like and take after?").

When presenting problems are approached directly by the therapist, there is the risk that a member of the family will "resist" change because the symptom affords a level of security for one or more members of the family. The use of a mythical child opens a door to a new concept of reality, where the symptom or habitual interaction must be different simply because of the expanded composition of the family. ("What would you say to your child about your arguing? Which of you would be first to comfort the child? What would happen if that were reversed?")

One way to cope with defensiveness is to conceptualize the child as a source of confusion and unpredictability. With the injection of the mythical child, the resulting confusion of roles, boundaries, and hierarchies allows the couple to set aside their perception of reality and temporarily adopt a different reality in which to play. As their therapeutic work progresses they can then be free to adapt to a reality that is mediated by the confusion and openness represented by a healthy fantasy.

Of course, the same procedure of working with a mythical child can be applied when one is working with a couple that actually has a child. In this case, the "mythical child" is more connected with the fantasy to enlarge the "sibling floor." The addition of the image of a new child forces a family of three to reformulate a new organization with different alliances, opportunities, and responsibilities. By adding a mythical child, the therapist could confer with the real child and get information at many different levels. The following are examples of issues that could be addressed:

a) *Subsystem Hierarchy*—The therapist could explore how responsibilities and distribution of care and nurturing might be organized differently if the real child has an older or younger sibling.

b) *Gender Stereotypes*—The therapist can obtain a picture of how people get close to one another according to their gender. Thus, questions could be addressed that ask the real child to guess the gender ramifications of a mythical child. For example, the real child could be asked, "Do you think if you had a sister that she could reach Mom? Do you think your brother would know when Dad feels alone and needs someone close to him?"

c) *Family Myths*—The real child can be helped to expand his/her fantasies about family anecdotes, playing "as if" he/she were a sibling. The therapist might ask questions like, "Could brother/sister help you to reconnect your mother/father with his/her parents? If you are a team of two, what would your brother/sister think is the problem between your mother/father and his/her families?"

d) *Separation Anxiety*—The image of another sibling can help the therapist understand and locate the deep fears around separation. "If your parents split, it might be easier for everyone; one kid would take care of one parent and the other could do the same with the other parent. How would you two choose?"

Introducing an "as if" discourse allows the adult to listen more objectively to the content and affect presented by their child. Through the creation of this "make-believe" story, the child's voice can reach the parents with less defensiveness and more spontaneity than by answering direct questions in an adult fashion. The "imaginative" child can allow the real child to express his/her concerns, fears, and needs much more openly because he/she doesn't have to take responsibility for responses that belong to another sibling. In addition, it introduces a context of playfulness, which is often lost with families in crisis. By enlarging the family unit, the therapist can help each individual to regain his/her own personhood.

CHILD AS CONSULTANT IN MARITAL THERAPY

Previously, I have described how a child can enter a marital crisis or difficult separation process by performing a variety of symptoms. This event can be considered a "physiological" response of the family system to excessive tension on the horizontal level: the parental dyad. If these tensions and disturbances become an integral part of the child's personality and family constellation, then this could become a chronic psychosomatic or behavioral disorder. However, in this section I would like to describe an aspect of my work with dysfunctional marital relationships that do not result in visible symptomatology of the child. In this case, the child is included in the process of couple therapy as a healthy resource.

In the diagnostic phase of marital therapy, we observe the couple at different functional levels. Therefore we like to meet each partner:

a. with his/her family of origin,
b. alone,
c. and with their children. We even feel that it is important to observe how a couple interacts with a newborn.

Through the years, we have organized these meetings as a basic diagnostic proceeding before starting couple therapy, divorce therapy, or mediation. Of course, we are very flexible in proposing this step-by-step process, especially in situations of severe struggle between the partners. Sometimes we reverse the order: We include the kids at the first meeting and then, with their help, schedule the family-of-origin meetings.

Although we have had some "resistance" to this diagnostic process, we have found that its success depends mostly upon the security of the therapist in proposing it, as well as upon his/her capacity to keep emotional distance from family dramas.

The medical model provides a useful metaphor for initiating this type of diagnostic process. Patients usually do not consider "resisting" a doctor when he/she requests blood tests, urine tests, x-rays, etc., to check their health. Similarly, we request kids, parents, etc., as routine procedures in our research laboratory to study the quality of relationships and perceptions of the trigenerational system. Besides, it is very useful to observe which request (to come alone, with the kids, or with the family of origin) produces the most anxiety, concern, or enthusiasm.

Generally, inviting parents and siblings for a joint session is the most painful and scary proposal, perhaps because of the implicit admission of failure or an unsuccessful marriage. However, requesting children frequently elicits less "resistance" in the couple. The reservoir of hope is often located in the next generation, while people tend to see their past as the territory of blame, guilt, and abandonment.

But, there are circumstances when couples "resist" bringing in their children as therapeutic consultants. Naturally, if there is abuse, we can expect that parents would want to maintain this secret. Sometimes, parents feel ashamed to show their faults in front of their child or fear that the child could be aligned with one partner against the other. If the partners have had problems in their sexual life, they could "protect" the child by deeming it inappropriate for the child to join the session. Or, when kids are adolescent, the couple might feel reluctant to invite them for fear of their judgments. But in all these circumstances the therapist can play with parents' resistance by introducing an "as if" reality.

For example, the therapist could ask: "If the child were here, how would you talk about this secret? How would he/she respond to you if you were able to disclose your fear? Or how would he/she suggest to be not used as a weapon between you two? How would the child see your relationship differently if you began to show tenderness and concern with each other? How would your adolescent child judge your behavior if he/she would be here? What would he/she say? What would need to happen in the family to change his/her negative perception of you two?"

When this is done, adults can feel at one level more free and understood as their fears and needs become more overt. At another level, this creates a curiosity about the child's possible responses. Although the child is not present, the "presence" of the child in their dialogue enables the parents to reconsider their refusal to include the child directly in the therapy.

Following is a clinical anecdote that illustrates how a child can be a consultant in a marital therapy. Sara, a woman in her 30's, felt very depressed about her role in her marriage. The therapist chose the issue of depression as a starting point in the dialogue with her 12-year-old son, Jerry. With the help of the child consultant, the therapist temporarily removed the issue of depression from the marriage and transported the topic to an intergenerational context. The child adeptly noted mother's unfinished issues of nurturing and care related to her family of origin. Later, the therapist was helped by the child to dislocate the extreme dependency of the husband in his family of origin.

Therapist: Where did your Mom learn to become depressed, from her mother's side or from her father's side?

Child: From my grandma... In all the family pictures she never smiles and she always wears dark!

Therapist: So, we are luckier: your mother doesn't smile, but at least she likes colorful dresses.

Child: Mom always chooses beautiful tee shirts for me and my father!

Therapist: Do you think your grandma was wearing dark at your age, in primary school?

Child: I don't know. Mom, how was grandma dressed in school?

Mother: (*very moved as we are touching profound areas of darkness and light*) My mother stopped going to school when she was very young. They were very poor at that time and she used to help her parents in a small fruit-shop. She used to wake up very early in the morning and she never had time to take care of herself. She didn't have time to take care of me either when I was a child. I don't remember her playing with me when I was four or five years old.

Therapist: (*to the child*) You didn't know about this, did you? So your Mom might be depressed because she has to care about everybody, too, like your grandma. She has never had the possibility to be a "little girl," and lean on other people's shoulders. She probably wears nice colors to attract some attention from the outside, but she does not feel colorful inside. Who can help her to feel bright inside?

Child: Dad and I can help Mom.

Therapist: So maybe we have to recharge the batteries of the marriage, to get the light back. Sometimes, it is good to go back and take energy from other sources. Maybe you and me together could make an invitation to grandma to come and see if she has any energy left for her daughter.

Child: Perhaps Mom could help her to dress more colorful when she comes.

Therapist: (*to the child*) Did you see how your father becomes more alive when we enter Mom's depression and look for more light? Does he really think that Mom is the family barometer?

Child: When Mom is happy, Dad becomes very humorous and he plays with me and we have fun. But when Mom is depressed and has a headache, he sleeps in front of the TV for hours or hides behind the newspaper. He looks very old.

Therapist: When did he learn to depend so much upon women's mood? From the time he was in his Mom's belly, or later?

Child: (*laughs and starts to tease the father*) When, Dad, when, Dad?

Therapist: So you can help me in two directions: eliminating Mom's depression and Dad's dependency. Perhaps we have to see how your Dad behaves when there are no women around. We can have a meeting only for men: you, me, Dad, his father, and his brothers. What do you think about this idea?

Child: I think they will come with many newspapers. Grandpa has a lot of books too.

Therapist: So, you bring your comics and I'll bring mine. We will start as a reading session. When everybody has finished reading, we'll see how men in this family can learn to take initiative and to trust their guts...and Mom can rest, she can save energy if she is not compelled to give, to give to everybody.

The active collaboration of the child in the session enabled the therapist to send indirect messages to both parents, as a couple but even more emphatically as *children* reconsidering depression (wife) and dependency (husband). Both these elements were not born into the marriage, but have been carried into it from their childhood. Therapy became a co-therapeutic project as child and therapist realized that the damaged marriage needed to be revitalized first by the inclusion of other significant relationships that can provide hope and help.

Although the presence of children in marital therapy is useful in the diagnostic and preliminary stage of therapy, they can be included at any time as competent, sensitive consultants. For example, when there is an impasse in the therapeutic process, they can be very resourceful and give suggestions to the adults on how to change direction. Often, I have worked with them interchangeably behind the one-way mirror. Sometimes, they direct me over the intercom in my work with their parents, and sometimes I send them into the therapy room with a task to enact with their parents. Whether they are behind the mirror or in the room, they readily function as competent consultants or co-therapists.

During the termination stage, I frequently involve children in the evaluation of the marital therapy. I like to make a school-like context in which roles are reversed and kids give grades to adults for the progress they make in therapy. It is amazing to see how seriously parents perceive criticisms and positive comments coming from their own children. At the same time, I'm impressed by the natural ability of children to get right to the point, without diplomatic facades, and with a great sense of justice and honesty. I also like kids to evaluate the therapist and what he/she has been able to achieve with their family and in which areas he/she would have been able to do more or better. I plan with them how we can follow up the progress of therapy in the long run and if and when to meet again in order to determine whether therapy succeeded in entering their house.

Often, children's voices are ignored or become mute when their parents are in turmoil. Unfortunately, many therapists collude with the couple in the idea that children are better off if they are not included in the family "battle field." Through experience, I have found that this "protective exclusion" is, in fact, based on the indifference or incapacity to employ resources from children, to play with them, and to learn from their simple language. If we are ready to listen to them, children will offer information, hope, sensitivity, and a fervent desire to help the parents be more harmonious.

CONCLUSIONS

Within the context of family therapy, there exist several languages that need to be understood at some level in order for interaction/change to occur. The family has a language composed of many parts. These parts in dysfunctional families are often disconnected, and therapists need to understand that different situations will demand the use of different languages. For example, adults within a family will communicate at different levels depending on the recipient of the communication. Within an adult context, a more sophisticated level of communication will exist. In rigid families, the communication often consists of shoulds, duties, or loyalties. This style of language is very concrete and limits the option of "choice" from individuals. It is a language that is rich in abstract thoughts and words (Andolfi, Angelo & de Nichilo, 1989). This style of language can be especially intimidating for children.

Within an "adult-child" context, the communication is often direct and logical. Children, however, may not relate nor respond to injunctive language since the inner language of a child is more magical, creative, and playful. This unique language relies more on context, nonverbal expression, concrete images, and playfulness (Andolfi, 1979). It is a playfulness that is foreign to the parents. If the therapist elects to stay with one or two generations in the therapy, access to the family's myths may be difficult and could result in an extended period of time listening for symbolic material embedded in the language of the parents. Thus, aside from resolving the more obvious relationship issues, moving to three generations can have other benefits.

As grandparents are brought into the session and the family is enlarged, the grandparents bring the language of the "older" generation. The language has a romantic quality and is full of elaboration, based on history. This language may be difficult to challenge as it is based on their memory of their perception of a time when no one else in the room existed. Within this language comes the family culture, values, myths, and rituals. It is within this experience that the therapist can more easily access the mythology of the family.

Mixed with the languages of the nuclear and family-of-origin members is the very foreign language of the therapist. This level of communication is much different. It is a language that considers and operates on clinical theory, goals, objectives, responsibilities, logic, and strategies. It is a language that often ignores and distances children. Through his or her language, a therapist may connect with adults because their communication style is similar. This is a tenuous position for the therapeutic process because the parental failure to handle the identified problem may leave the parents feeling incompetent. If the therapist has all of the answers, the result is that the therapist becomes the competent parent, but not an effective therapist.

The therapist can create both connections and confusion by rapidly shifting between the language of the therapist, parent, grandparents, and child. This requires a great deal of flexibility, playfulness, and symbolic thinking on the part of the therapist. So, the therapist must learn how to act as a translator for the different ways of thinking and communicating between the family members. He or she must be capable of encouraging interaction among adults, yet must consider the child as a person with full rights who can show and convey their thoughts and feelings in a personal way that is not inferior to the adults' (Andolfi, Angelo & de Nichilo, 1989).

If psychopathology inside the family can be imagined as a synthesis of an intergenerational gap, filled up by the child for the adult, the most convincing follow-up of a therapy with a child is to discover that the child has succeeded in becoming a child again...and a good therapist recognizes a real child. A child is a real child when he or she does not need to think for his/her parents any more nor be attracted by what they do or do not do, because at this point the adults go to the "upper floor" and the child speaks with his or her own voice.

ACKNOWLEDGMENTS

I would like to thank Marcia Sokolowski and Jerome Zake for their help in editing some sections of this paper from my teaching about the child as consultant in the Practicum held in Rome, June 1993.

REFERENCES

Andolfi, M. (1979). *Family Therapy: An Interactional View.* New York: Plenum Press.

Andolfi, M., Angelo, C., & de Nichilo, M. (1989). *The Myth of Atlas: Families and the Therapeutic Story.* New York: Brunner/Mazel.

Andolfi, M., Angelo, C., Menghi, P., & Nicolo-Corigliano, A. (1983). *Behind the Family Mask: Therapeutic Change in Rigid Family Systems.* New York: Brunner/Mazel.

Minuchin, S. (1974). *Families and Family Therapy.* Cambridge: Harvard University Press

Selvini-Palazzoli, M. (1990). *Paradox and Counterparadox.* New Jersey: Jason Aronson.

Whitaker, C., & Keith, D. (1981). Symbolic-experiential family therapy. In A. S. Gurman & D. P. Kniskern (Eds.), *Handbook of Family Therapy.* New York: Brunner/Mazel.

6

The Family of Origin as Therapeutic Consultant to the Family

David V. Keith

The ancient Greeks saw the future as something that came upon them from behind. They gained a sense of where they were going from looking at where they had been. In our unconscious thinking, we do the same. Our origins are the foundation for our orientation to the present, for our reality. We look backward at our family history, both consciously and unconsciously to guide our fantasies about where we are now and where we are going. Of course, there is a reciprocal influence between present and past. The present colors how we understand the past and what we are likely to see when we look at it. In that sense, the clinical history is mythological or poetic, a compelling blend of fiction and fact.

CASE ILLUSTRATION

A 42-year-old auto mechanic was referred to the author by an internist for a psychiatric consultation because of chest pain, part of a cluster of anxiety symptoms. At 18, he began working as a mechanic. Through much of his life, he worked 16-hour days and became owner of an auto repair center with 10 hydraulic hoists. He was very successful. An important part of his history revealed that his father had been very successful in the scrap-metal business. When his father was 43, the bottom suddenly fell out of the scrap-metal market. He went broke, lost his spirit, and never regained it. My assumption was that this man's anxiety was, in part, the result of anticipated failure in his near future, an unarticulated fear that his life would follow the same path as his father's.

One family member gives only a limited and distorted description of his or her family. Family members, individually, can describe only their transference to the family; they know only their fantasy of the family. A multigenerational group is required to simultaneously describe and enact the complex system of past/present, person/event/thing relationships that I think of as a family. In a family-of-origin consultation interview, the family comes together to talk about the past and present of the family. The interview is a free-associative, that is, meandering group stroll through the labyrinth of the family history. The interview accumulates symbolic/historical information in the here-and-now experiential process of the family (how they operate as a multigenerational group) (Keith, 1989).

When the expanded family of origin enters the therapy room, there is a shift in consciousness, with psychosomatic implications. If there is a three-generation group in the room, with grandparents talking about their grandparents, there are, symbolically, five generations present. The spirits of the past become present in the present. The ancestors' spirits are part of the structure, part of the creativity, and part of the pathology of the present living. These spirits are included in the anecdotes and stories of the family members.

Family therapy is an effort to potentiate the multigenerational family's capacity for self-healing. The therapeutic process usually begins with an attempt at disrupting growth-inhibiting pathological processes. But even more crucially, the therapeutic process can uncover the fragments of health in the family that support the continuing growth of the family and its members. This consultation interview with the expanded family is often beneficial both for the family to gain a sense of adequacy, and for the therapist to uncover the dangers hidden in the family. But what is endlessly fascinating to me is that *there are shifts in the dynamics of the family without any conscious translation or interpretation of events.* It matches Winnicott's (1971) observation about play therapy, that therapy of a deep, ongoing kind proceeds without any interpretation.

CASE ILLUSTRATION

Judy forced her husband, Chuck, to come in for couple therapy when she discovered his brief affair. They had no children. Both were graduate students, age 29. At the beginning of therapy, she was very disorganized by her emotional pain. He was a covertly angry, unwilling participant, motivated by her threat to divorce and by her deep emotional distress. As therapy proceeded, their anxiety diminished, they learned to control their distress. But the adjustments were tentative, there was little change. He kept himself in control and reasonable, maintaining a distant, anonymous quality.

Chuck was the fourth of six children. He was a strong, athletic man, but identified with his mother and two sisters. He was a man with many maternal features. He admired his mother, but characterized his father, a retired railroad engineer and farmer, as an emotionless nonentity, who barely spoke and spent his days reading mystery novels. It did not occur to me until later that Chuck had become a mirror of the father he passively despised.

Judy, likewise, had an ambivalent relationship with her family of origin. We had conversations about arranging for the families to come in. She was reluctant, worried they would come in to mock her. Chuck was sardonically amused by the therapist's suggestion. He did not like being in therapy, and the idea that "Mommy and Daddy" come in made him even more disdainful.

But, much to the author's surprise, in the fifth month of therapy, Chuck brought his parents, without previous announcement, to the 15th interview. They were visiting from their home some 400 miles distant. He had portrayed his parents accurately. Mother was strong, intellectually alive, and interested in her family. She was philosophical in a warm, restrained, rustic way. It was as if her hard, rural life continued to add to her vitality. The father said little, seemed in a different world, but was not toxic. I introduced the purpose of the interview and started them talking about the family background.

Dad contributed little. The interview was flat. But at one point, mother told a poignant story. It sounded initially like a complaint about the father's noninvolvement, but developed into a rich, appreciative sketch. When Chuck was a young boy, Father would go to the barn in the evenings to tinker in his shop. Chuck and his sister frequently went with him. They had the first TV for miles around. Father constructed it from a do-it-yourself kit. Mother made fun of her now antique virtue when she told how she had been against TV and made Father keep his "wonder-machine" in the barn, where father, Chuck, his sister, and the kids from the neighborhood would gather to watch it in their secret enclave. There were other components to the interview, all delivered in sparse, cautious, rural language with understated affect. When it ended, I was not sure we had touched upon the whole-family mythology and wondered if there would be any effect.

At the next interview, two weeks later, Chuck mentioned the story cited above. He had not remembered anything about his father. In the days following the consultation interview, his memory portrait of his father expanded, recalling when together they had repaired the doors on an old shed and pruned and cleaned up the shrubbery around the house. He shared few details, but emphasized his surprise at how much he had enjoyed his parents' visit, which contrasted sharply with his usual distaste. Over the next two interviews, Chuck's guarded demeanor faded and signs of a previously absent personality emerged. He became interested in himself and his marriage, and quit treating me like a probation officer. He took a job he had been equivocating over, and decided he had had enough of graduate school. The couple ended therapy after four more months. I was disappointed that Judy had been too apprehensive to invite her family. Four months after they ended, I received a phone call from Judy with the happy news that she was pregnant.

Something happened during and after this consultation interview which allowed Chuck to become more invested in himself and his marriage. What is important to understand is that there was no plan, no attempt to fix. There were comments on the experience, but no translation or interpretation. The therapist's job was chiefly to provide a time and place for an experience. Then a series of changes emerged over the next months. This is a fascinating, common result of these family-of-origin consultative interviews.

The "something that happens" is the result of primary process experiences. Thus, I would like to give some impression as to what I mean by "primary process," an elusive concept at best, and how it relates to family consultation interviews.

PRIMARY PROCESS: A PARTIAL EXPLANATION

Primary processes are the activities of the unconscious. Likewise, secondary process thinking is expressed in consciousnesses. If we were to consider the relation of conscious to unconscious activity in the mind, we might use an iceberg as an example. Consciousness, the more visible part, makes up 10–20% of the volume, 80–90% is submerged and invisible (Bateson, 1972). The unconscious is difficult to picture or describe. Is it possible to use rational discourse to describe nonrational processes? What follows is a brief attempt to do so. I will divide the territory in two: a region of symbolic perception and a region of organized practice.

Primary process expresses itself in those inchoate pushings and heavings, the unholy madness that Freud described as the Id, with its instinctual drives. The material there is not inaccessible, but it is just difficult to understand with secondary process. It appears in dreams, metaphors, art, religion, intoxication, psychosis (phobia), humor, and play.

Primary processes are expressed symbolically. Symbols are relatively stable and repeatable elements of perceptual experiences that stand for some larger meaning or set of meanings. Symbols cannot be entirely or explicitly defined, since their essential quality draws life from a multiplicity of associations, subtly and, for the most part, unconsciously interrelated. *The symbol and things related to it are joined in the past; they are activated and elaborated by experience.* Symbols may be personal, shared by a family, or related to several generations of family experience (Bagarozzi & Anderson, 1989).

There is no concept of time in primary process thinking. It is always the present. There is no such thing as a logical sequence of events. Before and after do not exist. Past and future collapse into the present. Thoughts, ideas, or concepts are not subject to mutual contradiction. There is no good and evil, back and front, male and female, me and you. Thus, there is no morality, no DSM-IV. Primary processes substitute psychic reality for external reality. Whatever occurs psychically is real. There is no distinction between what is fantasized and what actually takes place (Bagarozzi & Anderson, 1989).

In the example above of the garage owner, the sequence of success followed by failure that he experienced from his father's experience polluted his experience of his own success. His anxiety was stimulated by an unconscious symbolic experience.

Next, I want to use a slightly different, but not contradictory, perspective on primary process from Gregory Bateson. He speaks of an *organized region of submerged practices or processes* that allow us to conduct most of our living without conscious intention. Patterns of thinking and behavior are submerged in the unconscious for the sake of economy in living (Bateson, 1972).

There is an analogy with computer programs. Bateson (1972) speaks of "algorithms of the heart," making a comparison with the complex equations that are the basis for computer programs. These are equations that take in data, organize it, and proceed toward an end. For example, algorithms are the equations making up the computer program that works out airline schedules. He is suggesting that these algorithms underlie our living experience. We do not think our way through situations. The algorithms of the heart guide.

These submerged patterns allow us to conduct much of our living without conscious intent—for example, driving a car, playing tennis, conversational style, how to be sick, how to get well, how much personal distance is necessary, how to celebrate Christmas, what to do when a baby is born, what to do about pain, to mention a few. These algorithms of the heart come from our family, and they can be partially accessed and sometimes modified by the family consultation process. But they are rarely consciously apprehended.

Patterns of thinking and behavior are stored in the unconscious for the sake of economy in living. Again, it is analogous with a computer programming system. For example, when I play tennis, I am guided by unconscious patterns (my program). I play with little conscious decision about where to move and how to respond. If I take a lesson to work on my forehand, the intrusion of consciousness may throw off my game for a few weeks until the new patterns are integrated into the unconscious program.

Secondary process delimits reality so as to make the world more understandable. Secondary process accomplishes that by obscuring or cutting some of the circuitry. It serves some necessary purpose for our adaptation and survival. Thus, in this sense, "...we create the world that we perceive, not because there is no reality outside our heads, but because we select and edit the reality we see in order to conform to our beliefs about what sort of world we live in" (Bateson, 1972, p.vii). Secondary process has little ecological awareness and unchecked is likely to be destructive.

Bateson (1972) suggests that primary process experiences repair these secondary process interruptions of larger circuits. Experiences that reconnect the whole include art, religion, experiences with nature and animals, and play (especially with children). I would add here that family reunions give access to primary process. They put us in touch with patterns that help us understand ourselves better, but not in a conscious or cognitive way. The experiences remind us that we belong to a larger We, our multiple-generation family. This awareness establishes a framework for the "something that happens" in the family of origin consultation.

An important and often overlooked component of family therapy is acknowledgement of the family We, an intangible hologram submerged in the unconscious. When the We is acknowledged, it is possible to learn more about the I. Membership in a We enhances the integrity of the I. If there is no We, the I's identity is weakened. An absent, or weakened We may be compensated for by external structure (rigid religious practices, preoccupation with a physical illness, overinvolvement in role functioning, financial or social success). In my thinking about families, it is this multigenerational We that plays a part in impeding or potentiating healing.

Primary process is accessed by metaphors. Patterns of relatedness are best acknowledged metaphorically; the vehicles are anecdotes and stories. The family is a metaphor for itself (How to be a We). The patterns of relatedness in a family background are guides for relatedness or for understanding distress in the present.

So, I hope it is possible to see that the "something that happens" in the family-of-origin consultation interview is unconscious and related to primary process. Primary process refers to the nonrational components of our mental life, and pressure from the unconscious leads to distortion of our living patterns. However, primary process also refers to patterns that guide our living. Thus, I may feel it is important to murder my father so that I can have my mother all to myself, but the patterns that interfere with my desire to get rid of father are also in the primary process; somehow, I learn to avoid murdering my father in the same way that he avoided murdering his.

The family We is also in the primary process world. And when the family is together, there is automatic access to the family unconscious. Health depends upon access to primary process experiences. In the next section, I will describe how primary process is lived out in the family group psychosis.

THE FAMILY GROUP PSYCHOSIS

In these next paragraphs, I want to discuss a concept important for further appreciation of the "something that happens" in these family interviews. When the family gets together, they enter an emotional hot tub. I refer to the experience as a "family group psychosis." The word "psychosis" may be overly strong, but it helps define the "something that happens." Psychosis is a poorly defined word describing a psychosomatic (whole person) state in which a person's powers of self-observation are compromised. It is nonvoluntary, and has little to do with whether or not the state continues.

I wish to discriminate between the clinical psychosis that occurs in an individual and the family group psychosis that is, in fact, part of normal family living. The individual's psychosis is a socially identified experience in which he is overwhelmed (panicked) by subjective experience, personally isolated, ambivalently extruded from an intimate relationship (family), and objectified by the community (a doctor makes a diagnosis). A polarization evolves (We are normal. You are sick.) isolating him with his subjectivity.

The family group (existential) psychosis refers to a powerfully subjective realm, outside the intellect, where social propriety is in abeyance and unconscious factors dominate. The subjective experience is powerful, but it is multipersonal, in the context of group experience. It is usually culturally invisible, that is, blended into the fabric of the community so that it does not become a named phenomenon. When a family group psychosis is visible, it has been culturally choreographed into a ritual such as a baptism, wedding, funeral, or wake. Even though the anxiety can become quite high, the group behavior is within the bounds of what the community regards as normal. The individual psychosis probably *begins* in the same way. But when the group anger, pain, or anxiety becomes too high, a scapegoat may be nominated, elected, extruded, and isolated. The crucial difference, of course, is that the family psychosis belongs to a group. Family reunions, the celebrations of Christmas, Passover, Easter, births, deaths, and weddings collapse the structure of living, put social propriety in abeyance and bring a family close together.

CASE ILLUSTRATION

An orthopedic surgeon's son was having problems in school. In the diagnostic interview, we learned of an old congealed conflict in the marriage plus a standoff between the surgeon's wife and his parents. Family therapy began with the nuclear family, the two-generation unit. The boy's symptomatic behavior diminished and the marriage was showing renewed signs of life after five interviews. The surgeon's parents and younger sister, age 32, came for the sixth interview. We scheduled two hours. His family was rigid and self-admiring; the interview began with a description of how normal and appealing they were. But the momentum disappeared after half an hour. The two hours passed slowly with virtually nothing happening. It was both boring and disappointing.

At the next interview with the surgeon and his wife, he commented on his disappointment with the consultation. He was annoyed with us for not having been more active and not having pushed harder. He went on to describe post-interview events in a free-associative way. His parents stayed for the weekend. He had an unusual extended discussion with his father; his mother interrupted them and he objected. This led to a dispute between the surgeon and his mother, after which his parents withdrew to their room. He went on to say that while his parents were pouting, he felt a great burden lifted from him. He felt as if they were children and he had been protecting them for years. Since the dispute, he had been sleeping better than he had in years.

By our observation, his demeanor in the interview was very different. He seemed larger, more full of himself, less obsequious. He had made an existential shift. An existential shift is one outcome of an existential psychosis. It results in a change in freedom. It occurs as the result of therapeutic experience, formal or informal. He was unaware of a change in himself, but we could see it. There were reasons for the change; there was just no way for us to delineate them. He had been a subject of a family group psychosis, which is the crucial, albeit implicit primary process result of the extended family interview (Keith, 1989). The process probably began in the organization of the interview. There were high expectations because the sister was herself a family therapist. An inexpressible group anxiety rose during the interview. Some delusions about themselves seemed to be crumbling and fading. The high anxiety and disappointment then led to the confrontation at home, and the surgeon felt himself relieved of a longstanding, unnoticed burden.

ACTION METAPHORS: FAMILY CHOREOGRAPHY

The primary process world of the family is revealed in several ways. The most accessible is in the family anecdotes and legends that make up the family history. Another important way that primary process is accessible is in the interactional patterns that appear as action metaphors (dances) in the family interview. An unconscious interaction occurs that is an example of relatedness. A common example would be where the therapist is interviewing the grandfather about his family, and the grandmother repeatedly corrects him. This pattern suggests that what he says is of questionable validity in the eyes of the family. The following illustration is slightly more complex.

CASE ILLUSTRATION

The Smiths, a family with two sons, 17 and 15, were in therapy because the 15-year-old was engaging in small-scale juvenile delinquency, flirting with getting kicked out of school and being sent to the youth detention center. The father and mother had developed a manufacturing business into a success worth several million dollars. Both came from middle-class backgrounds.

Mr. Smith's father and mother came in for a consultation interview. The grandfather was an unemployed salesman with a bold, cocky manner, still boasting of WW II adventures in the Marine Corps. His son's business success far exceeded his own. Much of the story of the family background had to do with how difficult the grandfather's childhood was, how tough he had been on his sons, and how they had benefitted from a home modeled on the Marine Corps. He was proud and self-admiring. In the middle of the interview, the grandfather told a story about how his son, Mr. Smith, wanted to buy a car at age 16. Grandfather recalled showing him how stupid he was to think he could manage owning a car. The father looked humiliated by this story, and grandfather sneered as he told it. It was not just a story; it was a spontaneous, condensed reenactment of the event itself. Mr. Smith, who was usually rather cocky and polished himself, looked hurt, defeated. I commented on his affect. "No," he said, "I like to hear Dad tell those old stories."

In the six weeks after this interview, the 15-year-old's antisocial behavior came to an abrupt stop. He discussed the change at a later interview. "When I saw how bad my Dad was treated by his Dad, I decided I didn't need to do what I was doing if I was hurting him too. I don't want to be like my grandpa."

This is a picture of an action metaphor. It had the quality of a dance. As the grandfather told the story, his sadistic pleasure at belittling his son showed through, and as Mr. Smith listened, his pain was visible. Interestingly, Mr. Smith never did acknowledge that he had any pain about the situation; such acknowledgement would be against the rules of the family (and of the Marine Corps).

IMPACT OF CONSULTATION ON THERAPIST'S RELATION TO FAMILY

When I participate in a family-of-origin interview, it leads to changes in my thinking about and behavior toward the family. Noel Keith (unpublished) describes two patterns of play with children in family therapy: play as therapy (the "something that happens") and play as revelation (what the therapist learns from observing the play). The most important component is the therapeutic part of the experience. The following example illustrates how the consultation interview is like revealing play and changes the therapist's interaction with the family.

CASE ILLUSTRATION

The Olsen family was filled with contradiction; they had high visibility and were admired by the community. They were psychologically minded and gave the illusion of closeness. But the interior of the family was chaotic and filled with painful duplicity. The 22-year-old daughter was hospitalized after a serious suicide attempt and continued to be dangerously self-destructive. Our intensive therapy with the family was helping keep the daughter alive, but accomplishing little else.

Mr Olsen was a somewhat rigid, but human, political science professor. Mrs. Olsen was a successful realtor, much admired in the community for her leadership and support of the city's Art Museum. Her image in the community was majestic. In this family, however, she was an elusive Queen of Hearts who ran the family with a manic-depressive emotional style, intimidating everyone in the style of a petulant 13-year-old. Her self-centeredness obfuscated and trivialized family discussions. The family was terrified of her and her moods, but she thought of herself as weak and felt disregarded. She viewed her husband as uncaring and domineering. We never saw that side of him, but kept looking for it, assuming he was displaying his best manners in front of us.

An important part of Mrs. Olsen's family history was the suicide of her brother some 30 years previous at the age of 24. By innuendo, she blamed her own mother for the suicide, often describing her as toxic and uncaring. She viewed her father as long-suffering, dominated and emasculated by her moody, witch-like mother.

After four discouraging months of work with this family, Mrs. Olsen's parents, visiting from the West, came in for a 90-minute interview. Our experience of the grandparents did not fit with mother's projections. Her mother was very apprehensive about the meeting and wanted to talk about the suicidal, anorexic granddaughter. Her husband interrupted, corrected, and sarcastically mocked her with subtlety borne of 52 years of marital martial artistry. Grandmother appeared frightened and in endless reaction to her husband's demeaning understructure. In an attempt to support her, I playfully flirted with the grandmother and wondered if she had any plans for how to get even with her husband for 50 years of endless sarcasm. She said, with resignation in her voice, "I no longer notice."

At one point, Grandfather teased the author about being a psychiatrist. I love humor, but I could feel sadism and viciousness in his teasing, despite the sugarcoating of humor. My patients, i.e. his daughter, son-in-law, and granddaughter, were amused. I must have been double-bound, because I did not take the liberty of straightening him out about how demeaning I found him.

At the next interview with the Olsens, as they talked about the parents' visit (in and out of the office), I mentioned my experience of Mrs. Olsen's parents and the way it contrasted with what they had described. But they did not hear what I was saying. All still saw Grandfather as the victim of his impossible wife. I saw him as sadistic, castrating, and crazy-inducing.

This example shows how the family consultation interview can be like a Hall of Mirrors where images are confused with the real people. The image of "good, reasonable people" in "good, reasonable families" is difficult to dispel even in the face of very serious problems. In many families, the images are maintained by distortions of reality. In the case above, for some reason, it was safer to pretend the grandmother was dangerous than to acknowledge the sadism of the grandfather. The consultation interview gave me a way to see past the images.

The interview helped me to understand a complicated problem in my relationship to Mrs. Olsen which was related to her transference to her own family. By viewing her husband as uncaring and domineering, she was probably confusing him with her father. But her husband was not dangerous in the way Grandfather was. I had been taking a gently confronting posture toward Mrs. Olsen, but after the consultation I made it clearer that she hungered for nurturing. Her depressions and caustic outbursts came from hunger. As I became more warmly mothering of her, she calmed. I enjoyed Mr. Olsen's warmth. Their daughter's self-destructiveness faded gradually, and a playful warmth emerged in the marriage and family.

TIMING THE CONSULTATION INTERVIEW

In essence, a consultation interview with the family of origin is useful in the beginning or middle stages of family therapy. I usually involve the family of origin in crisis intervention with families, but in those cases the expanded family is a patient, not simply a consultant. While the process has much in common with the consultative process, it is different. I will not discuss crisis intervention in this chapter.

Beginning Stage

I do the first part of the first interview on the phone. As I get a brief sketch of the history including people who are involved, I ask about the availability of the grandparents. "What do they think ought to be done? Would they come in and talk about it?" This introduces the idea that when I talk "family" I am talking about an actual three-generation group, not just a conceptual construct. With most families at this point, a three-generation interview is not a demand but a strong suggestion that induces a reorientation in their thinking about the family troubles. In the following situations, I will insist that three generations be present for the first interview.

1) *History of Failed Family Therapy.* A father calls for an appointment, indicating he seeks help for his son. They have seen two previous therapists, and tried a halfway house. Or, a couple is seeking help, their individual therapists did not help nor did the marriage therapist. It is essential that something be done to change the format of therapy so that the new therapy project does not become a copy of the previous therapy attempts. It is important that therapists use the power of their newness to change the anxiety focus, to expand the symptoms. In these cases of previously failed therapy attempts, I would not want to begin if the family-of-origin members were not available to attend the first or second interview.

2) *Uneven Anxiety Within the Family.* The father is angry and upset about the son while the mother does not see a problem. Her brother, the airline pilot, was also like that at age 14. The presence of the background family will help redefine the pain behind the pain.

3) *Lack of Agreement on the Problem.* The mother is preoccupied with the daughter and has turned her back on the father. The father, on the other hand, is trying to repair the marriage and diminish the conflict about the daughter. The family of origin helps delineate the network of distress the family is facing. It is of note that this lack of agreement is frequently associated with a problem in the grandparent's generation, such as depression, physical illness, or marital trouble, where the emotional impact is underestimated.

4) *The Family Is Preoccupied with an Objective Reality Problem.* This may be a problem such as physical illness, allergies, learning disability, or coronary artery disease. When a family senses danger or too much pain in acknowledging distressing components of their subjective world, they focus on problems that seem less ambiguous, less personally dis-

rupting. A great deal of ambiguity and many symbolic concerns are packed into reality problems. When some peripheral members are included, they have less anxiety about specific situations and thus more freedom to speak of the unspeakable. They see less of the symbolic danger. Also, the larger group is able to bear more pain without paralysis.

Use of the family-of-origin consultation in the beginning stage is in the interest of *building* a therapeutic alliance. In the middle stage, it occurs in the interest of *deepening* the therapeutic alliance.

Middle Stage

The reader may have concluded, correctly, that any course of family therapy should include a consultation interview with the family of origin. The consultation experience is most profound in this stage of therapy. The indications in the middle stage include: 1) Family Wants a Ph.D. in Family Therapeusis/Preventive Medicine Project, 2) Impasse, 3) Crisis Occurs, 4) Therapy is Failing.

1) Family Wants a Ph.D. in Family Therapeusis/Preventive Medicine Project. This suggests a family who come in for an inventory of "where we are," or they say, "Bill is having trouble in the ninth grade, but we think it is a family problem." The implication is that there is little or no conflict about the family trouble, but only a wish to add to the richness of family life by consulting with the larger family.

2) Impasse. Therapy has been useful; the initial symptoms have been helped, but the family continues to feel they are stuck and wishes to go further. Sometimes this is manifested in uneven anxiety in the parents. The case of Judy and Chuck cited earlier is an example of this problem. He was ready to quit; she was frightened about ending.

3) Therapy Is Failing. The treatment effort is clearly not going where the family wishes to go. The therapist can acknowledge his/her failure to provide enough security for them to move into a more honest expression of their self-doubt or the therapist may see the failure as the result of too much pressure for change. Sometimes, the family chooses to end at this point. However, in most cases, when the therapist acknowledges his/her failure, it allows the family clearer access to their desperation and to the self-doubt that lies behind it. The initiative switches from "What are you going to do for us?" to "What can we do to salvage the project?" At this point, an interview with the family of origin is of benefit and results in a renewed investment from the family.

4) Crisis Arises. The earlier case example, in which the grandfather humiliated his businessman son, was stimulated by a middle phase crisis. We had suggested that the father's family come in very early in therapy. For one reason or another, this did not occur. The interview described came about when, after a period of improvement, the son who was in trouble went joyriding in his mother's car without permission and was arrested for shooting his pellet gun in a public place. The parents felt discouraged and hopeless. "We thought we were getting somewhere," the mother complained. The therapist replied, "I think you are getting somewhere, but the changes make it difficult for him. I believe it would help if you both got your parents to come in." "How would that help?" asked Father. "Do you recall at the first phone call when you told me that your first therapist asked your son what an ideal father would be like, and you were surprised that he had no answer? When you told me that, my first thought was to wonder how you, Dad, would answer the same question. My belief is that you are struggling with your own father, but you forgot about it." "So what will happen if they come in?" queries the father. "I don't know, but, whatever it is, it won't happen if they don't come in."

Whom to Invite

When I speak of the extended family, I mean vertical and horizontal extensions. It is best to have the full family of origin present for the consultation. I do not like to have one grandparent when both are still living. It changes the process and usually results in a less productive experience. It is also helpful to have at least one of the parents' siblings come so that the consult extends beyond the parent-child triangle, which is present with only one person from the second generation.

It is important to have family members to whom a lot of negative or ambivalent affect is attached. When they are not there, they automatically increase in importance as the family talks about them and focuses anxiety and anger upon them. With that person present, the anxiety level is raised so that something significant is more likely to happen. Anger tends to clarify differences and make a move for resolution of those differences more likely.

INVITING FAMILIES

The following is designed to provide guidance in implementing the family consultation when you are convinced it is worthwhile. Let us say that you have seen a family six times and would like to get the family of origin in for a consultation. What follows are samples of dialogue that help to set up the interview.

"Where do we go from here?" asks the family. "I think you would feel you got a lot more out of therapy if your background families could come in for a consultation interview," answers the therapist. "They don't even know we are in therapy." "This would give you a good way to tell them, and the purpose of the interview is not for them to know more about your problems or why you are in therapy, but rather to help you get a better sense of where you come from and how you got to be like you are. They may even have some advice on where to go from here."

Another scenario begins with acknowledgment of an impasse. "I am worried that we are headed for failure and suggest that you get your background family involved," says the therapist. "My mother would come, but I don't think I can get my father." "Tell them they are coming in as consultants, to help *me* help you. I don't want them to be patients. And by the way, I will get a co-therapist to come in for that interview to improve my vision. My investment in you might cause some blindness about your parents."

Generally, it is not a good idea to divide the generations. If the grandmother will come but not the grandfather, it is best to postpone the interview until both are available. The presence of one parent adds to the content, but something vital from the process will be missing.

"I raised that question with them just after the second interview. My mother and father will come, but my sister won't." The therapist then responds, "I suggest you ask her again. Tell her it is important to *you*. If she has any questions, you can tell her to call me so that I can explain what I am doing, and she can ask questions about the components she is uneasy with."

There is a common situation where a couple are in therapy and the wife's family has been in, so the husband reluctantly agrees to invite his family. "Be sure to invite them in a way that says you want them to come. With your capacity for passivity, I am concerned that you will covertly tell them not to come while you are inviting them. Would any of your siblings be likely to attend?"

It helps if the whole family comes rather than just the grandparents. When there is at least one other representative of the second generation, it gives a much fuller sense of the family rather than just the single triangle (mother, father, son). That is, if your patient's father and mother come in, you can learn something about the father-mother-son triangle in the family. If your patient's sister comes also, more relationship triangles are added, plus a clearer picture of the family generation gap. The range and depth of the discussion increase significantly.

It is my belief that the extended family should be included in the course of family therapy with every family, but the family has veto power over the suggestion. They don't have to do it. Therapy does not have to be successful. The therapist, however, is free to turn down any configuration that the therapists view as not helpful. The family may wish the interview to fail rather than upset some important member of the family. For example, grandmother will come but grandfather refuses. I am inclined to say, "I don't think we should meet. His unwillingness gives the sense that it is too dangerous and I think it would be a waste. You do not need a failure like that just now."

Before starting therapy, you can make the three-generation interview a condition of beginning. However, once the therapy process has begun, it is an error to *demand* the family consultation. At that point it becomes an elective adjunct. The family has to weigh the *value* of having the interview against the *danger* of having such an interview. In the same way, the family has to decide what secrets can be exposed in therapy or at what costs the secrets can be maintained.

THE FAMILY ARRIVES

When the family of origin comes in for the first interview, the beginning is easy because all are in the same place. However, when they come in later in the therapy, the family of origin's appearance is always awkward. It reminds me of the dinner party where the guests have started eating. When more guests arrive late, the dinner has to be interrupted and then restarted.

When the outside family arrives, they are undoubtedly anxious and wary. It takes little imagination for them to know they have been talked about. If you are new at doing these interviews, you may be surprised by your feelings toward the family based on what you have learned. Be wary of what you have learned and how it affects your own feelings, because these feelings arise from your protective caring for and/or identification with your patients. Be at your social best at the beginning, but be prepared to do the serious work of supporting the family's effort to repair. Bear in mind that you are in *your* office; you make the rules and visitors have to follow them. The family know a good deal about the family, but you are the expert in psychotherapy. Younger therapists are sometimes intimidated by grandparents. In your head, place yourself in the position of parent to the oldest member.

I am routinely surprised by the physical appearance of family members. Usually, they are much smaller and older than I imagined from the family projections. As I indicated earlier, the projective process can be softened if you include a co-therapist.

When all are seated, I begin by introducing the purpose of the interview. "Let me tell you why I suggested this family interview. I have learned over the years that the kind of problems we see are best helped by our helping the family get together to talk about themselves. People know more about families than professionals know about families. I asked you to come in so you can help me help this part of your family get more out of their living. The idea is to talk about the family, what it is like and what it has been through over the last generations. The interview will be more rewarding if you talk about those things you feel uneasy talking about."

Then, I ask the highest ranking, emotionally most distant member to begin. That is usually a grandfather. I have tried different patterns as I go along over the years, but consistently the most useful idea is to talk about the family of origin, not to focus on the nuclear family in treatment. And although this may sound sexist, I also begin with the senior ranking man, not because I think he is the most important person in the family, but rather because if he doesn't get involved in the beginning he will inevitably stay out and defer to the emotional picture painted by the women in the family.

The pattern that I use most at present is to ask the grandfather what his parents were like or what his grandparents were like. "What kind of family did you grow up in? What can you say about your parents' marriage?" It may seem ridiculously irrelevant at first, but when Grandfather is talking back a generation, he is generally less guarded than he would be if he was talking about his own marriage or his relationship to his children. In some strange way, being irrelevant helps get into more useful territory. As the interview continues, it is helpful to ask, "What was your family like when your children were growing up?" or "What was your son, Bill, like when he was a little boy?" One reason to begin further back is so that everyone is getting fresh information. If the interview begins with a discussion of your patient's nuclear family of origin, the grandfather may talk about something you already know about.

The idea is to focus on *relationships*, emphasizing the idea that the family is not a collection of individuals, but rather a network, a pattern of relationships. "What was the marital relationship between your father and mother like?" "How did your mother get along with her mother-in-law?" "How did your mother meet your father?" "How did you and your wife meet?" "How did your parents feel about your plans to marry her?"

Talking about relationships of less immediate significance gives more freedom to think and talk about relationships of the present. There is less defensiveness and more spontaneity, less second-guessing. Grandfather is describing his parents' family. But simultaneously, he is painting a portrait of the family of the present, especially on a process level. As the background is filled in, they begin to move to those relationships which are more relevent to the present. The discussion of past relationships is like a projective psychological test. The past is basically a metaphorical description of the present, or as I suggested earlier, the present shapes the story of the past.

As the interview goes along, try to add to the intrafamily stress. If Grandfather died young of a heart attack, ask, "Who was to blame?" When they say, "Well, of course, we had our share of problems, everybody does," or, "Yeah, I had the same trouble when I was a kid," the therapist should ask, "Is there a story about it? What did you do? What did your mother say about it? Do you think your father was disappointed in you? Does your family blame you for the divorce?" These kinds of questions, if the family takes them on, adds to the symbolic richness of the interview. When the interview is successful, it frequently turns into a storytelling session where I have little to do. I begin to think I almost understand intimacy in some of these sessions.

The family process will decide how much can happen or how successful the interview will be. I often find myself feeling anxious or disoriented when these interviews begin. But I know it is usually not helpful to push. I almost routinely say after 20 minutes or so, "I am concerned this interview is going to fail, because it feels like you are being too careful with each other. Do you have any idea what you are so frightened about?" Or, "Do you have any idea what you are avoiding?" Ask the second generation if they intended to sit back and watch or is there something they want to know.

If the interview goes well, the family may find itself in a territory that is ambiguous and painful. When a confrontation arises, the therapist's responsibility is to pay attention to the process, to comment on and critique it. If the grown-up daughter is angry with her mother, the mother may try to deny the reason for her daughter's anger. Therapist: "You sound like you don't want her to be angry. It may be that you saw the situation very differently, but you can't deny her anger about it or her interpretation of it."

The success of the interview is not dependent upon the therapist's questions or on how the therapist pushes. Success is based upon the family's desperation about themselves. The therapist takes responsibility for the success or failure of the interview. It is the therapist's job to provide enough security so that the family can deepen their honesty.

There are times when the family of origin interview is like a symphony. The diverse sounds of family members harmonize because the family has the sense of themselves as a whole. The therapist has the freedom to sit back and listen. However, most family-of-origin interviews are like jam sessions or hootenannies. They may never start, or they start and lose momentum, or they ramble around picking up and leaving behind a variety of themes. When they go well, I recall why I am so enchanted by working with families.

ENDING THE INTERVIEW

As indicated earlier, the outcome from these interviews, like most psychotherapy, is difficult to assess. The outcome is idiosyncratic and often goes undiscussed and basically unobserved. The therapist has little sense of what happens that is important for the family in these interviews and attempts to summarize will often be reflections of his/ her own family. What is most important goes on in the family's unconscious. For this reason, it is important not to summarize the interview for the family. Frequently, at the end of the consultation interview, the family will ask the therapist to summarize the experience. Always refuse. They generally are asking you to clarify their confusion. If they are confused, it means something important happened and they should take it seriously and not try to get someone else to explain it. Likewise, when the family comes back and asks what you got out of the interview, say "Not very much, how about you?" The effect of these interviews is like a time-release medication—it goes on over a long period of time. The therapist's effort to summarize the interview may undermine the healing process that should take place in the family since they adopt the therapist's experience of the interview and diminish their own.

As to whether there should be a second consultation, I generally leave that up to the family. Very few come back a second time.

CONCLUSION

This chapter divides itself in two parts. The first speculates on how the family of origin consultation works. Having the family together for a conference provides a unique experience. The history obtained from the group is different from the history provided by an individual family member. A crucial difference is in the expanded access to the family unconscious, which I am playfully/seriously referring to as a "family group psychosis." The family consultation is important because it helps the therapist better understand the nuclear family. In addition, I believe these consultation interviews are implicitly and powerfully therapeutic, and have an impact on the primary process structure of the family.

The second part of the chapter was designed to be a brief field guide for setting up and conducting a family consultation interview.

Often, a session in this primary process hot tub brings the exhilaration of a renewed sense of unity. "We feel like Us, and it feels good." However, with other families a sense of desperation occurs with the awareness of the fact that we are who we are. We have met the enemy and it is Us. The family is able to avoid deeper levels of desperation by not acknowledging itself as a group, and thus avoids reliving painful, dark days of the past.

When there has been too much pain in the family, real or imagined, it can be difficult to get together. The grieving that looks so necessary from the outside, is not available inside. Or, as often happens, the family is able to acknowledge they cannot get much from the background family, their primary process sense of identity is revised by the experience, and they will have to take responsibility for their own destiny. Family loyalty considerations supersede the initiative for therapeutic change. Family therapy is more likely to fail when the family does not have the family's permission to change (Whitaker, 1976). In effect, a consultation with the more powerful or more vulnerable powers-that-be in the family of origin gives the therapist permission to take on the job of symbolic foster parent. Convening the family of origin gives permission not only to continue therapy, but also to bring about needed change. When the interview fails, it does so because the family is not giving permission to go ahead. Something from the shadowy recesses of primary process whispers of danger or pain in change. There may be no overt decision, but the family discontinues after this interview.

I have been teaching and writing about family therapy for over 20 years. I find my description of the process to be less and less adequate. However, my investment in, and enjoyment of, this work constantly deepen. Every time I had a family in for a consultation visit during the writing of this paper, I added something or changed something, or began to think I was leaving out a crucial essence. A family's participation is a complicated process, yet a simple one. I learn more each time. Family therapy to me means working with a three-generation group.

The inclusion of a multigeneration group has a constant impact on how I see my work as a family therapist. There is an impulse for health in a family that can be activated in a time of need. Those of us who work with families too often overlook the symbolic integrity of the family, which leads to the capacity to function with administrative effectiveness on its own behalf. The impulse for health can be disrupted by family disputes, "holy wars" and the methods of mental health professionals. Grandparents can be very supportive of families or they may be toxic to growth or change. In any case, convening extended families gives clarity to the patterns that effect our patients (Keith, 1989).

ACKNOWLEDGMENTS

The author wishes to acknowledge the extensive assistance provided by Noel Keith in the preparation of this chapter.

BIBLIOGRAPHY

Bagarozzi, D. & Anderson, S. (1989). *Personal, Marital, and Family Myths.* New York: W.W. Norton & Company.

Bateson, G. (1972). *Steps to an Ecology of the Mind.* San Francisco: Chandler Publishing Company.

Keith, D. (1989). The family's own system: the symbolic context of health. In L. Combrinck-Graham (Ed.), *Children in Family Contexts* (pp. 327–346). New York: Guilford Press.

Keith, N. (1992). Integrating therapeutic play into family therapy. Unpublished manuscript.

Whitaker, C. (1976). A family is a four dimensional relationship. In P. Guerin (Ed.), *Family Therapy: Theory and Practice* (pp. 182–192). New York: Gardner Press.

Winnicott, D. (1971). *Playing and Reality.* New York: Basic Books.

7

"With a Little Help from My Friends": Friends as Consultative Resources

Russell Haber

I first asked friends to attend a family therapy meeting in a consultation session with my wife, Karen Cooper-Haber, Ph.D. She asked me to consult on a case that involved excessive fighting by a middle school child. The family therapy was helping with family problems but did not substantially modify the child's behavioral problems at school. I asked Karen to request someone from the grandparent generation to attend the consultation session. In my head, I heard Carl Whitaker's words that adding somebody new from the therapist's side, clients' side, or better yet from both sides can bring forth new perspectives and help break a therapeutic impasse.

I began the session by having father's mother talk about her family of origin and procreated family. Grandmother described historical patterns that contained the distinct message that one should not trust outsiders and that the eldest, adult son was expected to take care of his parents. Since the father's parents had gone through a bitter divorce and were in poor health, the legacy of caretaking was particularly difficult to enact. Consequently, the father's sense of responsibility to his two families did not allow him the luxury of time to socialize. In addition, the father discussed his inability to have close relationships when he was a teenager. Thus, there was a parallel process between the lack of sociability of the father and his son.

At the end of the session, I asked the father to help his son learn how to socialize so that the son could emerge from this family pattern, "the family well." Additionally, I suggested that Karen bring the child's peers into subsequent family sessions to check the progress of the father's ability to get his child out of the family well.

Later, Karen conveyed that they had the family-peer session and that the child was enrolled in a school counseling group. She said that the father had taken the initiative to help his son develop friendships and that they had obviously been successful as the boy had made several friends. The feedback from the teachers affirmed that the child was friendlier, more outgoing, and had abstained from further aggressive behavior.

The confluence of friends and family in family therapy made perfect sense—the resources of the family helped foster better friendships and the resources of the friends helped alleviate family and developmental impasses. Therefore, I became much more attentive for opportunities to assess and involve friends as resources for individual and familial growth. Serendipitously, I had a run of one-child families with various school and behavioral problems. The various, repetitive scenarios involved two adult parents who had failed in some aspects with their child and had recruited an adult therapist to work with the family. Usually, the child would unenthusiastically accompany the parents to the family therapy meetings. Consequently, the sessions predominantly involved three adults speaking the 'mature' language of therapy. The adults contemplated why the child was being inappropriate and how they could help the child be more socially compliant to parental/societal expectations.

I remember feeling at one point that it was essentially unfair to have three adults and only one child deal with a developmental problem. Precipitously, I asked the child to even the sides the next time and bring in two friends so that we could have a three-on-three game of helping the development of the family. The child liked the idea and to my surprise the parents were very receptive to the viewpoints of the child's friends. We three adults were very interested in experiencing the exchange between children in the midst of an adult arena called psychotherapy. I felt that these "only" children needed a critical mass of other supportive children so that they would be more willing to honestly (differentiatedly) express themselves rather than just impulsively react to the demands of the adults. Table 1 summarizes the differences between child-child versus adult-child relationships on eight dimensions. The generational perspectives provide a relationship based on differences that indeed make a difference (Bateson, 1972).

Table 1
Child-Child Versus Adult-Child Relationships

Dimension	Child-Child	Adult-Child
Rule-setting	Egalitarian	Authoritative
Time orientation	Present	Future, Past, Present
Nature of relationship	Autonomous	Dependent
Choice of relationship	Voluntary	Involuntary
Goal of relationship	Satisfaction	Purposeful
Values: Dress, Music, etc.	Similar	Different
Developmental stage	Similar Tasks	Generation Gap
Context	School, Play	Work or Home

Initially, most of my work with peer consultants involved preadolescent and adolescent friends (Haber, 1987). Perhaps my bias toward the influence of youthful friends reflects 1) the preponderance of free time to play with friends in these stages of life, 2) the impressive socializing influence of peers at a very impressionable period of life, 3) the intense need for friends as a means to begin the process of greater autonomy from the psycho/social/economic dependence on the family.

However, there were other less obvious reasons for limiting friend consultants to children and not adults. Primarily, I was at a stage in life in which I had little time and energy for friends. I was family, career, and financially oriented. Additionally, my parents did not have many close friends outside the family, so I did not have a model for integrating adult friends into the family. My priorities seemed to match the values of my responsible, adult clients who preferred to focus on their marriages, children, and making ends meet rather than struggle with their capacity for nonfamilial intimacy and recreation. Therefore, it took some time to learn from preadolescent and adolescent friendships before I felt free to expose, explore, and include adult friendships in the therapeutic arena. This chapter will discuss a generational and life cycle perspective of the family and exemplify how adult friends can help resolve marital and family therapy impasses.

THE THREE FLOORS OF THE FAMILY STORY

Maurizio Andolfi often uses a metaphor that describes the three generational floors in the household: The children live on the bottom floor, parents on the middle floor, and grandparents on the top floor. In addition, the attic contains the artifacts of the ancestors. Each floor has different views, goals, customs, language, jobs or activities, physical capabilities, relationships, and perceptions and priorities concerning the past, present, and future. In addition, each floor has rooms or spaces for the males and females that reflect differences based on gender rather than generation. Despite the proclivity of dual-career families, females have remained more attentive to the activities and aesthetics within the home, whereas males are usually less preoccupied with the home and more concerned with outside matters. Each floor needs more or less attention at different points of the family life cycle.

The grandparent floor is a complex floor because it comprises two family systems with different family values, expectations, and practices. The adult floor contains the marriage (assuming the parents have maintained their marriage) and links the bottom and each spouse's top floors, which represents a major challenge. Carl Whitaker concisely described the marital dilemma, "It's really just two scapegoats sent out by two families to reproduce each other.... The battle is which one will it be" (1982, p. 368). Therefore, it is important to note which family members visit the grandparent floor and how often. Frequently, one set of grandparents may be very important while the other set has minimal influence or involvement.

If the parents get divorced, the structure of the house becomes infinitely more complex. Certain rooms may become vacated and other rooms or spaces may be filled by stepparents, other siblings, and more grandparents. There is much more coming and going in divorced homes to accommodate various visitation schedules. Although divorce changes the physical living arrangements, the noncustodial parent is a ghostly presence in the minds of the children. Besides divorced homes, there are other complex familial arrangements that could include foster children, friends, exchange students, child care workers, and other non-kin members. Each of these individuals will change the organization of the home and bring unique histories and perceptions into the family.

Although the structure of most family houses contains bedrooms, kitchen, bathroom, and perhaps places to recreate, they have diverse structural designs and very different interior designs. Some houses do not have any closed doors, others have areas that are off limits to the different generations. Some are geared for the activities of the children while others are oriented for the grandparents. Some have at least one parent home most of the day, whereas others barely have the parents home at all. There is no single, inherently "correct" architectural design for the family home, but endless possibilities for best using the resources and variables that comprise the group that is considered the "relevant" family. When there are sufficient and unresolvable problems among residents on the floors, between the floors, or with the household member and the community; the family may look for professional resources to resolve the impasse.

THE GENERATIONAL POSITION OF THE FAMILY THERAPIST

Usually, the marital or parental floor makes the request for therapy. Once this request is made, the therapist has many decisions about exploring the floors of the home. Should the therapist initially join the floor of the children, parents, or grandparents? Should the therapist explore the attic? Should the therapist temporarily align with one parent or one of the children? Should the therapist request the grandparents to come into the therapy? Should the therapist join the seriousness of the parents, the playfulness and irreverence of the children, or the respectful distance of the grandparents? Should the therapist agree to see a member of the household individually in therapy? Should the therapist push for the family to bring in the noncustodial parent and grandparents? The answers to such questions will invariably expose the therapist's accommodation to the different floors.

Family therapy, inherently, is a multigenerational therapeutic intervention. The importance of the present generational structure (Minuchin, 1974) and the historic transgenerational relationships and patterns (Bowen, 1978) to family health and pathology have been clearly articulated. Furthermore, several family therapy models (Bowen, 1978; Satir, 1987; Winter & Aponte, 1987) suggest that the therapist's emotional and chronological position in his/her family of origin facilitates or encumbers the therapist's exploration and connection to the different generations and genders in the household. For example, a therapist who was a parentified child from a single-parent family could have a learned tendency to become a co-parent when working with a single-parent client family.

Similarly, the gender roles and patterns learned in a therapist's culture or family of origin could be unwittingly transmitted by "therapeutic" alignments, communication patterns, or conceptualization of the problem. For instance, a therapist whose father was frequently out of control might shy away from issues in a family therapy that could provoke father's strong feelings. In such a case, the therapist would unwittingly reiterate a family rule to compensate for father's emotional frailty.

Additionally, the therapist's past and present position in the life cycle in his/her procreated family could also significantly influence the therapeutic process (Simon, 1989). For instance, I have immediately favored a nine-year-old boy because he would remind me of my son. Likewise, a therapist might overempathize with a beleaguered parent of an adolescent if he or she was raising a teenager. Therefore, the focus of changing the rigid proclivities of the therapist may be more instructional, at times, than attending to theories, strategies, and techniques (Haber, in press; 1990a).

If a therapist regularly prefers one floor over the other two, then the therapist's position in the family house will be evident to the different generations. The children may assume that the therapist is always in the marital bedroom or the parlor on the parental floor. This perception of adult bias by children is typical since the therapist usually belongs chronologically to the parental generation and is being paid by the parents to assume responsibility for helping the family. The agile and creative therapist, however, is one who can move up and down the stairs to the different floors with all or most of the family members. When this occurs, the generation gap becomes less obvious as the family members learn to perceive, understand, and communicate with each other's reality. In this scenario, the family could truly become mutually resourceful.

Is the goal, then, that the therapist become a multigenerational and gender chameleon? Could a therapist play with the kids, be "bad" with the teenagers, work hard with Mother, try to pave Dad's way back to the family, and provide a place for the grandparents to share their stories and wisdom gained from life's experiences? Such a therapist would be individually polemic and over time systemically neutral. However, I can act "as if" I were a teenage girl by being interested in appearance, distracted with adult or serious topics, absorbed into pop culture, oblivious to the distant future, but I wonder if I actually pull it off. At best, I think I can spend 10 to 15 minutes in a female teenager's room without knowing what to do, how to do it, and, generally, how to be in that world. I may even have that same type of awkward experience with an adult male dealing with a different life cycle or cultural issues. Although the furniture in the room may look familiar, I still may misunderstand the subtlety and meaning of the different objects in the room. Therefore, it is important for therapists to be mindful of their experiential and perceived position in the family genogram. Does the therapist mostly belong on the grandparent, parent, or child floor; and what is the nature of the relationship (older, younger, close, distant, competitive, sympathetic, etc.) in the various rooms? This position will undoubtedly illuminate gender, generation, and culture limitations.

There is an alternative to becoming a chameleon, ignoring our limitations, or chronically cohabiting in one of the rooms. Friends can be recruited as consultants to the family therapy to help bridge generational, gender, and cultural issues that are beyond the therapist's purview. Since friends resonate in the rooms where they are welcome to congregate, their presence quickly influences one floor of the home and perhaps transforms the entire family home. Different personalities of the family emerge in the face of the social exchange with friends. The peer contact allows the inhabitants of each floor the freedom to speak the same social language without attempting to translate one's psychosocial reality to the language of a different generation. The play and social intercourse prevalent in friendships offer insight into the life cycle preoccupations of each floor.

FRIENDS AND THE FAMILY LIFE CYCLE

Whether child or adult, it is friends who provide a reference outside the family against which to measure and judge ourselves; who help us during passages that require our separation and individuation; who support us as we adapt to new roles and new rules; who heal the hurts and make good the deficits of other relationships in our lives; who offer the place and encouragement for the development of parts of self that, for whatever reasons, are inaccessible in the family context. It's with friends that we test our sense of self-in-the-world, that our often inchoate, intuitive, unarticulated vision of the possibilities of a self-yet-to-become finds expression (Rubin, 1985, p. 13).

The nature of the universe is that we encounter the opportunity and the task of changing houses and floors. Children grow up, spend more time out of the house, and then roam around the neighborhood. Adolescents' territory extends farther away from the house. Young adults frequently move away from the family home. When they marry, they negotiate with their spouses how to build and decorate their house based on their mutual dreams. When they have children, they move to the second, parental floor and encounter parental responsibility. Their parents now become grandparents and move to the third floor; knowing full well that someday their deeds and creeds will be merely memories or material goods in the house or will perhaps be resigned to a chest stored away in the attic.

Life-cycle theory (Carter & McGoldrick, 1989) demonstrates the interplay between the floors during the transformation of one of the floors. For instance, the turbulence of adolescent separation occurs as the parents deal with midlife issues and the grandparents face retirement and aging concerns. If the family also confronts other traumas such as divorce, chronic illness, job loss, or premature death, the stress exponentially reverberates throughout the family system. For example, if mother and/or father are caretaking an infirmed grandparent on the third floor, their absence and concern will readily affect a child on the bottom floor.

Families frequently enter therapy when developmental and unexpected stresses are too painful or difficult to resolve in the family. The therapist's job is to help the family members better use their resources to leave the predictability of the impasse and meet new developmental challenges. However, the therapist should also be open to the possibility of enlisting resources from the social context of the family. Friends are ideal consultants for life cycle dilemmas due to their ability to:

1. *Provide developmental markers.* They can experientially understand and convey the developmental issues of their friends. Also, they can compare the other generational family members' reactions to their family responses.
2. *Bridge generation gaps.* They decrease defensiveness by their support and affirmation of their friends. Additionally, friends frequently exert positive peer pressure by their expectation of appropriate social behavior. Their presence bridges generation gaps by increasing communication.
3. *Promote perspective-taking.* Due to their trustworthiness, friends can often help one another reflect on and reconsider maladaptive behaviors more than family members or professionals can.
4. *Show a different picture.* Since friends have a mutually selective, non-obligatory relationship, their portrayals are usually more realistic, positive, and healthy than the family's preoccupations with dysfunctional behavior.
5. *Extend the therapy into the social milieu.* Friends can help family members meet therapeutic goals outside the meetings.
6. *Consult as problem solvers.* Friends can provide resources and insight that may be unknown to the therapist and the family. Therapists should not underestimate the homespun wisdom and creativity of nonprofessional resources. Additionally, the admission that the therapist needs help induces the family to search for new resources and resolutions.
7. *Challenge family or therapist enmeshment.* The ritual of recruiting a friend into the family therapy challenges the fantasy that the family or the therapist can provide all of the resources.
8. *Work on their friendship.* Dysfunctional relational patterns that are present in the family may be replicated in the friendship. Also, rigid friendships may malevolently affect the family and prevent

individual development. Therefore, on occasion, the therapist may ask the friend to temporarily leave the role of the consultant and deal with these patterns.

Medical researchers are finding that too often their interventions, intended to fight a disease entity, actually suppress the body's own capacity to cure itself...Just so, we (psychotherapists) may discover that in many cases our most effective interventions will be to potentate the healing powers of the intimate network rather than to administer directly to the observed dysfunction (Broderick, 1988, p. 221).

FRIENDS AS CONSULTATIVE RESOURCES: FROM IDEA TO REALITY

Stage I. Pre-interview: Setting the Stage

First and most important, the friends should be a live presence in the therapy room before their attendance is requested. They become manifest through the reflection of their meaning for and influence on the different family members. If a therapist has never discussed the systemic impact of various friendships, the family should be concerned about the necessity of inviting that particular person.

It is often necessary to explicate the temporary, consultative role of the friend in order to give the family a clear boundary about the degree of involvement of the friend. The family may decide to restrict discussion of certain topics in the presence of the friend. The family's right to confidentiality should be respected, especially since the friend-family meeting usually focuses on how friends can positively enhance the development of the individual and the family.

Stage II. Establishing the Friend as a Consultant

Despite careful preparation about the roles and goals of the consultation, the initial moments of the friend consultation frequently have an air of uncertainty, anxiety, and expectancy. Since this is generally a new experience for the client family and the friend (who may be altogether unfamiliar with the process of psychotherapy), the therapist initially needs to play the role of the host. This involves orienting the friend in jargon-free, clear, and direct language about the concern of the therapeutic system and the rationale for the decision to include friends in the therapy. The depth and breadth of this introduction depend on the implicit and explicit agreements between the family and the therapist regarding the disclosure of content.

Following the therapist's orientation, members of the client family can elaborate on the problem, the process of the therapy, and their hopes for this consultation session. This stage is critical because it not only delineates the focus of the consultation, but elevates the friend to the role of consultant.

Stage III. Weaving the Consultation into the Therapy

The procedures depend upon the individual family members, the consultant, the identified problem, and the relationship of the client system to the therapist. Later in this chapter, two case studies that exemplify different roles of adult friend consultants in marital and family therapy will be presented.

Generally, in Stage III, the therapist asks the consultant to further explore the developmental impasse from his/her unique position. This could include asking the consultant to discuss 1) the perceived motivation that surrounds the developmental and generational problems; 2) how the consultant friend and his/her family handle similar developmental issues; 3) the nature of the friendship; 4) the behavior of the client friend outside the family context; and 5) other matters that they consider relevant for the therapeutic relationship.

In addition to being in a "meta" position, the friend could enter the process of the therapy by engaging the family members in dialogue, sharing fantasies and play, and through physical or emotional support. The homespun wisdom of friends should not be underestimated. Frequently, they are more direct, succinct, and emotionally responsive than trained therapists.

Stage IV. From Consultant Back to Friend

In the final stage of the friend consultation session, the therapist should implicitly or explicitly shift the friend from the hierarchical position as consultant to the egalitarian role as friend. This shift restructures the previous therapist-friend consultative alliance into a new partnership that mutually validates the friendship and the therapeutic relationship. The therapist should also focus on the relationship of the friend and the other family members. Optimistically, their relationship will have become more cohesive as a result of the consultation.

The therapist could facilitate these processes by summarizing the session and thanking the consultant(s), requesting the family and the friend to avoid discussing the consult for 48 hours—thus, marking a boundary between the therapy room and their social existence, discussing the nature of confidentiality, directing discussion of the differences between therapy relationships and friendships; acknowledging the strengths of the client family (courage, openness, etc.) and the strengths of the friendship, and suggesting recommendations based on issues covered in the session. The goal is for the friend to be naturally therapeutic as a friend rather than being a professional.

In some cases, such as a suicidal crisis or substance-abuse problem, friends may be mobilized to continue a therapeutic role for the friend. They can be a tremendous help for an overwhelmed family. In these cases, their presence may be needed in future therapy sessions. The ultimate therapeutic goal, however, would be to transform caretaking friendships into differentiated friendships.

Stage V. After the Consultation

The consultation provides a view of the friend and the family from a different lens. This view can remain in the therapy room as a reference point long after the consultation. For example, a single parent, described as hiding her vulnerable feelings, was asked whether she shared her sadness and frustration before she lost her temper. The voice of her friends became a challenge to solicit understanding and support rather than to avoid her feelings. This message was equally important for her teenage daughter who could more clearly see her mother through the eyes of friends.

The peer consultation should be examined for any deleterious effects. There are several potential problem areas to note: 1) Does the friend resume a role-appropriate relationship with the family members? 2) Does the friend suffer any personal/emotional distress due to issues raised during the session? 3) Do the family members feel overly embarrassed or vulnerable about having exposed themselves in the consultation session? 4) Were there any unforeseen consequences or fallout from the consultation session? These problems may be addressed with the family or in a follow-up interview with the friend.

CLINICAL APPLICATIONS

An "Intervention" for Leaving Home

I inherited a client family from an intern who was finishing his year-long internship. The intern had been providing individual therapy to a 22-year-old engineering student who had been the valedictorian of his high school. The student came to therapy when he stopped attending classes. He and his parents were alarmed because he had experienced two unpleasant years in the U.S. Army after academic failure at a different university. The intern had two family therapy meetings with the student's parents, who were both high achievers and the oldest children in their families of origin. Both parents had fathers who were described as incompetent alcoholics. The parents were very worried that their son abused alcohol and drugs, suffered from poor self esteem, and had no academic or vocational goals. Their son, Dave Jr., asserted that life would be fine if his parents would stop worrying and leave him alone, although with continued financial support.

In a joint interview with the departing therapist, Dave Jr. and his parents described a tremendous generation gap. The parents lectured, threatened, and became very angry with Dave Jr.'s irresponsibility, while Dave Jr. defended himself against their controlling remarks through passive withdrawal. Both generations felt misunderstood. I accepted the case and suggested that each family member bring friends into the next session so as to promote greater understanding of one another's perspective. Whether it was the newness of a different therapist or the family's deep sense of frustration, the family readily agreed to recruit new resources for the therapy.

Three friends of the student, one friend of the father, and the mother's mother, sister, and friend attended the next session. The large kin-social network resembled a substance abuse "intervention" team (Johnson, 1986), a strategically planned meeting of kin and network members organized to confront the denial system of a substance abuser and press for a treatment plan (often at an inpatient treatment center). Although the parents suspected substance abuse, the intent of this meeting was not limited to a substance abuse intervention. The goals were to assess the severity of substance abuse, provide social support for each of the family members, and bridge the generational gap.

Dave Jr.'s friends clearly said that he was not a substance abuser or heavy drinker. They said that his drinking was similar to their social group. They were concerned, however, that he was doing poorly in school and was in immediate danger of flunking out of school. One friend related several difficulties with his own father and that it had been important for his father to prove his trust by giving up control. Mother's sister also revealed the difficulties she had experienced with her son at the leaving home stage.

Sister: I think Patti and Dave (Dave Jr.'s mother and father) need to get into the situation where they don't have to control Dave Jr. I don't know how they could get to that since he is still dependent on them and still needs for them to help him financially...the control is what I think they need to let go of. I think that's what happened when we let our son go and he was able to turn it around.... *Mother's friend and father amplified their fears of letting go.*

Mother's friend (in response to Dave Jr.'s friends' assertion that his parents should back off): It's real easy to say you have to let go as long as we think that you are safe and out of harm's way. But when we fear for your actions and what those actions may lead to, then it is hard to let go.

Father: Letting go would be a simple task if I wasn't scared to death, if I didn't think he would break society's law and end up dead, in jail, or otherwise compromised.

After father tearfully discussed the pain caused by the distance and rebuke of his own father, the therapist commented on the importance of his relationship with his son. The rebellion and emotional distance that Dave experienced with his father were being created in a similar way with Dave Jr. Dave denied that he feared a similar cut-off of the father-son relationship even though their communication was becoming more polemic and less frequent. The following passage illustrates how the therapist reframed the school failure as the means for father and son to need one another. Dave Jr.'s best friend, Steve, disagreed with this hypothesis and represented Dave Jr.'s position, but the therapist and the grandmother highlighted the dilemma of becoming more autonomous.

Therapist: Maybe he does not want to let go. Maybe he wants to keep his father involved. Is that a crazy idea?

Steve: I haven't thought of it that way. I think you're incorrect.

Grandmother: I wondered about that, Steve. I wondered about that. (*everybody laughs*)

Therapist: What do you think about that?

Grandmother: I'm not going to answer this for both of them. Don't cut that string completely, but let it go, let it go, let it go. How about that Steve?

Steve: Never let the string go completely.

Grandmother: Don't let it go completely.

Therapist: I don't see it as a string, more like a chain that's wrapped around your father.

Steve: I don't believe that.

Grandmother: For you Dave Jr. it is. (*A loud clap of thunder occurs after grandmother's statement—totally unplanned*)

Therapist: I told you it's the truth.

In this dialogue, Steve represented Dave Jr.'s position while the grandmother and I reframed the rebellion. This allowed both the parents and Dave Jr. to observe the dilemma of autonomy from a more objective position. This distance allowed them to see their controlling-irresponsible polemic positions from an angle that both shared, more successful autonomy for Dave Jr.

The friends provided greater reassurance to the parents that Dave Jr. was acting more responsibly toward school than in the previous months. Additionally, they had less fear that he had a substance abuse addiction. Finally, the friends and family members supported the integrity of the individuals and the family as a whole. Their support and energy helped Dave Jr. and his parents adopt a less defensive posture with one another.

Although new content was not revealed during the session, it became a demarcation for new behaviors for the parents and Dave Jr. Although the issues of monetary support were discussed in the first therapy, the parents became more clear about their limits for financial support. Shortly thereafter, Dave Jr. got a job. Additionally, he had a more industrious attitude toward school. The family reflected a more cohesive and congenial attitude and decided to terminate therapy three sessions (three months) after the intervention.

Friends Aiding Recovery from an Affair

Tony and his wife, Sheila, physically separated after Sheila's one-year affair was discovered. They entered therapy in the hope of reconciling their marriage. Sheila said that she had an affair to fill the void in her marriage. She had lost respect for her husband after she repeatedly discovered him lying. Tony never felt good enough for Sheila and fabricated stories to make up for his inadequacies. The more she pulled away, the more he became insecure and the more he engaged in falsification. The less honest he became, the more she pulled away, and so on. The goal of therapy was to break this cycle by increasing the level of honesty and intimacy in their relationship.

Their friends, Lynn and Mike, were referenced quite frequently in the therapy meetings. Lynn and Mike lived out of town, but the two couples traveled together and spent many weekends at each other's homes. Lynn and Mike were described as having many personal and marital parallels to Sheila and Tony, including having gone through the process of recovery from an affair. Since their affair happened several years ago, they were living proof that a relationship could survive an affair. The consultation took place one year (19 interviews) after the beginning of the therapy. Tony and Sheila had resumed living together several months before this interview.

The session began with Sheila's complaint that Tony was not direct with his question about whether or not he should go to the store to buy beer. She felt "crazy" when Tony displayed such dependent behavior. Lynn defended Sheila's feeling of craziness.

Therapist: How does Tony's indirectness translate into becoming a psychiatric problem.

Lynn: When Tony does that, it feels to Sheila that she has to take all the responsibility for whatever happens. It got to a symbolic level...(*speaking in Sheila's voice*) "I have to make all the decisions. Please don't be weak, please make that decision yourself." I feel like Tony walks on eggshells a lot with Sheila and wants to please her. So he didn't make any decisions for fear that he would make a mistake.

Mike: I've been there. Tony and I have paralleled quite a bit in what we do...Sheila could have stopped it and broken his habit by not getting into it and just asking him to make the decision for himself. You (to Sheila) push his buttons like he pushes yours. It's definitely a two way street....I perceive Lynn going crazy the same way that I perceive you (*Sheila*) going crazy. When you (*both women*) become emotional and critical, I can't keep up with you. I am not a verbally defensive or offensive person. I can't keep ground. I have to let her run out.

Sheila: (*nodding her head understandingly*) So you get panicky? And you used to lie?

Mike: Yeah.

Sheila: (*laughs and tenderly shakes Tony*) So help him. I watch Lynn still do that to you.

Mike: And I panic the whole time she's doing that. It's still there and that's one thing we're still working on. I still have the panic. Sometimes I let her run her course or sometimes I say shut up and let me finish.

In itself relatively unimportant, the beer episode seemed like a nonthreatening entrance into the rigid underlying patterns. Lynn and Mike's alignment with Sheila and Tony along respective gender lines helped clarify the motivation behind Sheila and Tony's position. The beer episode became a forum to explore the existential issues of responsibility and support. Sheila and Tony could watch their "alter egos" engage without the pressure of interaction.

Later in the session, Lynn tried to get Tony to understand the motivation behind's Sheila's sarcasm. This did not work. Sheila, feeling Lynn's support, became very emotional.

Lynn: (*to Tony*) You're right, her parents are extremely sarcastic, they are biting. I know you are not used to that. But why is she choosing to access that? Because Sheila is not like that. Why would she choose to be sarcastic and hurt you?

Tony (*without answering the question, he directs the question to Sheila*): I'd like to know why you feel like you have to get sarcastic. That bothers me, that's a low blow.

Sheila: I know that bothers you.

Tony: Why?

Sheila: I get sarcastic when I am out of other resources.

Tony: (*almost in disbelief*) Do you know it when you get sarcastic? You know you're getting sarcastic and you do it on purpose.

Sheila: I do it because it's what I have left.... When I try being nice and being the good wife (*Tony interrupts*), when I try being nice and I try using new language (*Tony interrupts again, Sheila continues in a loud anguished voice*), I'm exhausted, Tony, just listen to me for a minute. (*with anguish and tears*) I have tried behavior mod, I have tried being nice, I have tried what our therapist has suggested, I have tried being more covert, being more conscious, I have tried everything I know and it still doesn't work, and sarcasm is my final straw. I have nothing else. I don't know what else to try. I am so tired, I am so fucking tired. (*Sheila starts weeping*)

Tony: I understand that you are tired.

Sheila: You don't understand it. You have never understood it.

Tony: What you are saying is that I don't get tired.

Sheila: I didn't say that.

Tony: Are you saying that I can't relate to what you're going through, because I haven't gone through it?

Therapist: Tony, how do you understand her tears right now?

Tony: The tears are definitely of frustration, but you know I'm tired, too.

Therapist: The question is do you want to understand her tears or do you want her to understand your frustration? I think if, simultaneously, you have your panic and she has her tears, it will escalate. I think you need to choose to focus on her tears or your panic.

The session has moved into the couple's impasse—the mutual frustration of Sheila's expectations and Tony's inadequacy. Sheila and Tony continue their attempt for a simultaneous solution of both getting their needs met rather than sequentially establishing a quid pro quo relationship. Lynn and Mike have both tried, in vain, to bridge the impasse. Rather than force a bridge, I saw the impasse as an opportunity to explore the chasm of the affair. I felt that Lynn and Mike were ready and able to discuss their exploration of this dangerous territory for Sheila and Tony.

Therapist: When Tony talked about his fear of becoming vulnerable, the issue of the affair, getting hurt, his not being enough for her became alive for me. I wonder what reactions you two have regarding the issues of vulnerability and the affair. How do you see it operating in their relationship?

Lynn (*to Sheila*): As much as we have talked, I don't think I have talked to you directly about the affair's effect on Tony. This is another common ground that we have. Even though we have worked through the affair, and I chose to tell him against the advice of my therapist, I don't know how that feels on the other end and perhaps I don't want to know because it is so painful. So I can understand how Tony is feeling vulnerable but I don't feel adequate to respond. (*both couples are holding hands and the mood and tones are soft*)

Mike: Tony and I have talked some about it....I still have a lot of anger about it and from time to time it surfaces.

Therapist: How do you see the issue that we just experienced with Tony, about opening your vulnerability. It looked to me like he was involved in self-protection rather than receiving her.

Mike: I didn't see it as protection as much as him wanting to hurt her. It wasn't vulnerability, but he was pissed.

Lynn: The reason that I told Mike about my affair is that I needed him to know how desperately I loved him.

Sheila: You needed him to know how desperate that you were.

Lynn: Yeah, that I would have allowed that to happen, how incredibly removed I was. We were living in the same house but I was carrying on a different life. I guess it was through me being honest that we were able to gain our intimacy.

Therapist: Was it difficult for him to connect with you very deeply without the fear of getting hurt again?

Lynn: I feel like he took me back rather readily. We regained intimacy much more readily than I would have thought.

Therapist (*to Mike*): Can you tell about that from your process?

Mike: Part of me accepting her so readily was that I blamed her affair on myself. It wasn't till later that I got angry with her. I remember specifically telling her that I thought of it very often, and she was shocked....And I still feel to this day that I can't fully trust her. Her knowing that I don't trust her helps me, that I have admitted that I don't trust her.

Therapist: They (the friends) have traveled through a process that you are travelling through, maybe at an earlier stage. I think they have shown some of the stages that they have gone through to work through the affair.

The session concluded with Mike and Lynn's support for Tony and Sheila as individuals and optimism for their potential as a couple. The session clarified Nick's dilemma of how to be both assertive and empathic of Sheila's position. The session also provided a forum of their coping mechanisms—sarcasm and withdrawal. Lynn confronted Tony and Mike confronted Sheila on these dysfunctional coping mechanisms. In the past, when Tony had gotten angry, he shut down because he learned to fear his anger. However the affair has forced him to confront his anger and choose to be responsive to the marriage.

In a follow-up two years after the cessation of therapy, Sheila described the impact of the session with Mike and Lynn as consultants.

I am aware that our friendship with Lynn and Mike is unusually intimate. There is really nothing I would feel like I had to hide from them. We all accept each other totally so the therapy felt safe to me...no matter how deep it had to go.

The greatest impact for me was that their presence allowed us to dip deeper into the pain of our truth. We played out a major theme in our relationship...Sheila gets needy, Tony withdraws. Which comes first, who knows? Their presence and active support allowed me to feel it again and deeper. Actually it was awful...Tony left me emotionally and I felt totally abandoned. I was incredibly nauseous but it was like the truth of that theme hit me like a bullet. I felt my desperate neediness...with Lynn's help I could dip deeper into that without putting my usual defenses of anger and bitchiness.

For both of us, the presence of Lynn and Mike and their experiencing that with us only drew us all closer. Since then, they have been able to confront us and challenge us when they see us in this cycle.

We still get trapped in the cycle at times, but not for as long and not as intensely. The joint session illuminated this cycle and began my conscious journey toward working it through. I doubt I could have/would have let myself dip deep enough into myself without the support of our dear friends.

The two clinical examples illuminate the unique vantage point of friends. In the first example, the family's friends articulated the existential struggle of the leaving home process. In addition, the young adult friends' challenged the parent's portrayal of a major substance-abuse problem. The second example showed how friends can promote marital intimacy by challenging dysfunctional patterns, expressing support for the individuals and the couple, and sharing their own personal and marital struggles. In each case, the friends became catalytic consultants to the therapy. Their vista remained in the therapy long after the interview.

CONCLUSION

The family in psychotherapy gives the therapist a key to the front door of the house. The therapist comes to the door with his/her ideology, professional code of ethics, and previous professional and personal experiences. Once inside the home, the therapist needs to understand the structure of the home and join the occupants of the rooms on the different floors. Then, the therapist and the family can join forces in the task of restructuring the home.

This chapter suggests that the therapist and the family consider the role of friends on each floor. Friends can help the therapist and family to better understand a) the internal design of the home, b) the external view of the home, and c) the vibrance of the home. Friends can make the home more supportive and expansive. Since friends are the naturally selected psychotherapists for the different rooms of the home, the professional psychotherapist should consider seeking their council.

REFERENCES

Aponte, H. J. & Winter, J. (1987). The person and practice of the therapist: Treatment and planning. In M. Baldwin & V. Satir (Eds.), *The Use of Self in Therapy*. New York: Haworth Press.

Bateson, G. (1972). *Steps to an Ecology of the Mind*. New York: Ballantine Books.

Bowen, M. (1978). *Family Therapy in Clinical Practice*. New York: Aronson.

Broderick, C. B. (1988). Healing members and relationships in the intimate network. In R. M. Milardo (Ed.), *Families and Social Networks*. Newbury Park, California: Sage Publications.

Carter, B. & McGoldrick, M. (Eds.). (1989). *The Changing Life Cycle*. New York: Allyn & Bacon.

Haber, R. (1987). Friends in family therapy: Use of a neglected resource. *Family Process*, 26, 269–281.

Haber, R. (1990a). From handicap to handy capable: Training systemic therapists in use of self. *Family Process*, 29, 375–384.

Haber, R. (1990b). Family and social network members as lay consultants. *Journal of Strategic and Systemic Therapies*, 9, 21–31.

Haber, R. (in press). Response-ability: Therapist's "I" and role. *Journal of Family Therapy*.

Johnson, V. (1986). *Intervention: How to Help Someone Who Doesn't Want Help*. Minneapolis: Johnson Institute.

Minuchin, S. (1974). *Families & Family Therapy*. Cambridge: Harvard University Press.

Rubin, L. B. (1985). *Just Friends: The Role of Friendship in Our Lives*. New York: Harper & Row.

Satir, V. (1987). The Self of the therapist. In M. Baldwin & V. Satir (Eds.), *The Use of Self in Therapy*. New York: Haworth Press.

Simon, R. M. (1989). Family life cycle issues in the therapy system. In B. Carter & M. McGoldrick (Eds.), *The Changing Family Life Cycle*. New York: Allyn & Bacon.

Whitaker, C. (1982). Gatherings. In J. R. Neill and D. P. Kniskern (Eds.), *From Psyche to System: The Evolving Therapy of Carl Whitaker*. New York: Guilford.

8

The Impact of Multiple Consultants in the Treatment of Addictions

Jim Guinan and William Jones

Family therapists are well aware that family members are intimately involved with the addictive experience of one of their members. Addiction, however, is a problem that usually cannot be confined to the family and extends itself to the larger community. The purpose of this chapter is to articulate an important reminder, namely, that therapists need to be aware that community contexts are involved in the therapy, and that these "others" may function very much like consultants. That is, they are involved administratively in the counseling process, they influence the therapeutic relationship, and they have a significant impact on the outcome of treatment.

In the treatment of addictions, the use of multiple consultants—whether they are called family members, monitors, co-therapists, co-workers, extended family, etc.—has become customary. These "consultants" may even be viewed as an essential component in the development of addictive pathologies, and they certainly are heavily involved in the treatment.

Human beings live in a community of relationships. They are conceived as a result of relationship; born into dependency relationships; and grow and mature in a constellation of familial, peer, and community relations. Thus, the nuclear family is only one system and may not even be the most important system in a given individual's life.

In a previous article, I have described three "families" that interface in an individual's life (Guinan, 1990, p. 12). First, there is typically a readily recognizable close or *home family* that consists of parents, children, or significant others. It may be a conventional, intact, nuclear family, a single-parent family with one or more children, a blended family, a three-generation family, or long-term live-ins of one or both genders. It may even include caretakers or persons living in the same building or neighborhood. Second, there is a *vocational family*, which consists of friends, colleagues, and acquaintances from the school or workplace. Third, there is the *social family* that includes those people who have contact with the person around religious, athletic, recovery, or purely social activities.

Since people develop and participate in several systems, behaviors and, therefore, pathologies exist in and are supported by several interactive systems. Specific behaviors may be confined in one system (e.g. a person who is mean and irritable at home but warm and friendly at the workplace), or may cross the borders of one or more systems (such as the person who takes frustrations and irritations of the job out on family and friends). Since we do not treat people in a vacuum, persons from other systems are likely to enter the therapeutic process either by invitation or invasion. In any case, their presence needs to be recognized.

These planned or unintended consultative relationships can and do influence the client and alter or govern the entire therapeutic process. The structure of such multiple consultations and how consultants become "present" in the therapy, along with the principles governing such multiple consultations make up the remaining focus of this chapter.

THE "PRESENCE" OF MULTIPLE CONSULTANTS

Most addictions counselors assert that the first step in the treatment of addictions must include the addict's achievement of "clean and dry." That is, the patient must be free of the chemical presence of the addicting substance or behaviors. To achieve this status, the client is often required to complete inpatient treatment or detoxification, see a physician, attend support groups, elicit the active participation of other family members, bring other "consultants" into the therapeutic process. The multiple consultation process described in this chapter recognizes that these "others" do become part of the therapeutic system. They can be viewed as consultants to the therapy and even brought into the therapist's office to facilitate the process of change. These multiple and ongoing consultants contribute not only to the therapy of the client, but also to the client's family and social life style as well.

The position espoused here is that the inclusion or encroachment of additional persons into the therapeutic process can and usually does define the parameters of the therapeutic process and will determine the outcome of the therapy. This is true whether the "others" serve as consultants or as multiple-therapists, whether their presence is intentional or accidental, whether they are physically present in the consultation room or only present to therapist and/or client outside of the office, or whether such persons are recognized as part of the therapy or ignored.

The frequent failure of forced referrals is an excellent example of how unacknowledged consultants can affect the process and outcome of therapy. For example, a judge may "sentence" a convicted person to see the therapist. When the therapist fails to acknowledge that the judge is now present with the client in the therapy, then the therapist may become indistinguishable from the judge in the client's eyes and is met with the same resistance and antagonism. In a similar manner, probation officers, physicians, or family members become active consultants to the therapeutic process and need to be recognized as such.

Frequently, therapists view such outsiders as interferences or at least view them as extrinsic to the therapy. We, however, prefer to recognize that such "others" are, in fact, allies, and when accepted as consultants, they can strengthen and intensify the therapeutic process. An illustration may help.

Mike was a 38-year-old craftsman in a fabrication shop. His supervisor, with whom he had a long-standing antagonistic relationship, suspected that he was alcoholic and drank on the job. The supervisor demanded that Mike see the Employee Assistance Program (EAP) counselor. The EAP counselor referred him to one of the authors (JG) with a request for feedback following an evaluation. In an initial interview with JG, it became clear that the supervisor was seen by Mike as an enemy who was "forcing" the therapy as a punishment, and that JG was simply viewed as part of the punishing system. However, because his job was in jeopardy, Mike did agree to see BJ, the other author, for counseling.

Notice that in this case there came to be one therapist, BJ, but there existed at least three consultants: JG, the EAP counselor, and the supervisor, all of whom were involved in the treatment and needed to be dealt with before the therapeutic relationship between Mike and BJ could develop. In this case, JG agreed to participate directly in the therapy only when Mike, his spouse, or

BJ requested his presence, and agreed to communicate to the supervisor only that Mike was seeing a counselor. In this fashion, BJ was able to remain free of the negative transference associated with the "punishers," and was able to develop a therapeutic alliance with Mike and his spouse. JG also was able to report to the supervisor, thereby fulfilling the requirements of the referral source. In the ongoing treatment, each of these persons was involved and frequently spoken of, but by clarifying the nature of each of their respective involvements (identifying the consultant's contribution), the therapy could proceed more smoothly.

Guinan (1990) described an approach to the treatment of families of chemically dependent persons that utilizes multiple consultants as an integral aspect of the program. Agencies, other counselors, sponsors, attorneys, family members, pastors, friends, and co-workers are recognized as part of the treatment team and may be invited to actively participate in the therapy. Since addictions may exist in only one of the families mentioned previously (such as the social or home family), assessing and intervening in the interactions of the eco system can best help the addict meet his/her therapeutic goals. The process of coordinating all of the players in the addict's life directly confronts the denial of the addict and the intimate others. Even so-called antagonistic consultants, such as drinking buddies, have been found to help the treatment system, understand the addict, and even support the therapeutic goals.

A TYPOLOGY OF CONSULTANTS

Multiple consultative relationships can exist or be described as having a *direct, ancillary,* or *fantasied presence. Direct Presence* means that the consultant is physically present during the therapeutic interview. Direct Presence involves face-to-face meetings with the client, therapist, and consultant(s) and is usually structured by the primary therapist. This is the usual mode of co-therapy, multiple psychotherapy, and family therapy. Such Direct Presence may occur at every session, be periodic, or be a one-time experience. Such consultations are frequently recalled by the client years later as a pivotal intervention in the therapy (Whitaker, 1989).

Ancillary Presence refers to the fact that outsiders are frequently part of a therapeutic system even though they are not physically present. Referrers who request feedback on the therapy, HMOs who require information or authorize payment for sessions, police, court workers, attorneys, or employers who instigate the treatment and expect results in one form or another are all ancillary consultants.

These "others" are frequently present in some fashion as they often exercise real power in the addict's life or therapy. They may even govern the therapy, especially if not recognized (as in the case of Mike's supervisor). However, by including the ancillary consultant into the therapy either directly, or at least by negotiating with the client how the ancillary consultant is to be present, the therapist increases the probability of the ancillary consultant being an ally to the therapy. (Again, in the case of Mike, JG became an ancillary consultant who dealt with the ancillary and fantasied presence of the supervisor and the EAP counselor while BJ was then able to become the primary therapist.)

There are also forced referral situations wherein the consultant is usually seen as an outside or antagonistic force. In such cases, viewing the external person or agency as a consultant to the therapy may overcome or at least lessen the disturbance. Keeping in mind the principles of multiple consultation, it is necessary for the therapist to speak openly with the client about the quality of relationships between the therapist and the consultant(s), and especially of any interactions between the therapist and the consultant(s). This may be accomplished by allowing the client to listen in on telephone conversations or read correspondence between therapist and ancillary consultants. In some cases, the presence of the ancillary or fantasied consultant becomes so noxious or obstructive that the therapeutic process is frozen. When this happens, it is usually necessary for the therapist to process his/her frustrations or helplessness with the obstructing consultant(s). If that is not feasible, it may be necessary for the therapist to call in a consultant whose direct presence would allow the therapist some resolution to the frustration/helplessness.

Referring persons, as in ancillaries, are always "present" for the initial sessions and may stay for the whole therapy. Other examples of ancillary consultants are previous therapists, support groups, or treatment agencies that are still actively involved in the therapy. Similarly, family members who may not be able to come to every session maintain their presence in an ancillary manner, as was apparent in the following case.

JG received a telephone call from a woman who expressed concern about her father. The woman spoke at length about how her father drank far too much and how she, her two sisters, and two brothers felt helpless and worried. The father, Frank, was a political bigwig and had already told his grown children he would never attend AA or go to a treatment center. An appointment was arranged through the caller with a request to bring as many family members as possible. The five adult children all showed up and together planned a family intervention. Each of the children (ages between 27 and 37) promised to serve as consultants if only the father would agree to treatment.

In these initial sessions the identified patient was present only in fantasy, while JG called in BJ as direct consultant. But clearly Frank was present as evidenced by the individual children each expressing concern for his toughness ("You couldn't say something like that if he were here"), and his vulnerability ("We better not even tell you his last name or his political position").

Following the second session, the five adult children, with directions and guidelines from the therapists, conducted their own "intervention" by demanding to talk to the father together. Thus, the familial change had already begun because they had expressed that they were individually either too angry or too afraid to talk with him alone. Frank came to the next session and it quickly became apparent that his drinking was out of control and that his "special need" for confidentiality was part of his denial system.

Within the perspective of this chapter, one may assert that in this case the community as a whole was operating as a fantasied consultant that had to be held at bay. The therapists used the community as a fantasy consultant for the good of the therapy by repeatedly reminding Frank of his need to remain in control and how both the alcohol and the public opinion could be controlled by his sobriety. Now his entire family, including in-laws, were committed to his sobriety. They had monitored his drinking with alarm; now they could each be part of a team (of ancillary consultants) that would monitor and reinforce his abstinence.

Fantasied Presence, as with the community in the case of Frank, refers to a consultant who may never have been physically present in the consultation room, yet exercises an enormous influence on the therapeutic process and its outcome. While ancillary consultants are usually mutually recognized by therapist and patient, as happens in a referral to another therapist, a fantasied consultant is usually not acknowledged initially as having anything to do with the treatment, and is usually denied as having importance. In the anecdote described earlier, Mike's supervisor is one example of a fantasied consultant who would have controlled the therapy in a negative way had he not been recognized and responded to. Addicted persons especially tend to have people in their lives such as a spouse, a sponsor, or even an "old drinking buddy" who is with them in many ways, especially when talking about certain issues related to their addictions. It is proper to describe these as "consultants" because they can exert heavy influences upon the client's symptoms, behavior, and therapeutic compliance. The therapist's task in such cases is to recognize and utilize the fantasied presence in ways that can make them positive consultants. For example, asking clients how their sponsor, friends, etc. might feel about their recovery or "slips" can be a way of recognizing and enhancing the presence of a fantasied consultant.

The ancillary consultant having some "reality power" in the therapeutic process demands that the therapist take heed. A reality power (like authority to put someone in jail, deciding whether or not the treatment will be paid for, or having the authority to prevent a family member from participating) insidiously enters and contaminates the therapy. The fantasied consultant, on the other hand, is usually present only in fantasy, has no reality power (except when unrecognized), and can be used by the therapist as an ally for the good of the therapy.

One can readily conclude that the introduction, discovery, or identification of a consultant in the therapeutic relationship is always a significant event (Dreikurs, 1950; Papp, 1980; Warkentin, Johnson & Whitaker, 1951). Consultation is rarely, if ever, a one-time event. Direct presence becomes a fantasied presence when the consultant is no longer directly present. Ancillary presence has a way of hovering over the therapy throughout its duration. Fantasied presence of outsiders remains part of the addict's ecology. Therefore, it can be argued that all consultation becomes an ongoing and lasting part of the treatment. This influence is enhanced when the consultant's direct presence is intermittent or continuous (Whitaker, Malone & Warkentin, 1956).

PRINCIPLES OF MULTIPLE CONSULTATION

In most psychotherapy, and in every therapy dealing with addictions, there exists or will be created by the therapy a multiperson system of which the therapist-addict dyad is only one facet. When a consultant is called into a therapeutic relationship, the therapy proceeds only to the extent that the relationship between therapist and consultant(s) can nurture the therapeutic system. The energy, ideas, and caring of the multiple consultant(s) can transform the therapeutic structure into a therapeutic system.

The relationship between therapist and consultant closely resembles the relationship between therapists in multiple psychotherapy. When the relationship between consultant and therapist is limited or bound, the client cannot grow beyond these limitations. Whether the consultant is present in a direct, ancillary, or fantasied manner does not alter the importance of this principle. A case may illustrate this point.

Joe sought therapy, stating that he thought he might be a sexual addict. He reported that he had molested his 16-year-old step-daughter, Janet. The molestation reportedly consisted of fondling without sexual intercourse and had occurred periodically since Janet had been eight years old. Janet had told her boyfriend of the incestuous behavior and he reported it to the police who immediately involved the court. This precipitated Joe's seeking therapy. Thus, the therapy began with several ancillary consultants—the daughter, the boyfriend, the police, and the court—all present prior to the beginning of therapy. In fact, between the call for the first appointment and the time of that appointment, Joe's wife (Janet's mother) announced that she was filing for divorce; the county children's service board had the court place a police bond upon Joe that prevented any interactions (even therapeutic) between him and Janet. At this point, Janet became suicidal.

Joe was prevented by the police bond from engaging in family therapy, and his wife was advised by the children's service bureau to avoid speaking to Joe, even in therapy, and to actively refuse to participate in couples therapy. Joe expressed doubts that any therapy could help him and dropped out. At this point, the therapy may be considered a failure because of the absence of any therapeutic process or change. But, it is really a failure of the therapists to integrate or at least coordinate and redirect the negative impact of all the ancillary and fantasied consultants. So the story is not over.

Let us examine the process. The boyfriend, Janet, her mother, the police, the court, and the children's services board were negative consultants as they blocked structure of the treatment. In fact, there was no chance for treatment until these consultants were coordinated.

Several weeks later BJ contacted Joe for a follow-up. Joe had been sentenced to a work-release program in which he could work his regular job, but, had to reside in an institution. At this time, Joe sought to return to therapy. BJ contacted the staff at the institution and found that they would assist Joe's attorney in petitioning the court to allow him to leave for his sessions. Weeks later, the attorney sought and received permission for Joe to attend Janet's therapy sessions being conducted at the children's services agency (with BJ present as consultant).

Thus, by working with these ancillary consultants, arrangements were made that allowed Joe to continue therapy, and soon thereafter to be present with Janet and his spouse in the office of Janet's therapist. Note that now the attorney, the court, and the institution were working together as ancillary consultants to the family therapy. BJ could now function as ancillary to the family therapy and direct therapist to Joe. Rather than being antagonistic, the ancillaries became integrated into the therapeutic process.

In the initial phase of the case of Joe, there were simply too many consultants operating in too many oppositional directions to bring about a positive integration. As these antagonistic persons and agencies were "reframed" as consultants and contacted directly by BJ, a positive outcome became possible.

The principle of multiple consultation necessarily focuses attention and energy on the relationship between therapist and consultant. When the therapist is unable to perceive or respond to the presence of the consultant, then the therapeutic process becomes random, with the therapist and consultant operating sometimes in tandem, sometimes independently of each other, and sometimes in direct opposition. Ironically, it may even be a systems-oriented therapist who fails to recognize the influence of ancillary and fantasied consultants in the very therapeutic system that is being treated.

When the therapist is unable to integrate the impact of the various consultants, then an impasse in the therapeutic process will inevitably emerge and probably remain unresolved. When the therapist refuses to attend to the presence of a consultant in the therapeutic milieu, then the core issues that support the impasse are likely to be ignored. In those cases, even when relief is achieved, it is likely to be short-lived as the impasse reemerges. As the therapist becomes able to integrate the multiple consultants, the entire system of client-therapist-consultant(s) grows more resilient, nurturing, and mutually supportive.

The roles of the therapist and consultants in multiple consultation may disintegrate, or at least become very fluid. That is, the therapist may become therapist to the relationship between the client and consultant(s). This can immediately reverse as a consultant facilitates an interaction between client and therapist. But this too can reverse itself as the client speaks (becomes therapist) to the relationship between therapist and consultant. For example, in the case of the politician described above, much of the first session was taken up listening to Frank's "speeches." Finally, the oldest son blurted out to the therapist, "You're getting sucked into his bullshit just like everybody else!" By listening and responding to the son's consulting advice, the therapist could reinitiate the therapeutic process.

A healthy consultative relationship is one that helps the therapist get better at doing therapy. The ability and willingness of the therapist to seek help and communicate effectively with the consultant provide a powerful model for the client to imitate. It is very probable that the nature of addictions absolutely requires that the therapist recognize and respond to the system(s) of consultants that the addict uses to foster and maintain the habit. This model can teach the addict to recognize and cope with the differences and interrelationships with the systems of which he/she is a part.

The therapeutic relationship, like any healthy relationship, seems able to withstand anything except avoidance. Avoiding the ongoing events of the therapy, especially the presence of an unacknowledged consultant, confuses the client, the therapist, and the therapy. Open inclusion of all of the multiple consultants empowers the therapist and the client to more effectively deal with the therapeutic system.

SUMMARY

Consultation may be viewed as a form of multiple psychotherapy. While most therapeutic approaches do involve consultants in one form or another, the primary focus of this chapter has been to view consultants as those persons usually not included as being part of the therapy. These consultants may be direct, i.e. physically present in the consultation room, ancillary, or fantasied. The principle of multiple consultation stresses that regardless of the form of the presence of the consultant(s), the relationship between therapist and consultants(s) takes on an overriding importance in the process of the therapy. When the presence of a consultant is acknowledged in a therapeutic process, the therapy can be intensified and usually accelerated. Problems that arise between therapist and consultant(s) take precedence and may serve as a model of confronting, coping, and resolving issues that are presented by the client. This concept of multiple consultation can provide a clarifying method of keeping the therapist and the client coping with and processing the system of their relationships.

REFERENCES

Dreikurs, R. (1950). Techniques and dynamics of multiple psychotherapy. *Psychiatric Quarterly*, 24, 788–799.

Guinan, J. (1990). Extending the system for the treatment of chemical dependencies. *Journal of Strategic and Systemic Therapies*, (9), 11–20.

Papp, P. (1980). The Greek chorus and other techniques of family therapy. *Family Process*, (19), 45–57.

Warkentin, J., Johnson, N. & Whitaker, C. (1951). A comparison of individual and multiple psychotherapy. *Psychiatry*, (14), 415–424.

Whitaker, C. (1989). Personal communication.
Whitaker, C., Warkentin, J. & Johnson, N. (1950). The psychotherapeutic impasse. *American Journal of Orthopsychiatry*, (20), 641–648.

PART III

ELICITING COLLEGIAL RESOURCES FROM THE THERAPIST'S SYSTEM

9

The Referrer: Colleague, Client, or Pain in the Ass

Lars Brok and Rick A. Pluut

A referral to another therapist during an existing therapy can be viewed as a request for help by the referring therapist. The need for a referral occurs when the referrer feels unsure of his/her role in the therapeutic process. The referring relationship depends upon the stage of the therapeutic process at the moment of referral, the positions of the referring and consulting therapist in the work system, and the professional relationship between the referring therapist and the consulting therapist. The referring relationship can be a very effective one if well defined and collaborative; however, problems arise when this relationship is not well defined nor collegial. This results in what I call a "pain-in-the-ass" relationship.

Referral is a common procedure when therapists treat patients and patient systems for psychiatric problems. I have responded to approximately 200 referrals per year in the 12 years that I have worked on the admission ward and out-patient clinic of a general psychiatric hospital in the Netherlands. With most referrals, the referred patient or patient system has been in treatment for a considerable time with the referring therapist. Such referrals will be discussed in this chapter.

THE THERAPEUTIC PROCESS BEFORE REFERRAL

Since the timing of the referral in the therapeutic process needs to be carefully considered, I will briefly describe the phases of the therapeutic process in the original therapy system before any referral is made. These phases are contingent upon the various positions of the original therapist in the therapeutic system. To clarify these phases, I have further developed the diagrams of Andolfi, Angelo, Menghi, and Nicolo-Corigliano (1983, p. 83) and Andolfi, Angelo, and de Nichilo (1989, p. 144) regarding the therapeutic process (see Figure 1).

Figure 1a represents the situation *before* the onset of the therapy. The patient is central in the family (system) and is involved in every stressful relational triangle in the system (Andolfi, Angelo & de Nichilo 1989, p. 144).

The Wilson family wanted to commit their 15-year-old son who had been "unmanageable since he was two years old." The parents told us that all conflicts between them were about this boy and that his mother feared to leave him home alone. His sister blamed her poor relationship with her mother on her brother because he occupied all of her attention. All agreed that the 15-year-old boy "ruled" the family.

Figure 1b represents the formation of the first phase of the therapeutic system. The therapist obtains a central position in the system by linking with the patient's symptoms. The therapist enters the system by acknowledging and provoking the centrality and, perhaps, the logic of the symptomatology.

In the first session with the Wilson family, the therapist put the son on a throne (made by a chair on top of a table) and asked the family to discuss the pros and cons of this heavy job the son had as "ruler." At the end of the session, the therapist asked the father if he wanted to overthrow the government and help his son abdicate the throne. The father agreed. The therapist told him that he would give him a task that would help him, but first he had to be sure that the father was stronger than the son. He asked the father and son to engage in an arm wrestle. Father and son fought with great pleasure and father won easily.

Figure 1c illustrates the therapist's substitution of him/herself for the patient's centrality in the therapeutic system. In this phase, problems other than the patient's symptoms may come up for discussion and family members may adopt less stereotypical roles in dealing with stressful events and problem resolution.

In the next session, the Wilsons brought up the theme of being overloaded. All family members felt overburdened in their own

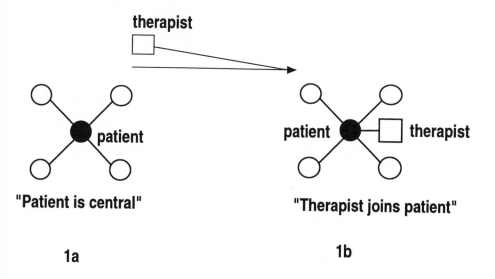

"Patient is central"

1a

"Therapist joins patient"

1b

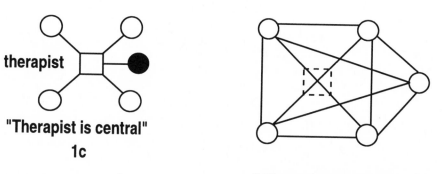

"Therapist is central"
1c

**" Therapist terminates, but
remains as a 'ghostly' presence."**

1d

Figure 1

way (the father at work, the mother at home, and the boy at school). The therapist became central by questioning each family member's motives to be overloaded. Issues concerning the parent's family of origin were discussed. The patient was no longer central and the symptoms soon disappeared.

In Figure 1d the therapy is officially ended. However, the therapist's (ghost) presence is still felt. If necessary, the therapist could be "materialized" again by the family (compare Andolfi, Angelo & de Nichilo, 1989).

We saw the Wilson parents for a follow-up consultation half-a-year later. This session took place on election day. The parents laughingly told us that they were determined that their coalition would remain in power and that the monarchy would have no chance of being reinstated. Thus, the therapist's influence remained in the family via the metaphor of the throne.

THE PROCESS OF REFERRAL

Many referrals occur when the therapist questions his/her role in the therapeutic process during a therapeutic impasse. Such referrals are often an appeal for help by the referrer rather than a request to take over the case (Zwanikken, 1979). Therefore, the consulting therapist should realize that this request for help/referral is an intervention by the therapist/ referrer in the therapeutic process. This intervention enlarges the therapeutic system by adding the consulting therapist.

The aim of the referring therapist is to restructure his/her position in the therapeutic system by creating an alternative reality: changing the interactional patterns, rules, values, and norms of the therapeutic system (Auerswald, 1985; Kantor & Neal, 1985). The role of the consulting therapist is central to the restructuring process in this system and is largely determined by the relationship with the referrer. This is similar to the relationship between the identified patient and the therapist (see Figure 1a) at the beginning of a therapy.

The referrer initiates this relationship by defining the problem. This problem definition is influenced by the role and position of the referrer in the therapeutic system, the phase of the therapeutic process at the time of the referral, and the referrer's perceptions of the consulting therapist's ability and ideology of therapy. It is important that the referrer clearly define the purpose of the referral at this time in the therapy. Thereafter, the referring and consulting therapists need to negotiate and mutually define their relationship.

The consulting therapist's goal is to develop a relationship that will provide additional information and help while maintaining the referrer's involvement. The following two types of relationships can accomplish this aim:

1. *The collegial relationship.* The referrer, in principle, remains in charge of the therapy and adopts a metaposition toward the consulting therapist. At the request of the referrer, the consulting therapist could provide a specific service within the framework of the ongoing therapy of the referrer. For example, the family therapist could ask a physician to prescribe medication to one of the family members in order to continue out-patient family therapy.
2. *The consultative relationship.* The referrer wants help to get unstuck and have the therapeutic process flow again. The consulting therapist could adopt a metaposition towards the referring therapist in the consultation process.

If the referring and consulting therapists do not clearly define their relationship, they can create what I call a "pain-in-the-ass" relationship. In this problematic relationship, the referring process often does not help create alternative roles in the therapeutic system, but rigidifies the already stereotypical roles.

THE PAIN-IN-THE-ASS RELATIONSHIP

Referrals that easily develop into a pain-in-the-ass relationship often start with a short message or phone call from the referrer to the consulting therapist:

Dear Colleague: I would like to refer Mrs. Holland to your admission ward with short notice. She has been on our ward for more than one year because of a borderline, personality disorder. A countertransference has developed with the nursing staff.

Dear Colleague: I would be grateful if you would take young man Stone in treatment. From nursery school and onwards, he has been in treatment with several therapists without success. I have seen his parents regularly for two years. The boy attended the sessions just a few times. His behavior was too difficult to handle in the sessions. The contacts with the parents were satisfying. The boy, however, remained unchanged. Probably a case of schizophrenia with mental retardation....

In each case, the referrer has circumvented the referral process by not including information about his/her position in the therapeutic system. The referrer has not taken partial responsibility for the continuance of the symptoms still existing in the therapeutic system. It is as if the consulting therapist has to meet a client system where a therapist does not even exist. Yet, the referrer gives clear advice about how to handle the case.

Selvini-Palazzoli, Boscolo, Cecchin, and Prata (1980) believed this type of referrer becomes an important family member, entangled in the family system. He/she becomes frustrated because all his/her efforts do not bring about any change while the family claims that he/she is indispensable for them. Although there is a referral, the referrer seems to obstruct the subsequent course of therapy.

Berg (1985) also described how these therapists not only refer, but dictate the treatment process. Like Selvini-Palazzoli, she emphasizes the unclarity of the referrer in the subsequent therapeutic system. Luyn and Vergouwen (1986) observed that such referrers wanted only to be relieved of the responsibility for their patients. The referrer views the consulting therapist as the rescuer. Peck, Howe, and Stackhouse (1978), on the contrary, interpret every application for referral as a request for consultation. They describe how quickly conflicts between the referring and consulting therapists can arise if one ignores the goals of the referrer.

A common feature noted by these authors is an undercurrent of irritation and complexity inherent in the referral process. I think that the basis for the irritation is the lack of communication between the referring and consulting therapists, which prevents a clear definition of their relationship.

Frequently, the following condition(s) obstruct the referral process:

1. The referrer is conspicuously uninterested in the consulting therapist.
2. The referrer presents a therapy plan that must be carried out by the consulting therapist. This plan or command, however, may include some of the following conditions:
   a. unilaterally decided by the referrer;
   b. very specific, although the referrer knows little about the prescribed treatment;

   c. referrer does not take any responsibility for the proposed treatment plan;

   d. the referrer could have done the treatment just as well;

   e. the proposed treatment plan is incompatible with the frame of reference and/or possibilities of the consulting therapist.

3. The referrer allows one of the patients to make the first contact with the consulting therapist.
4. The referrer gives little information about the therapeutic process, particularly avoiding information about his/her position in the therapeutic system.
5. The referrer describes the patient(s) as unchangeable.
6. The referrer suddenly refers because of a change in his/her frame of reference. For example, a psychotherapist changes the definition of the problem to an individual, biological problem and refers the patient for pharmacological treatment.

The consulting therapist can also contribute to the evolvement of a pain-in-the-ass relationship with the referrer by responding to the referral with:

1. strikingly little interest in the referrer;
2. immediate and unconditional agreement to the referral;
3. premature and unsolicited advice for the referrer to carry out. This results in ideas that:

   a. do not come about through consultation with the referrer;

   b. are very specific, although the consulting therapist has little knowledge of the method involved;

   c. include no co-responsibility of the consulting therapist for the implementation of the advice;

   d. are not compatible with the capacities or theoretical frame of the referrer;

4. a hierarchical position that makes it difficult or impossible for the referrer to stay in charge of the therapy. For example, the referrer provides all of the extra efforts such as traveling and time commitments.

Occasionally the consulting therapist gives the impression that he/she would like to help the referrer, but without being involved in the referring process. Mostly, however, it is the referrer who "charmingly leaves" the therapeutic system. I agree with Selvini-Palazzoli et al. (1984) that this usually indicates that the referrer has become more like a family member than a therapist. The therapist has become part of the patterns that confirm the central role of the patient. This position reinforces and perpetuates the symptoms. When the therapist can no longer handle the entanglement and therapeutic impasse, he/she looks for a referral source.

How can the consulting therapist handle this problem? If he/she is confronted with a therapist who plays the role of family member in the therapeutic system, then the consulting therapist could treat both the therapist and the other members of the system as clients in the newly formed consultative system. Usually, this does not concur with the way the referrer sees the problem. Selvini-Palazzoli et al. (1980) ameliorated this problem by inviting the referrer as a colleague while treating him/her as a client. In this way, they counterparadoxically responded to a referrer who, paradoxically, defined him/herself as a colleague, but behaved like a family member. The goal of this intervention was to put an end to the repetitive game between the family and the referrer. After the mutual dependence was broken, the consulting therapist could more effectively deal with the therapy.

I do not prefer this method because a collegial resource can become undermined. If the consulting therapist feels uncertain or insecure with the referral, then this needs to be explicitly addressed. This necessitates delaying the discussion about the problems of the client until the questions and problems of the referral are resolved. The consulting therapist should explore how to develop a mutually agreeable collegial or consultative relationship.

If the consulting therapist fails to metacommunicate about his/her relationship with the referrer, this could reinforce a taboo against such discussion. This may parallel the dysfunction that exists in the therapeutic system. However, a frank discussion about the role and relationship of the referring and consulting therapists may create tension. If the referring and consulting therapists cannot agree about the nature of their relationship in the therapeutic process, then they can request additional assistance from another therapist about their relational problem. If the referrer rejects this proposal, the consulting therapist should not accept the referral. Thus, the consulting therapist sends a clear message to the referrer that he/she cannot simply withdraw from the co-responsibility of the therapeutic impasse in the therapeutic system. The possibility of denying the referral disrupts the illusion of a magical solution and confronts the referrer with part of the responsibility for the impasse and the solution in the therapeutic system.

Therapist Peters referred Mrs. Jones for brief hospitalization "...to reduce her use of tranquilizers." The therapist had been seeing Mrs. Jones, together with her husband, for a considerable time in marital therapy. According to the referrer, the therapy was stuck because Mrs. Jones was so drugged by the medication that she could not be "touched" enough in the sessions. The consulting therapist agreed with the hospitalization without further discussion.

In this case, the consulting therapist did not clarify whether his help should be distinct from, or a part of, the ongoing marital therapy. Also, it was unclear why the referrer, at the time of the referral, found the medication of Mrs. Jones to be interfering with the therapy. Finally, nothing was said about the position of the referrer in the therapeutic system or about the therapeutic process. The consulting therapist assumed that there should be a change from an interactional approach to a medical approach.

Some days after the hospitalization, Mrs. Jones refused to cooperate with the plan to reduce her medication. She described her request for hospitalization as an excuse to escape an unbearable situation at home. The consulting therapist reported the patient's decision to the referrer and said that he wanted to discharge Mrs. Jones. The referrer became angry because he wanted his patient to remain hospitalized.

The patient, by refusing to reduce her medication and by describing her troubles at home, tried to involve the consulting therapist as an ally in the marital conflict. At the same time, she behaved as if the referrer did not have anything to do with the marital therapy. The consulting therapist wanted to stay out of the position as marital therapist, but got into a conflictual triangle with the referrer and the patient.

The consulting therapist persisted in his decision to discharge the patient. He told Mrs. Jones that she had to leave the hospital because she did not want to reduce her medication, and he referred her back to the original referrer to talk about her problems at home. Mrs. Jones immediately phoned the referrer to complain about the consulting therapist. She told the referrer that she would commit suicide if she had to go home. The referrer phoned the consulting therapist and told him to keep Mrs. Jones in the hospital because she was suicidal, and that he did not want to be involved as long as Mrs. Jones needed hospitalization.

Thus, this exemplifies a therapeutic system that is absolutely unclear about who is responsible for the therapy and who is in charge of the therapeutic system. The referrer, on the one hand, decided to hospitalize the client, but on the other hand, refused to take any responsibility for the marital therapy.

The consulting therapist, with great frustration, requested help from a colleague. This colleague arranged a meeting with the referring and consulting therapists. In this session, it became clear that the referrer felt stuck in the marital treatment. He felt obstructed because the husband was brain damaged and was unable to handle much stress. The session concluded with an agreement that the referrer would attend a session with the consulting therapist and Mr. and Mrs. Jones to see if and how the consulting therapist could help.

The consulting therapist needed help to change the pain-in-the-ass relationship with the referrer. The helping colleague asked the questions that the consulting therapist should have asked in the beginning of the referral process. Fortunately, the referrer agreed to participate in the process at this point. His willingness to be involved and the revelation of his position in the therapeutic impasse helped transform the relationship with the consulting therapist into a collaborative, consultative relationship.

The consultation session clarified Mrs. Jones' anxiety about her husband's condition and Mr. Jones' uncertainty about his intellectual functioning. Furthermore, it became clear that the referrer felt stuck in this problem because he could not find out the seriousness of Mr. Jones handicap. The consultation session concluded that both Mr. and Mrs. Jones should receive evaluation and treatment in the hospital. In addition, the referrer was placed in charge of the therapeutic program and continued with the marital therapy sessions in the hospital. The consulting therapist agreed to regularly inform the referrer about the clinical observations at the hospital. The treatment program addressed the cognitive functioning of the husband and the couple's division of roles.

The consultation session clarified the problem of the couple: their fear to address the issue of the brain damage of the husband. More importantly, it clarified how the referrer was stuck in the same issue. Thus, it became clear how the consulting therapist could help the therapeutic system. The hospital could lessen the tension in the couple by addressing the nature of the husband's cognitive functioning and the division of marital roles. The hospital could provide a supportive climate for the marital therapy of the referrer.

In the group program at the hospital, it became clear how cautiously Mrs. Jones handled her husband and how she tried to protect him against any stress. Also Mr. Jones' anxiety and fear of failure became evident. However, he increasingly participated in the different therapeutic programs (for example: creative therapy, psychomotor therapy, and group therapy) even though he had some cognitive problems. In general, he functioned quite well. His wife slowly gave up her overfunctioning role in the marriage. She began dealing with her family-of-origin problems concerning an incestuous relationship with her father. After some time, the couple decided to stop the group program. The task of the consulting therapist and his team was done. The couple continued the marital therapy on an outpatient basis. As the relationship between the couple became much more symmetrical and satisfactory, they successfully terminated the outpatient marital therapy.

This case study demonstrated a referral that began with a "pain-in-the-ass" relationship and, through a consultative relationship, ended successfully in a collegial relationship between the referring and consulting therapists. The following will further explain the collegial and consultative relationship in the referring process.

THE COLLEGIAL RELATIONSHIP

Here, as Figure 2a illustrates, the referrer is a competent colleague who is reasonably comfortable in the therapist's position in the therapeutic system.

In the course of the therapy, however, as shown in Figure 2b, therapeutic system A may lack imperative treatment modalities and therefore require assistance. In such a case, the referrer could initiate contact with a consulting therapist.

In Figure 2c, the referrer could request an auxiliary treatment while continuing the therapy. He/she may ask the consulting therapist for a hospital bed for one of the clients to add some safety during a stressful period in the therapeutic process, psychopharmacological support for a client, or some nonverbal therapeutic modality such as activity, movement, or art therapy. In each instance, the referring therapist would continue involvement with the client system.

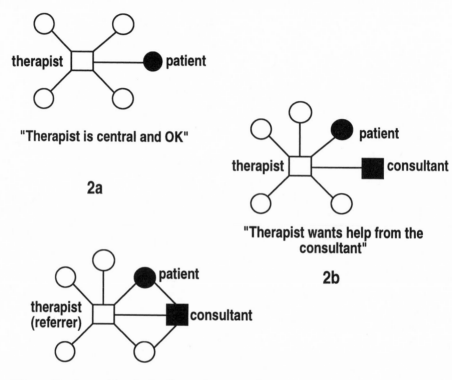

"Therapist is central and OK"

2a

"Therapist wants help from the consultant"

2b

"Consultant provides help, therapist stays in control of therapy"

2c

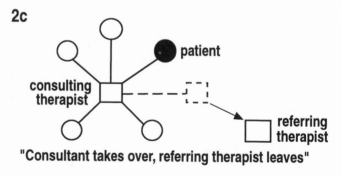

"Consultant takes over, referring therapist leaves"

2d

Figure 2

Figure 2d illustrates a different scenario where the referrer terminates his therapeutic involvement and the consulting therapist takes over the therapy as an extension of the referrer, following his/her "line" (Figure 2d). For example, after a successful family therapy, one of the members of the family could be referred for individual therapy to work out his or her individuation. Or, after a period of inpatient crisis intervention of an individual client, the patient or family members could be referred for outpatient family therapy.

Therapist Rick treated a family, consisting of the parents and two children, for parental disagreements about the education of the children. The therapy dealt with the rigid complementarity between the parents. Father adopted a stereotypically weak role while mother enacted a strong all-knowing role. The therapeutic process developed adequately, but the therapist wanted to approach the marital relationship more playfully and nonverbally. He requested that the physical therapist, Harry, work with the couple in the sports hall. Prior to the referral, there was a session with the entire therapeutic system and Harry. The marital problem and the division of roles between the therapists were discussed. It was clarified that Rick would remain responsible for the case and the family therapy while Harry would regularly report about the physical therapy in the family sessions.

In this case, the referrer asked the consulting therapist to take a well-defined position in the therapeutic system. Thus, the referrer is in a metaposition with regard to the consulting therapist. The task of the consulting therapist consists of the implementation of an assignment. The new consultation system, distinguished itself from the old therapeutic system by the addition of an assigned element. To maximize the chances for a successful, collaborative referral, one must pay attention to the following points:

1. The referrer and the consulting therapists should exchange information concerning their roles and positions in their work systems. Topics such as frame of reference, training, family norms and values, job position, responsibilities, and the treatment culture of the work place may come up for discussion. Cooperation could be impeded when the similarities and differences in these elements are not explicitly discussed (Green and Herget, 1989).
2. The position of the referring therapist in the therapeutic system has to be clarified. The referrer should give his/her view of the

problem, therapy, and the therapeutic relationships. The consulting therapist should assess the life cycle of the therapeutic system. Questions may include:

a. In what phase is the therapeutic process at the moment of referral?

b. How were transitions made from one phase to another? For example, could the referring therapist move beyond the exclusive focus on the identified patient and reach the existential problems of the family? Who resisted this change the most and how?

c. Did the structure of the therapeutic system change? For example, were formerly rigid bonds between allies broken?

d. Which topics were central and what is the major theme now? For example, symptomatic behavior, sexual rules, intergenerational loyalties, etc.?

e. Does the client system have some special impact on the referrer's position in his/her work system?

f. Who took the initiative for the referral and what is the attitude of the members of the therapeutic system towards this referral?

g. Are there any (unreal) illusions concerning the resources that the consulting therapist may add to the therapeutic process?

h. Does this referral influence the position of the referrer in the work system?

When the referring and consulting therapists come to an agreement, the basis for a conjoint session is formed. In this session, information about the division of roles and functions between the referring and consulting therapists can be mutually defined with the client system. The consulting therapist must be mindful of the referrer's goals for the referral and should not extensively probe whether the referral is proper nor attempt to supervise the referrer's vision of the therapeutic process. If this were to occur, the consulting therapist could preemptively assume a position that the referrer might not accept. If this were the case, the consulting therapist could instigate a "pain-in-the-ass" relationship with the referrer. To avoid such a development, the consulting therapist should explicitly discuss what he/she needs and can do in the referral process.

The referral may not materialize if, in the course of the referring process, it is decided that the referral is no longer necessary or that the consulting therapist is not suited for this referral. The referrer may also discover that a consultation session, instead of a referral, could best help the referrer redefine his/her position in the therapeutic system.

THE CONSULTATIVE RELATIONSHIP

In a consultation, usually the referrer is not clear about his position and role in the therapeutic system. Concerns about the therapeutic system could be related to the first (Figure 1b) or the second phase (Figure 1c) of the therapeutic process. In the first phase, the therapist has indeed acquired a central position in the therapeutic system, but has become entangled with the patient. Thus, this therapeutic system is too strongly influenced by the patient's symptomatic behavior. The therapist, in this case, could feel confined to a stereotypical role and rigid position such as the encourager of the depressive father, the sensible half of the impulsive adolescent, or the pacifier in a marital quarrel. The chronicity of such a role could result in a therapeutic impasse with increasing fatigue and desperation.

If the therapist succeeded in detaching from the patient in phase two, but did not succeed in helping the family become more autonomous, the therapeutic system would sabotage the termination process. The family could impede termination by repeatedly bringing up subjects that could be discussed without the therapist. In this case, the therapist might assume the position of guru, grandparent, or friend in the system. Another possibility in phase 2 could be that the discussion about the existential problems is too stressful. This could result in a return to symptomatology, not necessarily in the former identified patient. Consequently, the therapist may erroneously think that the therapy is a failure. In either case, the therapeutic system is at an impasse. The therapist at such an impasse could request a consultation, but more often decides to refer.

Depending upon the reason for the referrer's request for help and his/her position in the family system, work system, etc, the consulting therapist and the referrer may conclude it is better for the referrer to receive a consultation versus referring the case. The goal would be to form a temporary consultative system to modify the stereotypical role of the referrer in order to facilitate the transition to the next phase in the therapeutic process.

In the consultative system, the consultant takes a meta-position with regard to the referrer (Trommel, 1984). In the consultation process, the same phases can be discerned as in the therapeutic process; however they occur at a quickened pace. The consultant first joins the system by discussing the concerns of the referrer. Next, the consultant delineates the stereotypical role of the referrer in the impasse in the therapeutic system. The consultant, then, supports and provokes the role that the referrer needs to assume in order to help the family through the impasse. The consultant adopts a position that can help the referrer change his/her relationship with the client system. Finally, the consultant terminates the relationship with the original therapeutic system. Even though the consultant is no longer physically present, he/she remains present in the therapeutic system as a ghost.

CONCLUSION

The problem of the patient, contrary to what one normally thinks, should be of secondary importance in the referral process. The primary focus should be the referrer's request for help and his/her problem in the therapeutic system. This request and its relational consequences between the referral source and consulting therapist should be analyzed carefully and explicitly. If this doesn't happen, the referral relationship may remain unclear. This would increase the chance that the assistance offered by the consulting therapist will reinforce the existing, rigid patterns in the therapeutic system and probably those in the client system as well. Emphasis on the person of the referrer, position in the work system, and role and position in the therapeutic system is necessary to discover how the consulting therapist can catalyze an already "therapeutic" system.

REFERENCES

Andolfi, M., Angelo, C., Menghi, P. & Nicolo-Corigliano, A. M. (1983). *Behind the Family Mask*. New York: Brunner/Mazel.

Andolfi, M. & Angelo, C. (1988). Toward constructing the therapeutic system. *Journal of Marital and Family Therapy,* 14, 3, 237–247.

Andolfi, M., Angelo, C. & de Nichilo, M. (1989). *The Myth of Atlas*. New York: Brunner/Mazel.

Auerswald, E. H. (1985) Thinking about thinking in family therapy. *Family Process*, 24, 1, 1–12.

Auerswald, E. H. (1987). Epistemological confusion in family therapy and research. *Family Process*, 26, 3, 317–330.

Berg, I. (1985). Helping referral sources help. *Family Therapy Networker*. May–June, 59–62.

Brok, L. J. M. & Pluut, R. A. (1984). Gezinstherapie op de grens. In G. D. M. Schwencke (Ed.), *Groep en Systeem*. Jubilieumuitgave Nederlandse Vereniging voor Groepspsychotherapie.

Green, R. J. & Hegret, M. (1989). Outcomes of systemic/strategic team consultation: II. Three-year follow-up and a theory of "emergent design." *Family Process*, 28, 4, 419–437.

Kantor, D. & Neal, J. H. (1985). Integrative shifts for the theory and practice of family systems therapy. *Family Process*, 24, 1, 13–30.

Luyn, J. B. van & Vergouwen, H. H. P. (1986). Samenwerkingsverbanden vanuit systeemoptiek. In *Handboek Gezinstherapie*. Deventer: Van Loghum Slaterus.

Mazza, J. (1985). Commentary on article by I. Berg. *Family Therapy Networker*, May–June, 64.

Menicucci, L. D., Wermuth, L. & Sorensen, J. (1988). Treatment provider's assessment of dual prognosis patients: Diagnosis, treatment, referral, and family involvement. *The International Journal of the Addictions*, 23, 6, 617–622.

Peck, B. B., Howe, B. J. & Stackhouse, T. W. (1978). Network psychotherapy as a community consultation technique. *Psychotherapy, Theory, Research, and Practice*, 15, 1, 95–100.

Selvini-Palazzoli, M., Boscolo, L., Cecchin, G. & Prata, G. (1980). The problem of the referring person. *Journal of Marital and Family Therapy*, 6, 3–9.

Trommel, M. J. van (1984). A consultation method addressing the therapist-family system. *Family Process*, 23, 4, 469–480.

Zwanikken, G. J. (1979). Psychiatrische kliniek en eerstelijnszorg. *Tijdschrift voor Psychiatrie*, 21, 9, 481–488.

10

"Whose Pain Is It?": Consulting at the Interface Between Families and Social-Medical Systems

Yoel Elizur

During the last decade, family therapists have become more sensitive to the effects that larger social systems have on their work, and there is a growing search for ways to implement this insight into clinical practice and training (Schwartzman, 1984; Wynne, McDaniel & Weber, 1986; Imber-Black, 1988; Elizur, 1993). The psychosomatic family model (Minuchin, Rosman & Baker, 1978), likewise, has been challenged for being too narrowly focused on family dynamics (Coyne & Anderson, 1988). The general consensus is that disorders that affect both mind and body need to be treated as a product of a complex interaction among a multitude of factors, including biological, psychological, familial, social, and environmental (Elizur, 1992; McDaniel et al, 1992).

Nonetheless, there is a gap between theoretical development and clinical practice. Longitudinal observations on the actual field work of experienced family therapists demonstrated that therapists were mini-

The ideas described in this chapter have been developed and applied in the Kibbutz Child and Family Clinics, in collaboration with Mordecai Kaffman, its medical director. During 1987–93, the author established and directed there the Medical Psychology Department, a national center to which the different Kibbutz Clinics referred cases characterized by mind-body disorders.

mally aware of how much their view of cases, or their manner of intervening, was biased by the institutional setting and the larger social context in which their therapy took place. Family consultations, in these
cases, were better directed and more influential when they also dealt
with the ecosystemic dynamics (Elizur & Minuchin, 1989).

The consideration of multilevel dynamics is extremely important in
the work with families that have become chronically stuck around a
mind-body disorder. These systems are characterized by isomorphic
dysfunctions that reappear on many levels and reinforce each other.
Over time, the symptoms become embedded in numerous relationship
contexts that typically include all those people who try to help: physicians, therapists, teachers, counselors, good Samaritans. Over a period
of time these helpers can correctly identify many of the dysfunctional
patterns that maintain the problem, but they may not be aware of their
own part in the dance. Hence, the challenge for the consultant is to
chart out this complex territory and to creatively devise interventions
that will affect all the players in the system. Unless the consultation
deals with the major homeostatic-maintaining patterns and mobilizes
enough strengths on different levels of the system, it will not have
enough impact for changing the system. In such a case, there is also a
risk that the consultant will become a part of the impasse (Elizur, 1990).

This chapter will focus on consultations with a level of the social
ecology that has been defined by Bronfenbrenner as the *mesosystem*; a
system comprised of the interrelations among the various settings in
which the patient participates (1979, p.25). The emphasis is on the
interconnectedness of settings, including the attitudes and knowledge
existing in one setting about the other. Three interrelated questions will
be explored: What *psychosocial dynamics* are involved in the mainte-
nance of the problem. What are the therapeutic possibilities that can be
realized by *working with the social system*. And what are the *practical
means* for doing clinical work at this level?

The Social Ecology of the Consultation

Since the consultant is part of the social and professional context of
the therapeutic system, it is important to identify the setting of our
work and to acknowledge its influence on all of the participants, from
patients to consultants. The work takes place at the Medical Psychology Center of the Kibbutz Clinic in Tel Aviv, Israel, which has a program for dealing with the refractory and chronic mind-body disorders.
Ecosystemic interventions are a routine part of this program. Our
multidisciplinary team accepts referrals from all parts of Israel. Most of
our patients are kibbutz members, but in the last few years there is a

growing number of self-referred patients from the Tel Aviv metropolitan area. However, it needs to be emphasized that this paper is not a simple description of kibbutz ecological therapy. We deal with the same family/personal problems as do clinicians in other cultures. Like them, we fit our interventions to the particular culture in which they are applied.

CHARACTERISTICS OF CHRONIC MIND-BODY DISORDERS

The term *chronic* is used here in a descriptive way to designate systems whose functioning is limited by dysfunctional patterns of long duration or frequent recurrence. A *mind-body disorder* is characterized by the interweaving of physiological distress or medical illness with dysfunctional psychosocial dynamics. This can occur in practically all types of medical illnesses, including the traditional areas of psychosomatic illnesses, somatoform pain disorders, somatization disorders, and conversion disorders.

Since pain is the most common symptom, a case of chronic pain will be presented to illustrate some typical patterns of chronic mind-body disorders. Chronic pain is a major health problem that has been estimated to cost as much as 90 billion dollars per year in the United States alone (Philips, 1988). This figure includes the cost of treatment and the consequences of chronic pain, such as compensation claims, time missed from work, medication, and disability allowances. It does not include the suffering and the corrosive effects of this disorder on the patient and family's life.

The identification of dysfunctional mind-body patterns is a challenging theoretical and clinical task, especially as new scientific disciplines, such as psychoneuroimmunology, are revealing an intimate connection between physiological and psychosocial processes (Ornstein & Sobel, 1987). In looking for these patterns, we may be stimulated by the knowledge of different theoretical models. For example, Sternbach (1974) used a transactional approach to uncover patients' "pain games." They are identified by analysis of their goals, such as attention seeking, sympathy seeking, and avoidance of tasks.

Griffith, Griffith and Slovik (1989), in a noteworthy attempt to integrate family therapy with medical treatment, differentiate between six different mind-body patterns of symptom generation. They range from the simplest "neurobehavioral patterns" in which the family fails to recognize an alteration in the neurological functioning of one of their members to the most complex "mimicry patterns" in which patients generate symptom behaviors to communicate with others and regulate relationships. No doubt one can integrate and expand such different schemata by attending also to ecosystemic dynamics. This is a necessary step in the development of a multilevel approach, and it will be demonstrated in the following case. The initial focus on the patient will be widened to include family dynamics and the broader social context.

CRUSHED BY PAIN: IS THERE A WAY OUT OF CHRONIC PATIENTHOOD?

For Dan, age 44, pain has become the center of life. Four years ago Dan began to suffer from lower back pain. Numerous medical examinations indicated a degenerative change in the intervertebral disks; treatments included analgesics and rest. Although the acute pains decreased after a couple of weeks, Dan continued to complain of continual pains and felt completely incapacitated. Following his physician's advice, he remained in bed, eventually staying there for six months. All of his energies became invested in finding a cure. Since there was no medical solution, he began to experiment with other healing approaches such as acupuncture and reflexology. With each new healer, Dan's spirits lifted and he felt a little better, but this did not last more than a few weeks. Gradually, Dan's functioning at home, at work, and in his social life became minimal.

According to the DSM-III-R (American Psychiatric Association, 1987), this is a case of "somatoform pain disorder." It fits the following two criteria: (1) Preoccupation with pain for at least six months. (2) When there is related organic pathology, the complaint of pain or resulting social or occupational impairment is grossly in excess of what would be expected from the physical findings. However, life is ever more complex than diagnostic categories, especially when they do not include the interpersonal world.

Chronic pain within context

Dan (44) and Debby (43) have been married for 20 years and have two children; an adolescent girl (17) and a boy (8). Marital relations have been strained for a long time, and Dan's disability has considerably escalated the family tensions. Debby resented Dan's withdrawal from her and the children. She complained Dan has not shared household chores or other responsibilities since his preoccupation with his pain. Dan felt misunderstood, and his approach was to minimize and avoid the problems. Debby insisted on marital therapy, but Dan soon dropped out and Debby continued with individual therapy. As tensions escalated at home, their adolescent daughter made a suicidal gesture. Subsequently, they began family therapy. It helped to detriangulate the daughter from the marital conflict and gave attention to her school problems. But once her condition improved, Dan had no further interest in family therapy. The therapist tried to address the marital tensions and Dan's troubled condition, but Dan insisted that things would improve once the organic problem was resolved. He increasingly missed appointments and the therapist began to see Debby alone.

The therapist was stuck in a pattern that had defeated the previous therapy; her individual work became supportive and focused on Debby's complaints about Dan. She also experienced the conflictual pull of other helpers. On one side, the local kibbutz physician and one nurse took a gentle, understanding approach with Dan. In the other camp, there were nurses and friends who blamed Dan as taking advantage of his condition, virtually accusing him of malingering. Their coalition with Debby added fuel to the marital conflict.

The therapist suggested a consultation in the Center of Medical Psychology to rethink the direction of her work and to deal more specifically with Dan's condition. Dan was willing to try a new approach to his problems. At that time, he was feeling increasingly overwhelmed by his bodily dysfunctions. In addition to the backache, he began to experience chest pains and abnormally fast heartbeats that made him panic. Emergency room visits and tests showed that his symptoms were only anxiety-related.

Dan's case reveals many common characteristics of chronic pain and other long-term mind-body dysfunction (Roy, 1985; Kellner, 1986; Steinglass et al, 1987). Dan had been functioning at a depressed level with a high degree of anxiety. He entered the sick role, his self image deteriorated, and people in and out of the family related to him as incompetent. In such a stuck system, conflicts are not resolved; they are avoided by a focus on the physical problems. This pattern was described by Kaffman (1981) as monoideism: the intrapsychic and interpersonal fixation of attention into a monothematic track. Life revolves around the problems and there is a drastic reduction in joint activities that bring satisfaction and fun. As the rigidity increases, family members assume stereotypic roles and group functions that restrict their opportunities for self-expression and differentiation (Andolfi, Menghi, Nicolo & Saccu, 1980).

The Pre-Consultation Evaluation

The evaluation of such cases is a challenging task and the preparation that goes on before the actual consultation determines much of its impact. The consultant's goal is to create the conditions that will enable him/her to join and challenge the patient's problems. Reviewing the medical and psychological information helps organize the meeting in terms of whom to invite to the consultation, how to divide the session, and in what order to see the different subgroups. Semistructured questionnaires are sent to the adult patient, parents of young patients, nurse, physician, and school personnel when the patient is school age. The review of their written feedback creates a sense of their importance in conceptualizing and/or intervening in the case. A more extensive description of this important phase is provided in Kaffman's thought-provoking discussion of failures in family therapy (1987).

It is important to prioritize the consultation by pinpointing the most central dysfunctions that need to be dealt with in order to maximize impact. The evaluation and subsequent interventions are directed at all levels of the system, but the emphasis here will be on ecosystemic dynamics and their influence on the family and individual patient. Concepts of system theory, such as boundaries, detours, cross-system alliances, triangulations, myths, and life-cycle transitions are easily applied to this level of analysis (e.g., Imber-Black, 1988). In the following list, five of the most common ecosystemic dysfunctions in chronic mind-body dysfunctions are presented. They are all pertinent to Dan's case.

1. The never-ending treatment

Chronic patients often become chronic consumers of medical services and other healing approaches. Like a roller coaster, the lives of the patient and other family members move in cycles, ranging from periods of high hopes to the depressing realization that nothing has been changed by the last cure. These trips are exhausting and demoralizing, and they add to the family's financial burden. Many times there is someone in the kibbutz's infirmary who is "helping" the patient with more and more referrals. In this respect, Dan's case is typical in that "treatment tends to perpetuate symptoms rather than to abolish them" (Lyght, 1966, p. 973).

2. Sympathy and misery: An unwholesome complementarity

The monoideistic preoccupation with bodily symptoms and concurrent anxieties is usually sustained by close relationships with a friend, a nurse, or anyone else who has an empathic ear. Dan, for instance, has become used to visiting the infirmary a few times a week, or even more often when he feels in crisis. In such meetings, the emphatic "helper" reassures the patient, and for the moment both of them feel better because some of the anxiety is dispelled. But, over time, such a process increases both dependence and anxiety, and the patient feels less able to contain his/her anxieties alone. A variation of this pattern of a close, protective relationship could be with a member of the family. Consequently, a characteristic folie-à-deux type of system tends to develop with the formation of enmeshed family relations and a rigid boundary between the family and the outside world.

3. A restricted and increasingly isolated way of life

As the patient becomes less involved with social relationships and productive spheres of life, there is also a reciprocal avoidance by others. People get bored with complaints, resentful of increased self-centeredness, and angry with the helplessness that increases their own burden. Unfortunately, at the end of the self-reinforcing spiral, one finds that most chronic patients suffer from isolation. As a rule, the less involvement in social, intellectual, and physical activities, the more a patient's life feels like an empty shell with symptoms at the center.

4. A preference for somatotherapy over psychotherapy

Many patients with a psychophysiological disorder have a suspicious attitude toward psychotherapy, and the creation of a therapeutic alliance with them is difficult (Wickramasekera, 1989). One common reason for the resistance is related to the patients' belief that they need a medical cure. Consequently, they perceive the referral to psychotherapy as a challenge to the authenticity of the somatic symptoms. Additional resistance to therapy comes from family members and others who have accompanied the patient's previous "roller coaster rides" with special and promising treatments. They, too, feel suspicious of another hopeful helper who thinks he/she has "the way" to change a chronic condition. These self-protective attitudes often become a self-fulfilling prophesy that maintains a depressive atmosphere and the patient's low functioning.

However, the systemic understanding of "resistance" as a transactional pattern also needs to consider the therapists' part, including the unpalatable fact that therapists not only fail but also harm patients. The a priori resistance to the new therapist may be a sequel to such an experience. Too often therapists overburden chronic patients and their families by making unnecessarily stressful interventions without providing enough support. Individual therapists may not know the potentially disruptive effects of their work on family life, or be in touch with the needs of other family members. On the other hand, family therapists' bias of overemphasizing family dynamics sometimes leads them to make too great a demand of the family (Montalvo, 1986).

5. Triangles and coalitions in the mesosystem

In rigid systems, triangles that develop around unresolved family conflicts often involve the ecosystem. In one commonly found conflict pattern, there are "the 'heavy' and the 'understanding' styles of responding. Each contains some truth; each feels intuitively correct" (Elizur & Minuchin, 1989, p. 138). As usual, the different positions are related to different perspectives. The "understanding" may be family members, friends and sometimes members of the medical team who feel close to the patient and empathic toward her/his suffering. Others, who are more critical of the patient may also come from the family or "outsiders" who identify with the family members whose life is compromised because of the patient's demandingness. A similar position of criticism is sometimes adopted by physicians, nurses, and community members, who feel frustrated and annoyed with the patient's "nagging" for more help and his/her underfunctioning. In these situations, the solution endorsed by one of the factions is usually more of the same and therapists, who do not have a wide enough perspective of their position in the ecosystem, are inadvertently drawn into the dysfunctional dance.

INTERVENTIONS

Setting up the Consultation

After the pre-consultation evaluation of the case, the next step is to decide whom to invite for the consultation. My general policy is to involve people from all levels of the ecosystem that are relevant to the case. These individuals can be a part of the dysfunction and/or provide important support to the patient and the family. The family is always included, unless the children are too small. With older chronic patients, adult children who live away from home and perhaps their spouses are invited. Usually, the family group is seen during the first part of the consultation. The patient is not met alone during this part of the session, unless there is a specific request or special reason. The therapist participates in all parts of the consultation.

Medical and social systems representatives are invited to come an hour-and-a-half later. There are at least two people in this group; the nurse and a *coordinator*, who is appointed by the kibbutz in cooperation with the patient and the family. The coordinator is a kibbutz member who helps the therapist implement and coordinate the treatment plan by networking with the patient, family, and relevant social network and kibbutz systems. Cases do not come with a coordinator; the role is created at the consultant's suggestion once the review of the problem reveals that it is multileveled and well entrenched. The therapist brings this message to the family and the kibbutz, and helps them to find a suitable person for the role. It is understood that the coordinator will receive time consideration from the kibbutz for the community work that needs to be done.

Most families and kibbutzim will collaborate with this request, and in the few cases in which there is initial resistance, it usually comes from the kibbutz. In chronic and socially isolated cases, kibbutz officials sometimes feel that the patient has used many resources, or that the patient is malingering and has taken advantage of the community. Finding a coordinator is difficult when people do not like the patient or when kibbutz resources have already been overstretched in dealing with other problems. These problems are usually resolved when the consultant communicates clearly that a comprehensive pre-consultation evaluation has shown that a coordinator is necessary for creating change.

Physicians are invited, but usually do not come to the consultation. Unlike the nurse, they are not usually kibbutz members, and the organization of their work does not allow them to invest much time in one case. They are involved, however, through telephone and written correspondence. The nurse is usually the link between the therapeutic and medical teams, and she/he does the coordination of all medical issues and referrals.

These consultations are long, three hours on the average, and everyone is notified in advance. During this time span, the consultant has the flexibility to select different constellations of people. A short individual session of hypnotic relaxation may be added toward the end with patients who demonstrate motivation to disrupt the chronic cycle. This adds another half-hour to the consultation. In the end, there is usually a summing-up that includes all of the invited people.

Obviously, the setting-up of the consultation is by itself an intervention, which is done by the therapist in collaboration with the consultant. The preparations that are necessary to organize such a meeting, the expectations that are aroused while waiting for it, its unusual scope, and the anticipation that it will end with a comprehensive program for change give these consultations many of the characteristics of healing rituals. As Jerome Frank puts it: "The core of the techniques of healing...seems to lie in their ability to arouse the patient's hope, bolster his self-esteem, stir him emotionally, and strengthen his ties with a supportive group" (1973, p. 76).

THE CONSULTATION

The general objective of the consultation is twofold. First, to arrive at a common understanding of the problem with an emphasis on the way the system is coping with the mind-body problem. A therapeutic narrative is constructed as the consultant shifts the focus from the physical symptoms to the psychological factors that can be controlled. This change-oriented diagnosis becomes the basis for the second objective, to mobilize the patient, family, and larger social system to work together toward the commonly defined goals. Whenever possible, these goals are framed within a normalizing, temporal framework which is derived from the developmental stage of the family, the type of illness, and the adaptational tasks of the chronic phase (Rolland, 1987). The five points that were defined in the section on the pre-consultation evaluation provide a general framework that needs to be adapted to the specifics of the case. The use of this framework in constructing guidelines for change will be evident in the following description of interventions.

The creation of a collaborative therapeutic team

Two elements are mandatory for good teamwork: a clear and accepted leadership and the ability to closely monitor the implementation of the therapeutic program. The consultant and the therapist need to build their position of leadership, and this is done throughout the work. It is implied in the way that the consultation is set up, in the delineation of the therapeutic blueprints, and in the handling of ecosystemic resistances and conflicts.

In working with chronic patients, the coordinator is a necessary link for effective and economical implementation of the therapeutic program. The coordinator helps to transform ideas into concrete reality and monitors the outcome, so that the therapist can be kept informed of problems. Beyond providing vital support to the family and the work of therapy, the coordinator also helps the social system. He/she becomes the local expert for any unresolved problems in the community concerning the family. In this way, the coordinator helps the therapist to clarify everyday confusions and to deal with the common tendency of lay people to frame problems in terms of pathology.

Of course, the coordinator needs to be supervised and supported by the therapist. For instance, in one case the coordinator was approached by an educational team who were hesitant to discuss problems at school with both parents. It turned out that for a long time they had been discussing the issue only with the father who had been trying to protect his wife from "too much stress." The coordinator phoned the therapist and after their discussion she helped the team approach both parents. This helped the mother feel more competent and increased her participation in the parenting process.

The use of social resources in support of the family

A major task of the treatment team is to support productive activities of the patient and family instead of the preoccupation with the illness. This may mean encouraging and helping the patient find satisfying work, register for an interesting course in the local educational center, or explore other activities in and out of the kibbutz. In some cases, it is important to provide some relief for the overworked spouse or to find help for a child who is falling behind in school. In the most isolated chronic cases, a community network of people would be organized. They would visit the family and invite the patient to their homes, helping in this way to reinvolve the patient and the spouse in social and recreational activities. The creation of satisfying activities helps the patient and the family cope with the sense of emptiness that is often experienced when bodily complaints are moved into the background.

This direction discussed during the consultation has been previously attempted by most patients. Its failure was usually a result of not being a part of a comprehensive program that would provide patients with the intensive support necessary for breaking out of the multilevel cycles that maintain the chronic dysfunction. The task of the consultant is to initiate this process again, and to ensure its practical implementation through a collaboration among the patient, the family, and the community. Coordinators and other involved kibbutz functionaries can be quite creative once they understand the logic of this task, often coming up with suggestions that neither the therapist nor the patient had considered.

Collaboration with the medical team

The nurse acts as a link between the therapist and the medical systems, helping to control the roller coaster pattern. Typically, we need to intervene by decreasing the overinvolvement of the patient with nurses, physicians, and other experts. We try to reach an agreement that for a specified period of time, usually six months, there will be minimal contact between the patient and the medical team except for specified or other substantial medical needs. Usually, the medical team welcomes controlled appointments since they are frustrated and exhausted by the case. As one family physician wrote to us: "I have done everything possible, I have no more patience." The family, who often feel the same, tend to accept this intervention with relief. Since this is a drastic change in the life-style of the patient, the intervention needs to be done with tact and without blame. When patients resist this intervention, we accommodate by making an agreement that the patient will come to the infirmary for a checkup on a regular basis, once every two or three weeks, but not in between.

The supportive services of the medical team are used for a variety of interventions. With many patients, we prescribe exercise as a way of improving both their physical and mental status (Schocken, 1987). Some patients are prescribed antidepressants. There are also patients with a serious drug dependence, who usually overuse narcotic analgesics and/ or tranquilizers. With these patients, it is important to reduce the dependence gradually. With such interventions, it is necessary for our psychiatrist to have a dialogue with the physician, to get medical evaluation and follow-up.

Interrupting the monoideistic cycles

The adverse effects of focusing attention on pain and coping are explained to the patient and all others who come to the consultation. Usually, these effects can be demonstrated during the consultation. Dan, for example, was sighing deeply every couple of minutes and making strange coughing sounds during the initial part of the consultation. When asked, he explained, in very obscure terms, that these behaviors were helping him withstand his suffering. At my suggestion, Dan agreed to stop this practice during the consultation. Later, when he was fully absorbed in the conversation, it was pointed out to him that the decreased attention to the pain actually helped him. This observation was repeated after 20 minutes of hypnotic relaxation. Since Dan was obviously in a more receptive orientation at this point, a more detailed explanation was added about the important role of distraction in pain control. This helped to secure his cooperation for stopping the endless conversations with family members and friends concerning his pains.

In general, the Gate Control Model provides a useful framework for explaining the effects of psychological factors in mediating pain perception and exacerbating pain problems (Melzack & Wall, 1982). It helps to reduce resistance to therapy and to motivate the patient to use psychological resources to reduce the pain problem.

Hence, a critical guideline that is established very clearly during the consultation is to minimize the verbal and nonverbal communication about the disorder and related complaints. This point is included in the pact between the patient, his family and the social-medical environment that is represented by the nurse and the coordinator.

Dealing with resistance and conflict

The consultant takes the role of the expert who is sharing his knowledge and experience of mind-body disorders. He is straightforward, expecting cooperation and compliance, and using all the allies that can be found in the system. There is an understanding attitude toward the patient and family's plight, including an acknowledgement of the real nature of the pains. All the same, the emphasis is put on building up the patient's strength and improving the coping. Consultants who are familiar with the methods of hypnosis will also be able to use these means in the waking state by interspersing in hypnosis indirect suggestions that enhance the patient's motivation and cooperation. Such an approach elicits cooperation and a willingness to try the new approach to an extent that surprises many therapists who participate in the consultation.

There are some patients who want a "cure" and they will not settle for a way that does not promise quick relief. More often, resistance is overcome by psychoeducational methods, a persevering therapeutic attitude, flexibility, and negotiation. In Dan's case, once the therapeutic blueprints were explained to him, he reacted with relief. He understood the rationale, asked why he had not been told all this before, and declared that he would make all attempts to cooperate.

We have found that the inclusion of children in the therapy, including adult children who live away from home, helps in working through resistances. For example, when Dan was defending himself by saying that he did not talk so much about his pains, his daughter protested. With much laughter, a role play was arranged: the two children mirrored their father's verbal complaint, as well as the many nonverbal ways by which he drew attention to his suffering. It was easier for Dan to accept this point from them than from his wife. She was evidently angry at him, showing skepticism toward his "show" of motivation and framing his compliance as a proof that the problem was psychological, as she had been claiming all along. Evidently, it was necessary to deal with their conflict.

The first objective of the consultant in dealing with conflicts in the family and the mesosystem is to uncover the conflicts within a frame that highlights the way that they affect the patient's physical condition and are in turn affected by it. It is usually unrealistic to expect resolution at this stage. Therefore, the second move is to look together for a way to proceed with some temporary arrangement between the antagonists. In Dan's case, the uncovering of the marital tensions was shocking to him since he had avoided and minimized any problems. It became clear that changing the role of pain in the family could lead to the dissolution of the marriage. Moreover, when Dan asked Debby, his wife, if she would go with him to marital therapy, she refused, saying that it was his turn now to work in therapy.

This moment of high intensity proved to be a critical milestone. It was obvious that change would be taking a risk, but should Dan make the attempt there was a possibility for resolving the tension. The way was indicated by Debby, who said that she liked the idea that Dan, as a part of his reinvolvement with life, would plan some activities with the children and with her. In effect, Debby agreed to come to some therapy sessions "for helping with Dan's program," if indeed he would make sincere efforts to cope with the problems.

Clarifying boundaries between the family and the mesosystem

In many chronic cases, including Dan's, family conflicts "spill" into the mesosystem. Since the consultation is not only with the family, but also with members of the social and medical systems, the consultant can actually observe problems on this level of boundaries. This may be seen in open conflicts among family and non-family representatives, "innocent" questions of outsiders about the family dynamics, or remarks by family members that show their sensitivity to intrusion from the kibbutz. The consultant needs to deal with such problems directly and to clarify the boundaries between the family and the social system. Unless this is accomplished, the therapeutic program cannot be implemented in a truly collaborative way.

THE FOLLOW-UP

Like the pre-consultation preparations, follow-ups are an integral part of the intervention. Indeed, the author's experience in following-up Minuchin's consultations has elucidated that even the best interventions could be wasted unless they were monitored by the consultant

(Elizur & Minuchin, 1989). Hence, the idea of a follow-up is introduced at the initial stages of contact. The way of doing the follow-up is flexible, depending upon the participants' needs. Usually, a month or two later, there will be a meeting with the therapist and the family, or only with the therapist, during which new developments are reviewed and new issues are clarified. However, should it be necessary, another large meeting can be set up.

In most of our cases, the response to the consultation is positive. With some patients, the change is surprisingly quick, and when therapy continues, it is no longer centered on the patient's disorder. This type of response was seen in Dan's case. Within two weeks, he started returning to a full work load in a responsible position that demanded much traveling by car. The strange coughing noises were no longer heard after the consultation and Dan's morale improved. He began to walk an hour a day, sometimes with his coordinator or a friend, but also alone. Dan was surprised by the good effects of this activity on his physical well-being.

The relationship with the coordinator was a most significant support for Dan during the first couple of weeks. In their walks, they first focused on Dan's coping with his return to work. Later they discussed various ways for Dan to get more involved in social life. He decided to take up the challenging task of editing the kibbutz's local paper. He also became more involved in doing things with his children and with Debby. There was no more talk about the pain in or out of the family, no avoidance of chores, and no visits to the infirmary. For one month following the consultation, Dan listened daily to an audio tape for hypnotic relaxation and reported a significant decrease in his pains. After one month, he was rather busy in his various activities and no longer met with his coordinator.

Three months later, in a follow-up meeting of the couple and their therapist, neither the coordinator nor the nurse were included. There was very little mention of the pain; most of the session focused on marital issues. Evidently, the focusing of therapy on Dan during this time helped to forge a therapeutic alliance with him. Presently, Dan agreed with the consultant that the first phase of the work had been concluded, and that the major issue was the gradual distancing in the marital relationship. Dan had little insight into his part in the distancing process, and he was interested in more individual sessions for his own self-exploration. This seemed to fit Debby's feelings, too; she was experiencing more support in her everyday life with Dan, and there were some signs of warmth, but she also indicated that there was still much bitterness.

During the second phase of Dan's therapy, the focus was on his difficulties with closeness, and the many subtle ways that he used to reject

Debby and project the blame on her. This phase lasted three months, during which the therapist periodically met with Debby as well. Afterwards, they had two more months of conjoint therapy in which they learned to negotiate their different needs for intimacy. Therapy ended on a positive note, and the occasional pains that Dan sometimes experienced have moved into the background of life. A year later, the kibbutz nurse reported that Dan's physical symptoms continued to be minimal.

No doubt, many factors are involved in the success of this case. Dan was a patient with resources; he was highly trained, with a good reputation in the kibbutz, and so a good job was available to him once his condition improved. In addition, he had good friends, one of whom became his coordinator. His condition relative to other patients with refractory mind-body problems was not as chronic. Additionally, his frustration with all the healing approaches that he had tried before coming to our center made him open to a multilevel intervention. In other cases, there is a less dramatic response.

Nevertheless, a gradual process of improvement usually begins after the consultation. The therapist, aided by the consultant, needs to be persistent with the high tensions that arise whenever there is a relapse. In fact, improvement is often punctuated by points of crisis, which may frighten the therapist, family, and medical team unless they had been prepared in advance by the consultant. I have found it a good policy to tell people that, once their preoccupation with the pain is substantially reduced, they might have a difficult experience of existential emptiness. With some patients it later becomes a useful therapeutic frame for working on their difficulties. Others enjoy telling me that I was wrong, that they have had no difficulty in filling up their life with meaningful pursuits.

In a few cases, after an initial rejection of the program, some families returned later, more ready to accept our way of working. Undeniably, there were also cases in which we needed to be able to accept only a limited improvement. These are usually patients whose life has been characterized by persistent dysthymia and limited functioning.

CONCLUSION AND SOME CAVEATS FOR USING THIS APPROACH

Difficulties in the therapy of refractory mind-body disorders are often related to rigidity in the family and socio-medical systems' ways of responding to the disorder. Over time, these patterns can become well entrenched and intertwined with the physiological problem. Consultations need to impact the major multilevel dysfunctions. Additionally, it is necessary to provide enough support to the family when a chronic maladaptation is changed. This way of working can be more easily applied in the kibbutz, but I have applied these same principles with urban patients. Members of the extended family, friends, close neighbors, working partners, physicians, and community agencies can become important therapeutic allies once we learn how to coordinate their resources. In applying this approach, however, some caveats need to be kept in mind:

1. The consultant, even though he/she tries to observe the ecosystem from outside, is a member of that system. As in Escher's picture *Print Gallery*, the observer is also a part of the picture that he/she is observing. Hence, one cannot avoid experiencing some pull into colluding with dysfunctional patterns. The consultant needs to be aware of his/ her position in the mesosystem and to maintain differentiation by being alert to the pulls of the system. In this respect, it is helpful to achieve a sweeping view of the mesosystem in one long session that includes representatives of different systems.

2. Chronic mind-body disorders have some common characteristics, which we have highlighted, yet each case is unique and needs to be evaluated as such. The specific biological nature of the problem is always significant; it affects the course of the disorder and the psychosocial organization around it. A case of chronic pain was presented because it is a common characteristic that is shared by many disorders. In addition, the multilevel dynamics that evolve around pain are often found when there is a dysfunctional adaptation to other chronic mind-body disorders. However, there are significant variations in the adaptation to different forms of chronic diseases, depending on whether they are progressive, constant, or episodic. A useful psychosocial classification of illness has been presented by Rolland (1987).

3. A careful consideration of the biology of the illness is crucial during the diagnostic stage. Nonmedical therapists cannot work in this field without collaborating with a psychiatrist who is well versed in the medical aspects of the disorders. Moreover, some physicians will cooperate better with a psychosocial program when they have contact with a medically trained therapist. Therefore, teamwork is an important part of the therapist's own support system.

4. Because of the complexity of the problem, consultants will often need to use a wide variety of techniques that affect different levels of the system. Chronic systems do not respond very well to theoretical purists who, instead of adapting their approach to the needs of the case, will overfocus on one particular dynamic or overemphasize a specific

intervention. Even the length of therapy varies considerably; some patients will terminate after the first phase that is focused on coping with the disorder, while others will continue with any combination of family, marital, and individual therapy.

REFERENCES

American Psychiatric Association (1987). *Diagnostic and Statistical Manual of Mental Disorders, Third edition, Revised.* Washington, DC: American Psychiatric Association.

Anderson, C. M., & Stewart, S. (1993). *Mastering Resistance: A Practical Guide to Family Therapy.* New York: Guilford.

Andolfi, M., Menghi, P., Nicolo, A. M. & Saccu, C. (1980). Interaction in rigid systems: A model of intervention in families with a schizophrenic member. In M. Andolfi & I. Zwerling (Eds.), *Dimensions of Family Therapy.* New York: Guilford.

Auerswald, E. H. (1987). Epistemological confusion in family therapy and research. *Family Process, 26,* 317–330.

Bronfenbrenner, U. (1979). *The Ecology of Human Development.* Cambridge, MA: Harvard University Press.

Coyne, J. C. & Anderson, B. J. (1988). The "psychosomatic family" reconsidered: Diabetes in context. *Journal of Marital and Family Therapy,* 14(2), 113–123.

Elizur, Y. (1993). Ecosystemic training: Conjoining supervision and organizational development. *Family Process,* 32: 185–201.

Elizur, Y. (1992). Ecosystemic consultation: A case of epilepsy. *Family Systems Medicine,* 10: 135–146.

Elizur, J. (1990). "Stuckness" in live supervision; Expanding the therapist's style. *Journal of Family Therapy,* 12, 267–280.

Elizur, J. & Minuchin, S. (1989). *Institutionalizing Madness, Families, Therapy and Society.* New York: Basic Books.

Frank, J. D. (1973). *Persuasion and Healing, a Comparative Study of Psychotherapy.* Baltimore: John Hopkins University Press.

Griffith, J. L., Griffith, M. E. & Slovik, L. S. (1989). Mind-body patterns of symptom generation. *Family Process,* 28(2), 137–152.

Imber-Black, E. (1988). *Families and Larger Systems.* New York: Guilford.

Kaffman, M. (1981). Monoideism in psychiatry: Theoretical and clinical implications. *American Journal of Psychotherapy,* 35, 235–243.

Kaffman, M. (1987). Failures in family therapy: and then what? *Journal of Family Therapy,* 9: 307–328.

Kellner, R. (1986). *Somatization and Hypochondriasis.* New York: Praeger-Greenwood.

Lyght, C. E. (Ed.) (1966). *The Merck Manual of Diagnosis and Therapy.* Rahway, NJ: Merck Sharp and Dohme Research Laboratories.

McDaniel, S. H., Hepworth, J., & Doherty, W. J. (1992). *Medical Family Therapy: A Biopsychosocial Approach to Families with Health Problems.* New York: Basic Books.

Melzack, R. & Wall, P. (1982). *The Challenge of Pain.* Harmondsworth, Middlesex, England: Penguin Books.

Minuchin, S., Rosman, B. L. & Baker, L. (1978). *Psychosomatic Families: Anorexia Nervosa in Context.* Cambridge, MA: Harvard University Press.

Montalvo, B. (1986). Family strengths: Obstacles and facilitators. In M. A. Karpel (Ed.), *Family Resources: The Hidden Partner in Family Therapy.* New York: Guilford.

Ornstein, R. & Sobel, D. (1987). *The Healing Brain.* New York: Simon and Schuster.

Philips, H. C. (1988). *The Psychological Management of Chronic Pain.* New York: Springer.

Rolland, J. S. (1987). Chronic illness and the life cycle: A conceptual framework. *Family Process, 26*(2), 203–221.

Roy, R. (1985). Family treatment for chronic pain: State of the art. *International Journal of Family Therapy, 7*(4), 297–309.

Schocken, D. D. (1987). Exercise as a therapeutic modality: The exercise prescription. In J. A. Blumenthal & D. C. McKee (Eds.), *Applications in Behavioral Medicine and Health Psychology* (pp. 543–565). Sarasota, Florida: Professional Resource Exchange.

Schwartzman, J. (Ed.) (1984). *Families and Other Systems: The Macrosystemic Context of Family Therapy.* New York: Guilford.

Speck, R. & Attneave, C. (1973). *Family Networks.* New York: Pantheon.

Steinglass, P., Bennett, L. A., Wolin, S. J., & Reiss, D. (1987). *The Alcoholic Family.* New York: Basic Books.

Sternbach, R. A. (1974). Varieties of pain games. In J. J. Bonica (Ed.), *Advances in Neurology* (Vol 4). New York: Raven.

Wickramasekera, I. (1989). Enabling the somatizing patient to exit the somatic closet: A high-risk model. *Psychotherapy, 26*(4), 530–544.

Wynne, L. C., McDaniel, S. H. & Weber, T. T. (Eds.) (1986). *Systems Consultation for Family Therapy.* New York: Guilford.

11

Consultation as Evaluation of Therapy

Sara B. Jutoran

Act always so as to increase the number of choices.
Heinz von Foerster (1973/1982)

AN INVITATION TO CO-INSPIRATION

While studying with Maurizio Andolfi, I was invited to consult in the therapy of a couple who were Andolfi's patients. The couple and I were asked to make an evaluation of the therapy and of the therapist, my teacher. Without hesitation or prior information, I plunged into the rough waters of the session to perform the novel function of consultant to my teacher, while he remained as an observer behind the one-way mirror.

By allowing his therapeutic work to be evaluated by his student and patients, Andolfi reversed relational patterns and hierarchical roles in both the therapeutic and training systems. He thus added unpredictable elements in order to increase the system's complexity by establishing a reflexive process to comment on the therapeutic system. His observation of the evaluation enabled him to attain information about the patients' perception of his impact. Furthermore, the evaluation session not only increased the system's complexity but created additional discontinuity by allowing the patients to assess their progress towards their life goals.

The consultative examination of the therapy provides interesting feedback about the process/progress of the therapeutic relationship. The therapy could be thus defined as a progressing therapy, failing therapy, successfully finished therapy, a therapy which could use new methods, etc. The positive and negative behaviors of the therapist could also be assessed, i.e., supportive, creative, dramatic, impatient, distant, overly involved, etc. In essence, Andolfi created a different context for the therapeutic and the training systems to reflect upon themselves. Thus, Andolfi's reformulation of the functions of all the participants reversed his one-up position into a one-down position in both systems.

I shall consider, from the point of view of an observer who describes the consultation system, three different criteria which will bring forth different observations.

1. The observation of interactional processes permits us to describe a reversal of both complementary relationships in the therapeutic and training systems. The therapist-patients relationship was reversed into the consultee–co-consultants relationship; and the teacher-trainee relationship into the consultee-consultant relationship.

2. By observing hierarchical roles in the therapeutic system, we can perceive the therapist in the role of expert and the couple in the role of clients, while in the consulting system it is the consultant and the couple, as co-consultants, who take the role of experts as they evaluate the therapist's work. "Power is not something that one person or another has; it is a relation in which something is conferred to somebody..." (Maturana, 1990a, p. 64). Therefore, power is a concept that always implies two or more persons—one who confers power and one who accepts power. In this case, power was offered by Andolfi to his patients and student and was accepted by them.

3. According to Maturana, our emotions change as we move ourselves in linguistic interactions. The changing of our emotions changes our actions, which recursively change the course of our languaging and our reasoning. *Conversing* is therefore the intertwined flow of languaging and emotioning, and the flow of conversing is a *conversation* (1990b, p. 47).

Andolfi's proposal created an organization with specific functions and roles for the components of this system. Languaging in these different roles and functions triggered different emotions which resulted in a different network of conversations (Maturana, 1990b).

The shifting of functions, roles, and conversations by the components within the consultative system allowed Andolfi to expand and enhance his observations and reflections. Furthermore, by being behind the one-way mirror, Andolfi had more freedom and distance and less emotional involvement, while the couple, through my participation as consultant, was able to perceive and experience their therapy with more emotional involvement. Similarly, the inclusion of the couple in the training system established more symmetry in my relationship with Andolfi. His proposition, therefore, was, as Maturana (1990c) says, "an invitation to enter into a domain of co-inspiration."

AN UNUSUAL CONSULTATION

Gino and Anna are a middle-class couple. They have been married for 16 years. She is 36 years old and a housewife. He is the owner of a store and is 45 years old. They have two sons, aged 13 and 15. With respect to this therapy, they have had 11 sessions in five months, two sessions with their children and one with each family of origin.

Surfing on Latin American Waters

When I entered the session, I saw Gino as a formal and reserved man with an unexpressive face, and Anna as an attractive, refined woman with a sad look in her eyes. She said that my face looked familiar to her, and it turned out that she was born in Latin America. Since my homeland is Argentina, the coincidence of our common Latin American origin seemed to have facilitated a favorable atmosphere that was maintained during the rest of the session.

The Cold War

They both defined their problem jokingly, which put me off balance. On the other hand, their playfulness confirmed my first impression about good rapport and their acceptance of my role as a consultant.

Anna: We are here because we agree on everything. We want to find a method that will allow us to quarrel (*she laughs*).
Gino: We haven't found one yet. We agree all the more as time goes by (*he laughs*).
Anna: (*seriously*) It was a joke. We are here because for 16 years we haven't agreed on anything.

Gino: We don't talk. There's no communication between us.
Anna: It's more than that, there is a cold war going on.

Anna commented that a year and a half ago she decided to participate in an English course without telling Gino. She assumed that he
didn't want her to have other activities because of his fear of abandonment. When Gino found out that she had started studying English, he
left home for one-and-a-half months. He also left her on another occasion after an argument about his many business trips which she quite
disliked.

Cons: So, then it was your husband who left because you didn't like his
    going away on business trips, and again he left because he didn't
    like your going to English classes.
Anna: Exactly.
Gino: Let me explain. She has a much stronger character than I. We
    don't talk, we argue all the time, and I always feel in a lesser posi-
    tion. I have no weapons to defend myself and at a certain point I
    get exasperated. And when she says, "He left," I really feel I was
    thrown out. It was I who was feeling really bad. Today I got rid of
    the concept I had, that she must only work at home in the tradi-
    tional way. I don't think like that any more. Since I came here I've
    changed a lot. She has also matured....

Anna mentioned that when Gino came back home, he talked with
some friends about their problems, and they suggested Andolfi for
couples therapy.

Double Individual Therapy

They agreed that their relationship has not improved, but they considered therapy to have been beneficial on an individual level.

Cons: I would like to know what you think about the therapeutic pro-
    cess from the beginning up to now.
Gino: I believe this therapy is very productive, though painful for me.
    When we leave here there's no dialogue between us. We live as if
    we were a separated couple. Maybe this is part of the therapeutic
    process. At the beginning I came here to attack her position, to
    blame her for all these things that she has been telling you about.
    But afterwards, I felt guilty myself. I blame myself for having
    worked only for my family, never for myself. I haven't left a space

for myself. Gradually, I started seeing my sexual and affective difficulties, and although it was painful and it bothered me a lot, I realized that the therapy worked, because if the pain is there, it means that the wound is healing. All these things started moving inside me; they made me think a lot.

Cons: Do you think along the same lines, Anna? You said you never agreed, though.

Anna: Yes, I believe this therapy is suitable, but there are changes going on inside me that scare me. On one hand, I need to feel I exist as a person, independently from my husband, my children, my parents; that I can do things for and by myself. On the other hand, it scares me a lot as it would mean an important change in my life. I don't know if I'm strong enough to achieve this goal.

Cons: What do you think, Anna? Would you agree that this would be a double-individual therapy?

Anna: I believe this is the way it should be. One has to feel all right about oneself to be able to have a good relationship as a couple.

Gino: That's right. We are not working for the couple, but rather through it we are dealing with ourselves.

Their evaluation of the therapy allowed me to perceive the differentiation and individuation processes. They had moved from describing their conflicts in terms of mutual blaming and complaint to the perception of their own needs and difficulties and towards the discovery of their own potentialities. This shift enabled them to take responsibility for their own life rather than giving that responsibility to the other spouse.

Couple's Perception of Therapist

Cons: What do you think, Gino? Would you say Andolfi has then failed in this couple therapy?

Gino: I don't think so. If the therapy has succeeded in giving each of us strength to get somewhere, no matter what this may be, then it has not failed at all. On the contrary, I think Andolfi has done a good job.

Anna: This is the way it should be, I think.

Cons: Anna, what do you think Andolfi thinks, that he has been able to help both of you?

Anna: Seeing us today, I think he could think he hasn't helped us much as a couple. He has helped each of us as individuals, and I consider this very important, because he has made me evaluate what

I have done with my life. (*starts crying*) I've realized it hasn't been enough. I've always blamed others, my father, my mother, my husband, while I'm the only one to blame.

Cons: Sometimes a crisis is important in order to become aware of certain issues.

Anna: That's right. And now that I am 36, I don't know what to do. It makes me sad but not afraid. It is easier when you are twenty. I've realized that I didn't take certain decisions, always blaming the others. It's easier to hide behind certain things.

Their positive evaluation of Andolfi's work on an individual level, in spite of their negative perception with regards to their relationship, validated the goals attained and confirmed their commitment to the therapy.

Questions on the Future of the Couple and the Therapy

Cons: Do you believe, Anna, that there is a future for the couple?

Anna: I don't know... if one believes in miracles... perhaps. I don't know... if something could happen... Sometimes there are external factors that make people change their minds. Maybe... I don't know (*Her short disrupted sentences reflect her doubts; the tone of her voice expresses her frustration and pessimism.*)

Cons: And what about you, Gino?

Gino: Yes, even if the chances are one in a million I want to try. (*His colorless voice and his rigid posture do not seem to fit his comment.*)

Cons: Anna, would you be willing to do something here?

Anna: I don't know. It's as if I couldn't take all this anymore. I'm tired.

Cons: Your husband said that even if the chances were one in a million he would come here to work. What about you?

Anna: I'm afraid of...(*starts crying*) of being let down again. I'm scared.

At this moment Gino, hesitating, compares the consulting session with the therapy sessions. For the first time I remember Andolfi behind the mirror and feel rather awkward. My two roles—consultant and trainee—intersect. I feel myself involved in a triangle between Andolfi and Gino, who is trying to make an alliance with me.

Gino: I find... Andolfi... maybe I'm wrong...I don't know, but I find he has not talked with us like this, analyzing certain things, certain feelings like we are doing now.

Immediately Anna sides with Andolfi and reframes Gino's words.

Anna: I believe we haven't had a session like this with Andolfi because the sessions depend on the mood of each person. We are the ones that make the sessions. These things didn't come to light before, perhaps because it was not the right time.

From this moment on, the openness to unresolved issues led to an increase in emotional intensity. Gino stated that the overinvolvement of Anna's parents was a cause of his aloofness. Anna felt that Gino's unavailability in difficult circumstances caused her to turn to her father. Each spouse seemed locked in solitary confinement. Anna tried to hold back her sobs, but was overwhelmed by her pain. Gino, having lost all the color in his face, seemed petrified. The session's rhythm became slower, and the tension reached its highest peak.

Anna: You always stayed away. You were always absent. Are you ever present as a father? (*She speaks with growing pain. Her voice is becoming louder and her hands nervously grasp the handkerchief with which she is drying her tears.*)

Anna seemed to be spitting out the accumulated suffering of many years. I felt the impact of her accusations—maybe the presence of another woman allowed her to be more open. I tried not to give in to my impulse to side with her against Gino.

Gino: No, I think you didn't choose me as a father. You chose your father as father to your children. I was never close to the children because whenever you needed help you turned to your father (*He seems to have difficulties in expressing himself. His tone of voice hasn't changed. His face looks like a mask making it difficult to perceive the suffering his words convey.*)

Anna: You were never there when I needed you. Never. Whenever I wanted you to accompany me anywhere I had to call my father because if I asked you, you would tell me you had a shop full of people to attend. I remember asking you to come with me when my uterus had to be operated on, and you said you couldn't, so I called my father. How do you think I felt being there with my father? What embarrassment! I felt like a fool.

Gino: I can't remember.

Anna: You can't? But I can. When I asked you to come with me to choose the hospital where our child was to be born, what did you say?

"Take a taxi, go along with your sister." I remember crying my
eyes out in the car.

Gino: I don't agree with you.

Anna: Now I don't need you to accompany me anymore. Do you understand? (*Starts crying again.*)

Gino: I don't agree with all these things you are saying and I'm quite
willing to analyze them day by day.

During this entire sequence, Gino remained motionless. He was barely
audible and did not look at his wife. However, after further discussion,
as Gino seemed to be willing to work on these issues, I used my connection with Anna to arrive at an agreement.

Anna: I feel so tired.

Cons: It seems there are issues which haven't been touched yet.

Anna: That's right.

Gino: Yes.

Anna: To tell you the truth, I'm so tired I don't feel like solving them.

Cons: I don't know, at least in my country, you clarify certain issues
before taking a resolution.

Anna: Certainly. Some decisions are only taken once you have cleared
up everything; you don't take them out of the blue.

Gino: Exactly.

I considered this to be the right moment to restore the therapeutic
system. I left the room to talk with Andolfi behind the one-way mirror
where we decided to conclude the interview together.   '

Andolfi: Today you have shown great courage and I think the consultant has helped you achieve this.

Gino: Yes, I am happy.

Anna: So am I.

Andolfi: Maybe it is because I was behind the mirror, but I feel, more
than other times, a cemetery atmosphere, and I think you still need
to spend additional time in the cemetery... be able to plunge down
into the miseries of life. At this moment I am under the impression that you would rather escape from the cemetery than stay
there. (*to the consultant*) Are you in agreement?

Cons: Yes.

Andolfi: (*to the couple*) The consultant has quickly touched very important issues. From the beginning, the encounter with your South
American wife... it must have been something about the Latin spirit.

(*to the consultant*) Gino has been very quick too in admitting his errors. The swiftness of also reaching an intimate rapport.

Gino: It has been very touching. Some things reached me in a very special way.

Cons: I think it would be important to clear the way; if not, it would mean another escape.

Andolfi: Yes, but they have not breathed in this atmosphere of loneliness in the cemetery. I think they need to stand long periods of time there without the children coming along to enliven the situation. If they manage to do this, it will be quite clear to me how deeply they want to commit themselves in therapy, in order to come out of the cemetery and not spend their lives in it.

Gino: What about the consultant's words as to raking the pathway?

Gino's interesting metaphor, following Andolfi's intervention, reframed my previous statement in an attempt to restore my role of consultant in the presence of Andolfi.

Andolfi: Let's rake it, after all we are official rakers.

The pathetic feeling of death in the couple's relationship led Andolfi to prescribe that they experience these feelings in the cemetery so that they could aspire to the genesis of a different relationship. The powerful image of the cemetery highlighted the need to bury their lifelong positions in the relationship; it illuminated the need to face their open wounds and it challenged them to intensify their commitment to therapy.

As the couple left, I remained with the impression that important issues had been touched. I had the feeling that Gino and Anna had been able to connect with their voids, reaching for more complex levels of understanding. I was uncertain, as I guess they were, about their future as a couple, but I knew that through this path of uncertainty they would probably find their way out of their rigid and stereotyped functions.

ON CREATIVITY AND RESOURCES

Andolfi's proposal of a consultative evaluation created three levels of observation:

1. The couple's observation of the therapeutic relationship.
2. The consultant's observation of the couple's observation of the therapeutic relationship.

3. Andolfi's observation of the consultant's observation of the couple's observation of the therapeutic relationship.

Koestler (1964) coined the term bisociation as "the perceiving of a situation or idea...in two self-consistent but habitually incompatible frames of reference..." (p. 35). The possibility of being in two different roles and two different relationships simultaneously, offers two different frames of reference. The depth perceptions in the intersection of these two independent frames of reference can promote new emotions, meanings and behaviors. According to Koestler (1964), "the result... is either a collision ending in laughter, or their fusion in a new intellectual synthesis, or their confrontation in an aesthetic experience...the same pair of matrices can produce comic, tragic, or intellectually challenging effects" (p. 45).

In the process of this encounter a complex network of bisociated contexts is being created. Each of these contexts has a specific frame of reference with specific codes and rules, which are organized in patterns of ordered behavior. The simultaneous experience in two different frames of reference permits the "...transfer of the train of thought from one matrix to another governed by a different logic or rule..." (p. 95). Koestler considered bisociation as "the essence of creative activity" (p. 231), explaining that "the creative act... always operates on more than one plane...." It is a "transitory state of unstable equilibrium where the balance of both emotion and thought is disturbed" (pp. 35–36). "The creative act, by connecting previously unrelated dimensions of experience... is an act of liberation, the defeat of habit by originality" (p. 96).

The oscillation and intersection of functions and roles, previous and present, in the bisociated contexts trigger changes in the conversations through the changing of emotioning and languaging (Maturana, 1990b). This was evident when Gino, as co-consultant and patient made a past and present self evaluation of achieved change due to the therapy (see p. 184), while Anna doubted whether she would attain her goals (see p. 185). Gino and Anna's comparison of the consultation with the therapy sessions (see p. 186) made it more difficul to maintain my role of the consultant rather than become another therapist. My decision to include the therapist in the session (see p. 188) put him back in charge. Gino, however, confirmed the impact of the consultant when he referenced the consultant's optimism at the end of the session (see p. 189).

This rather unusual interview offered us the possibility to see the situation with different lenses, from different perspectives, and in different contexts. It enabled the components of the system to expand their own domains, to experience and construct alternative realities, and to bring forth new resources.

SECOND EVALUATION: ONE YEAR LATER

Pre-session

When I returned to Rome the next year, Andolfi requested a second evaluation/consultation in the continuing therapy with Gino and Anna. Andolfi told me that the result of last year's consultation was a noticeable, enduring improvement in the couple's relationship. He suggested that they write me about the changes they had achieved. The letters were never written because they didn't want to send them until they had fully succeeded in working their way out of the cemetery. Possibly, the thought of the unwritten letters maintained the presence of the consultant and the impact of the consultation interview.

During the year, Gino decided to leave the family business and branch off on his own. This decision, which tied him even more to his work, was resented by Anna, who felt more abandoned than before. On the other hand, Anna wanted to find an activity of her own, but was still feeling insecure in her ability to be more independent. Conflicting needs reappeared and the relationship became difficult once again, although with different nuances. Each spouse was now more centered on individual needs and difficulties. The mutual blaming had noticeably decreased, but they were both beginning to consider the possibility of divorce.

Although Andolfi and I agreed to conduct a second evaluation, we decided, due to the couple's current stress, to delay the evaluation till the latter part of the session. Thus, Andolfi once more created a new and different structure in this interview by including me as a co-therapist.

The Melting Ice

Upon entering the session I was surprised by how different they looked. Gino seemed much more alive and connected, and Anna looked more seductive and animated.

Cons: I can see you've changed.
Anna: For better or for worse?
Cons: You're different.
Anna: Separately or together? (*We all laugh openly.*)
Andolfi: How do you see them different?
Cons: They seem warmer, more assertive, more alive, especially Gino.
Anna: I have some news for you (*She looks excited.*) I've started a course on job orientation. It's for women who have never worked, like myself...(*Andolfi and I congratulate her with a handshake*).

Andolfi: (*to Gino*) Did you shake her hand?

Gino: No, but what she did is important. (*He does not seem to be too pleased with Anna's decision, but he shakes her hand while she looks at him naughtily.*)

Anna: I don't think things could be worse than what they are now. I must try a different way. If I had an activity, maybe I wouldn't feel his lack of attention, nor would I mind that he doesn't spend time with me, and I wouldn't expect everything from him. I was making his life impossible, so I took the decision to do something for myself. I started yesterday. I was terrified, my hands were shaking, but today it was not so hard. (*She talks with enthusiasm.*)

Cons: Gino, what do you feel when you see Anna's enthusiasm?

Gino: I think she has taken the right decision. (*He appears cold and detached, which makes me think that he is not too pleased.*)

Anna: During these past two weeks I realized that I never gave him the chance to understand what I wanted, as I was scared he would not agree with me. If I grow stronger and find the right path, maybe he will also change his attitude.

Andolfi: It's an open search, important. (*to the Cons*) Each one must be able to see his/her own voids, instead of seeing them in the other. I think Gino has also started to see them.

Gino: For me the most important achievement of this therapy has been the getting to know more about myself. (*I am surprised to notice that it is he who brings up last year's evaluation of the therapy.*) My ideas about who I am are clearer now and I think that the best thing might be to put an end to our marriage. The problem is that I don't have enough strength to do it. Today I feel the need to look at my personal problems (*His voice is much more colorful, his attitude is more relaxed and he seems to be in touch with himself*).

Andolfi: Why don't you allow us to hear those problems?

Gino: (*with growing suffering and in a very low voice*) The thing is I don't get satisfaction out of anything. Due to insecurity, maybe, or excessive responsibility, I don't know; the fact is I can find no way out. I have more work now, which implies more effort, and this is positive, but I would need someone in my family to appreciate it. I feel bad from the moment I wake up. (*He cannot carry on talking and begins to cry.*)

Anna watches him and cries too. There is a long silence filled with emotional intensity. Anna is surprised that Gino is crying; she says that she is worried about him, and remarks that he has built a wall around himself. She also mentions that he does not allow himself to enjoy life. I am surprised to listen to her concern for Gino which she did not show in our meeting last year. I reframe Gino's crying as the opening of the wall; Andolfi amplifies this and provokes Gino by commenting that until now he used to be an outsider, only accompanying Anna in the therapy, but today he is here. Gino reacts by trying again to make an alliance with me.

Gino: I can feel the consultant's presence a lot, both last time and today.

Gino's reference to last year's encounter gives me the opportunity to bring up the issue of the consulting session. To my surprise, for it had not been agreed upon before, Andolfi goes behind the one-way mirror. Thus, this second part of the interview becomes isomorphic to last year's consultation.

Cons: Do both of you remember our last year's interview?
Gino: Yes, of course.
Andolfi: O.K., I'm going behind the mirror. (*Andolfi exits.*)
Gino: For me it was like a space within the therapy. I felt you as a person who, in order to help, wants to enter into the essence of what is happening.
Anna: It was very important and I remember it quite well. I cried so much. But then I found strength to begin again, to try once more, and the marriage looked much better to me. So much so, that for a long time we were doing well. But four weeks ago, it was Andolfi who made me fall into a crisis when he said: "It's as if your husband had married another woman before marrying you and that woman is his job. You will always be the second." As from then, I haven't talked anymore and I started to look at myself from the inside. I saw my insecurities, and I discovered that I have missed a whole stage in my life.
Cons: I see. And what do you think, Gino, about our last year's interview?
Gino: I think that these interviews that we have once a year, allow us to let important things out into the open. It's like leaving one track to take another, to return to the first one later. It has been very important, it was a real dialogue between us, with great commitment; you came into our deep feelings. With Andolfi it's different, it's like going along a track that we don't know.
Anna: Yes, he gives a way, and then he hits. For example, he says one word to Gino, which relates to me, and when I go back home I

remember it and I think about it. When he spoke to me about my insecurities, it made me very upset, because for me it was Gino who needed help.

I find their description of the two different therapeutic styles rather unusual and quite interesting. Andolfi's presence behind the mirror does not make me feel uncomfortable this time, very likely because my relation with him has changed. On the other hand, Gino's comments show a different quality, which can also be noted in Anna's comments. There are no accusations, but mutual respect. I can also observe the configuration of different alliances as compared to the previous interview; consultant and therapist on one side, and both spouses on the other.

Gino: These last times Andolfi told me that I had so much rage inside me that nobody could even make me cry. Incredible coldness, he said. But in fact, today I was able to do so.

Cons: This is what I saw the minute I came in. I saw that the ice was melting.

Anna: Opening up is a risk, because the other person can say, "I like you or I don't."

Cons: The question is, if there is enough strength to take that risk.

Anna: I don't know.

Cons: Do you think Gino has changed?

Anna: Yes, but I'm scared he will close up again. Anyway, I've decided to go ahead, and if he accepts me like this, all the better, because I would prefer to solve everything without separating. He must accept me as I am, a woman who can make mistakes, but who can also take responsibilities. I have not yet achieved it, but I intend to head that way. Maybe we could both start again from the beginning.

Cons: This is not at all easy, it's a huge challenge.

Gino: I am scared too, because now, looking at our past, I don't want this any more. I'm scared of being the one who wants the separation.

Cons: It's interesting to see how things have changed. Now it is you, Gino, who wants to separate, and last time it was you who said, "Even if it's one in a million, I want to try." Do you remember?

Gino: Yes, I do.

Cons: Do you think you will continue with this therapy?

Both: Yes, whatever happens.

The possibility of evaluating the impact of the consultation one year later created an isomorphic structure with regards to the evaluation of therapy. In the consultation, the therapist was able to obtain information about his work with the couple. This interview allowed the consultant to get feedback about her previous meeting with them. Both evaluations punctuated different stages in the therapeutic process allowing patients, therapist, and consultant to review and verify the present status of this process.

The follow-up session was not our last meeting with Anna and Gino. We saw them once again a week later. There was an open and warm atmosphere with lots of humor and liveliness. The couple mentioned that some positive changes had occurred, and suggested the idea of a follow-up next year. At the beginning of this last session, Gino's words seemed to reflect the whole interchange of roles and functions when, assuming the role of therapist, he asked Andolfi and me playfully: "You look sad and tired, can we help you?"

One year later, Andolfi informed me that Gino and Anna were both doing quite well.

SUMMARY

The idea of creating a consultation team with clients in order to evaluate their therapeutic process offers new alternatives in the field of family therapy. It allows participants to expand their experience by viewing the therapeutic system through different frames of reference. The therapist's decision to interchange roles and functions validates each member's personal competence and potential. The freedom and responsibility of evaluating the therapy encourages new interactions, perceptions, and choices, thus bringing forth unpredictable domains of creativity.

Doors have been opened to glimpse other horizons or perhaps the same horizon with different lights. Possibly the traditional lighting effects will dull the new colors that may have appeared. Or maybe the new illumination will bring out the hidden colors never envisioned. In the delicate equilibrium between the familiar lights and the new ones, the prevailing lights will depend only on each one of us.

ACKNOWLEDGMENTS

I want to thank Maurizio Andolfi for having given me the opportunity to participate in this consultation, Humberto Maturana and Russ Haber for their assistance in the revision of the manuscript, and Mrs. Rita Kauders for helping me with the translation.

REFERENCES

Andolfi, M. (1979). *Family Therapy: An Interactional Approach*. New York: Plenum Press.

Andolfi, M., Angelo, C., Menghi, P. & Nicolo-Corigliano, A. M. (1983). *Behind the Family Mask: Therapeutic Change in Rigid Family Systems*. New York: Brunner/Mazel.

Andolfi, M. & Angelo, C. (1989). *The Myth of Atlas: Families and the Therapeutic Story*. New York: Brunner/Mazel.

Koestler, A. (1964). *The Act of Creation*. New York: Dell Publishing Co., Inc.

Koestler, A. (1982). *En busca de lo absoluto*. (Bricks to Babel II). Barcelona: Editorial Kairos.

Maturana, H. & Varela, F. (1987). *The Tree of Knowledge*: Boston: New Science Library.

Maturana, H. (1988). Reality: The search for objectivity or the quest for a compelling argument. *The Irish Journal of Psychology, 9, 1*, 25–82.

Maturana, H. (1990a). *Emociones y Lenguaje en Educación y Política* (Emotions and Language in Education and Politics). Santiago, Chile: Ed. Hachette.

Maturana, H. (1990b). Ontología del conversar. (Ontology of conversing). *Sistemas Familiares*, Año 6, No. 2, 43–53.

Maturana, H. (1990c). "Conversando con Humberto Maturana." Seminar organized by the Instituto de Terapia Sistemica, Buenos Aires, Argentina.

Von Foerster, H. (1973/1982). On constructing a reality. In *Observing Systems*. Seaside, Ca.: Intersystems Publications.

Watzlawick, P. Beavin, J. H. & Jackson, D. D. (1967). *Pragmatics of Human Communication*. New York: Norton.

Whitaker, C. A. (1986). Family therapy consultation as invasion. In Wynne L. C., McDaniel, S. H. & Weber, T. T. (Eds.), *Systems Consultation: A New Perspective for Family Therapy* (pp. 80–86). New York: Guilford Press.

Wynne, L. C., McDaniel, S. H. & Weber, T. T. (1986). The road from family therapy to systems consultation. In Wynne, L. C., McDaniel, S. H. & Weber, T. T. (Eds.), *Systems Consultation: A New Perspective for Family Therapy* (pp. 3–15). New York: Guilford Press.

12

Sequential Preventive Meta-Consultation (SPMC): A Model of Collegial Consultation in Systems Therapy

Noga Rubinstein-Nabarro

It is said that "the *wise* person avoids getting into situations that the *smart* person knows how to get out of."

Experienced family and marital therapists, trainers, and consultants have become adept and creative at using therapeutic consultation as a "rescue" method to help the family and the therapist "stuck" in a therapeutic impasse to get "unstuck." It seems, however, that "consultation" got stuck with "stuckness." It was only natural to put our first efforts into getting out of those difficult situations that made us sweat. However, we had, to a great extent, overlooked being wise—that is, using the creative potential of professional collegial consultation as a purposeful device to prevent getting into therapeutic impasse situations. The struggle that my colleagues and I (at *The Israeli Institute for Family and Personal Change* ["*Shinui*"]) had with the pitfalls of brief, impasse-focused, family-therapy consultation convinced me that this indeed was a worthwhile goal.

In this chapter, I advance the concept and structure of a form of collegial consultation with a focus on the creative-preventive possibilities rather than on the creative remedial, impasse-focused aspects. I choose the term *meta-consultation* because maintaining a meta-position is not only a desirable, but a necessary condition for this model of consultation. The general purpose of *Sequential Preventive Meta-Consultation* (SPMC) is to help the therapist prevent the therapeutic system from settling into ineffective patterns that may eventually lead to an impasse, as well as to maintain the developing change process. This may be achieved by the carrying out of the following five principles of SPMC:

1. Utilize the resources of *meta-consultation* to predict and unveil those patterns and problems—in the therapist, the family, and the therapeutic system—which, if not checked, may lead to impasse situations.
2. Expand the therapist's vision and flexibility and guide him/her to generate options and alternatives in understanding, planning and intervening so that ineffective or maladaptive patterns may be prevented or loosened.
3. Plan and structure the consultation in such a way that will enable the consultant to remain in a *meta-position* in relation to the therapy and therapeutic system throughout the sequential consulting process.
4. Take extreme care to maintain the centrality and status of the therapist with the family, so that changes can be made without jeopardizing the therapeutic alliance.
5. Plan the consultation sequentially as part of the normative process of therapy for the provision of continuous prevention and reevaluation of the consultative and therapeutic process.

PITFALLS TO AVOID

Three pitfalls of brief, impasse-focused consultation were particularly relevant to the development of my thinking about this model:

1. *The consultant's difficulty in holding a position that is truly "meta" to the therapeutic system, or parts of it.* The consultant who is called in to "rescue" the situation is in a dilemma, wanting to help the therapist but also feeling a responsibility to be helpful to the family in this short period of time. In cases where there is an audience involved, as in teaching situations, the consultant may be all too well aware that the audi-

ence is there to learn about his/her way of doing therapy. It may be natural, when consultation is a "one shot" deal, that the consultant will feel the need to experience and explore the family directly and intensively for maximum effectiveness.

Given the above, there may be a great likelihood that the consultant will conduct the consultation as a way of doing better therapy. The consultant may then become, albeit temporarily, an active member of the therapeutic system and, therefore, unable to be "meta" to the system. Minuchin (1986) identified additional dangers to be those of forming opinions and making interventions too quickly in such consultations.

2. *The consultant is often in a hierarchical position to the therapist because of his/her expertise or the mandate given to the rescuing position.* The therapist who is obviously in a "stuck" position with a family feels confused and insecure about his/her position. An "expert" consultant who had not struggled with the client family's difficulties may be looked upon as threatening or judgmental. These feelings may increase the therapist's feelings of incompetence and potentially prevent the therapist from best utilizing the gains and recommendations of the consultation.

3. *The negative effects of repeated impasse-focused consultations.* Because impasse-focused consultation interventions tend to be intense and powerful, repeated consults with the same family may augment the difficulty of preserving the status and centrality of the therapist. When a consultant is called in and becomes temporarily and intensively involved with the family, he/she raises the hopes and expectations of the clients for progress toward their therapeutic goals. This is even more so when the consultant is presented as an "expert." If the consultation is indeed useful and effective, the family will come back to the next session with more alternatives and a refreshed sense of hope. Let us assume, as is often the case with the more difficult cases, that this is not the last serious difficulty, or impasse that this system will encounter. If the first consultation was useful in moving things forward, more consultations may be requested. With the subsequent consultations two problems intensify:

(a) If the consultant, again, directly and intensively encounters the family, his/her involvement with and investment in the family deepens. A *meta-position* in relation to the family or the therapist becomes highly improbable. In addition, there is a heightened risk that the consultant will merely reinforce his/her previous views and hypotheses, thus, narrowing again the range of possible alternatives.

(b) Despite the above problems, consultation may still be, at least temporarily, effective. Besides specific useful interventions, a purposeful enlargement of the system changes it and may serve to loosen entangled interactions. The family may experience a "boost," a progress after each consultation, and may come to associate the better therapy and ful-filled expectations with the consultant and the "downfall" and disap-pointment with the therapist.

Encountering and recognizing these pitfalls as a consultant and teacher of family and couple therapy, I sought to avoid them in this model.

SEQUENTIAL PREVENTIVE META-CONSULTATION

Prevention

When the therapy is proceeding smoothly, the therapist and family naturally do not think there is any need for a consultant. Because the therapy is doing fine, both therapist and family tend to repeat the same patterns, and disregard potentially valuable information and possibili-ties. This narrows the view and limits the number of alternatives open for the therapy. The therapy develops the "problem of no problem."

A parable I once heard from an old Chinese teacher tells about people who are climbing a tree to pick an apple. They are very happy as they climb higher and higher and everything is going just fine. They are certain they will get the apple, but do not realize the apple is growing on the next tree. Simply stated, taking "right" steps does not necessar-ily lead to the right or best solution.

Periodic reassessment (before a state of impasse is reached) in the form of meta-consultation may be of vital importance to the therapy. Periodic reassessment encompasses examining things that are taken for granted or seem beyond doubt, challenging previous assumptions, and generating new alternatives. Since many therapists are too involved in the situation to conduct this reassessment themselves, a consultant in a meta-position could be extremely useful.

Periodic reassessment is needed most in the first and middle phases of therapy. In the first phase it is needed to avoid the emergence of problems created by forming opinions and hypotheses too quickly and rigidly. Consultation should help the therapist to acquire a more com-plete gestalt of the family and the problem. It should also help to evalu-ate and examine the therapeutic system for possible bugs that could become problematic later on, as well as to detect possible personal dif-ficulties that the therapist may have in dealing with the case.

Upholding the Meta-position

"It is quite wrong to believe that theories are based on observations. The opposite is the case. It is the theories that decide what we can observe."—Albert Einstein

A consultant could probably never be completely in a true meta-position. As soon as he/she joins the consulting session, he/she becomes a part of the system and its subsystems. This is a weak point in any therapeutic consultation. This "weak point" becomes even weaker because it is extremely difficult for an experienced, effective therapist not to slip into doing what he/she knows how to do so well: formulate hypotheses, categorize information, and intervene therapeutically. Many therapists/consultants find it difficult to refrain from making therapeutic interventions as quickly as the very first contact with the family.

In designing SPMC, six major conditions were established to enable the consultant to uphold, as much as possible, the *meta-position* in relation to the therapeutic system.

1. Elucidate clearly the consultant's role to the consultant him/herself, the therapist, and the family.
2. The consultant is not in a therapeutic role with the family. He/she does not have a direct investment in solving the family's problems; rather, his/her role is to help the therapist with them.
3. In order to avoid intense involvement, this consultation should take place during the "regular" course of therapy before an impasse has occurred.
4. The design of the consulting interviews provides a clear and consistent structure aimed at protecting the *meta-position* and the consultative process.
5. The consultant strives to take an *atheoretical position* while conducting the SPMC process. A "true" *meta-position* is an *atheoretical one*. Theoretical positions, although extremely useful, necessarily guide observations and dictate behaviors.
6. The consultant comes into the interview with minimal knowledge of the family and the therapy in order to maintain a fresh viewpoint and to avoid preconceptions about the family and the therapy.

The Role of the Consultant

In SPMC, the consultant is not in a training or supervisory role. It is extremely difficult, perhaps impossible, to maintain a *meta-position* while one is in a supervisory role. As a supervisor one must activate and apply his/her own theories, hypotheses, and what he/she estimates to be the "best" way of doing things. A supervisor is also in a position of responsibility to the family. In this consulting model, however, the responsibility for the success of the therapy, likewise the credit, lies with the therapist and the family, and not with the consultant and the family.

The consultant is not responsible for showing the therapist the "best" approach to the problem. There is no need to assume that the consultant "knows better." In the long run, his/her views may be just as "correct" or "incorrect" as the therapist's, since any way of looking at things is only one amongst many other possible ways. Every patient is different and every therapist is different; therefore, every patient-therapist relationship must be different. Thus, the consultant should facilitate a panoramic view, more of a meta-vision with many possible doors to choose from. This permits the therapist to pick the best option for him/herself until the next checkpoint.

The consultant's main role, consequently, may be described as a catalyst of ideas and viewpoints, a generator of alternatives, and a challenger of conceptions and categories. The consultant should expose elements in the therapeutic system and in the therapist's own personality that may be outside the therapist's awareness. The ultimate goal is to furnish the therapist with more degrees of freedom, thus helping to prevent fixed patterns that may lead to an impasse and allowing the therapist to intervene more fruitfully.

The consultant's main working tools are the *meta-position* and his/her own creativity in generating good questions. The section on structure further clarifies the practicalities of these principles.

STRUCTURE

In this chapter, I focus on consultation with one consultant because in everyday practice individual consultants are not only more available, but also more economical than a consulting team. However, the same principles may be adopted for a consulting team. The structure of the consultation in the different phases of therapy is always the same, although the specific content may vary. Each consultation includes three steps:

1. The therapist contracts with the family/couple for the consultation as a part of the therapy process and clarifies the consultant's

position. The contract needs to be briefly reasserted each time there is a need for a consultation.
2. A structured interview is scheduled with the family/couple. This step is carried out by the consultant in the passive presence of the therapist.
3. A structured consultation session takes place with the therapist after the family/couple interview.

The goals of the interviews are to evaluate the therapeutic system by discovering strengths and shortcomings, to predict and preempt future difficulties, and to reevaluate the effects of the previous consultation(s).

Contracting with the Family/Couple

The principle aim of the presentation of the consultant to the clients is to prevent the consultant from becoming a co-therapist, thus losing the *meta-position*, and thereby maintaining the therapist's centrality. The therapist should adopt the professionally responsible position that an ongoing consultation provides the best professional help for the family. He/she conveys responsibility to care for possible problems ahead of time, rather than waiting until the therapy is stuck. The consultant is there to help the therapist best help the family, but not to help the family directly. This also allows the therapist to receive the credit for using the consultation well. The consultant is presented as another experienced colleague and not as an "expert" who comes to "save" the situation. As Whitaker (1989) points out, a professional consultant realigns the therapist as part of the professional team hired to do a job.

The following is an example of how the consultation may be presented to a family during the therapeutic contract phase in the first interview:

I want to talk to you about an important resource that we use in the therapy work which we call "consultation." I consider it to be part of responsible professionalism to assume that I can make mistakes, fall into traps, and search for answers. Since we are dealing with human problems and I am human, too, I know that during the course of therapy there are plenty of traps we can fall into and that I do not have all the answers. Therefore, I plan to have a professional colleague (or perhaps a small team) join us for consultations a few times during the therapy. He/she will not be involved in the therapy except for consulting. Otherwise he/she may also fall into repetitive patterns.

It is important for us that the consultant maintain as objective a view as possible. So, his/her contact with you will be more formal and structured than mine. The main function of the consultant will be to help me think over things more clearly and diversely so that I can be most helpful. The first consulting session will take place near the beginning. As we continue the therapy, we usually have about two more if the therapy is going fine. We generally try to set the time in advance because we all consult for each other. Of course, all the rules of complete confidentiality equally apply to the consultant.

At our Institute, we charge one-and-a-half times the usual fee for the consultation sessions. The therapist and the consultant may split the fee, exchange sessions, or make another agreed-upon arrangement.

The Structured Interview with the Family/Couple: Evaluating the Therapeutic System and Predicting Future Difficulties.

In this interview the therapist may be in the room or behind the screen. The consultant should provide a comfortable and open atmosphere. He/she clarifies to the family/couple that the questions are meant to help the therapist be as effective as possible in helping the family and that the therapist has an opportunity to listen, observe, and learn as a bystander. The consultant makes no therapeutic interventions and gives no opinions, interpretations, or suggestions. He/she helps to clarify the questions and answers whenever necessary, and may also ask the clients to further expand on an answer. If there are hesitations on the part of the client, the consultant should convey a message that the therapist is brave enough and professional enough to deal with any criticism.

The consultant does not engage the therapist and the family in a discussion at any point during the consulting session. We have found it helpful to come to the session ready with written questions. This adds to the structured formality and further reduces the possibility of intrusion by the consultant into the therapeutic system.

Following are some sample questions that I have found to be particularly useful during the first consulting session. They are arranged, more or less, in a progressive order. Each member is asked for his opinion. The session generally lasts about an hour, depending on the number of participants.

Sample questions for the patients:
  1. Although you have had only a few sessions, can you please say what you found most useful in this therapy so far?

2. Can you please say what you feel or think was not useful so far?
3. From what you see (or have experienced) so far, what do you think will go well in the future? What do you think could become a problem in therapy?
4. How do you feel, or what do you think, about your therapist so far? (This, too, is an open question, but the consultant may add questions to help the hesitant client, such as: Do you think he/she is understanding your problem correctly? Is he fast, slow, or just right for you? The additional questions could be agreed on in advance with the therapist.)
5. How do you think your therapist feels about you, or what does he/she think about you so far?
6. With whom do you think the therapist will find it hardest to deal with in the future? Why?
7. Whose side do you think the therapist is on, if at all?
8. What are the three things that you think will solve your problems?
9. What do you think or feel about the way your therapist explains your problems?
10. What do you think are the traps that someone (an outsider) could easily fall into with your family?
11. Could you please think about what might be the traps that your therapist might fall into with your family?... Could you think of another one?
12. Is there anything you want to know from your therapist and did not dare to ask, or is there anything else that you are curious about?
13. Do you have anything you want to say about this interview?

These questions aim to accent and pinpoint areas of strengths and difficulties in the therapeutic system. The answers may shed light on patterned sets of interaction (feelings, thoughts, and behaviors) that may eventually lead to an impasse. They are not meant to give dry information, but rather to help the therapist recognize some of the possible traps ahead of time. In subsequent sessions, questions may change to permit an evaluation of previous consultations.

The Structured Interview with the Therapist

The questions in this session should expand the content of the interview with the family, illuminate new perceptions of the therapeutic system, and clarify the therapist's personal involvement. If the interview was videotaped or recorded, it may be helpful to refer back to relevant segments.

It is imperative that the consultant take a non-judgmental attitude with the therapist. The therapist should have the freedom to explore therapeutic and personal issues as much or as little as she/he desires. The idea is to stimulate and generate alternative ways of approaching the therapy.

The consultant, from a *meta-position*, has a more objective view than the therapist. Thus, there may be a temptation to talk about what he/she sees or to ask leading questions that will point in the direction of his/her thoughts, i.e., "What part do you think you played in the wife's refusal to come to the next session?" As soon as one does that he/she leaves the *meta-position* and enters a supervisory or advisory position, which could quickly become a pitfall for the consultation. An important feature of this model is to allow the therapist to create his/her own process and to feel that he/she is the one who is making the new connections. This facilitates the therapist's development as an independent professional, creates a greater commitment on the part of the therapist to the consulting process, and reduces the ambivalence and hesitations therapists often experience about seeking consultation and exposing their work.

Within this framework, the consultant has the opportunity to be unconstrained by the responsibility of having to solve a problem. He/she can be much more attentive to the therapist and enjoy observing the unfolding of the creative process. The mutual enjoyment of the process becomes a motivating force for further consultations and it works against burnout.

Sample questions for the therapist. The following are questions directed to the therapist that were found to be particularly helpful:

1. What did you think about what was said in the session?
   a. How else could you think about it? How else? How else?
   b. Find something else important in what was said.
2. If there were a non-professional person in the room what would he say about this?
3. If there were another professional in the session what would he/she say?
4. If your mother or father were there listening to what was said, what would they say about you... about the family?
5. If your child/ren were here, what would he/she/they say about what you might do with the child/ren or with the couple in this family?
6. If you could put a hidden camera at this family's home, what would be the one thing you would be most curious to watch and why?

   a. What would you be least curious to watch, why?

7. From what you heard, what do you think would give you most trouble in the next weeks, months? What else?

8. How could you prevent it?

9. How would you like to be a member of this family?
   a. Whom would you like to be the most?
   b. Whom would you like to be the least?

10. Let's look at the extended system: extended family, friends, work partners, school teachers, physicians, lawyers, accountant, housemaid, etc.... Assuming hypothetically that you could enlist anyone you want for any helpful purpose (does not have to be "right" therapeutically), whom would you want? What for? How would he/she/they be helpful?
   a. How could your answer affect your therapy in the future?

11. What is the wildest thought that you have about what to do with this family? What would happen if you did that?... and then what...and then what....
   a. What implications can that have for what you might want to do in the therapy? What else...? What else...?

12. Who is the member whom you dislike the most, or whom do you think will make things hardest for you? Describe him/her in 10 different ways (*if the therapist stays too narrow ask for more ways*).

13. What member do you think will be most helpful to you and why?
   a. Think of at least one reason why that might not be good?

14. What do you conceive to be the main problems in this family? Find different ways to think about them!

15. How will you change (if at all) what you do in therapy in the light of what you learned?

16. Please give me feedback on what this consultation was like for you?

A CASE EXAMPLE:
SEQUENTIAL PREVENTIVE META-CONSULTATION

The following case will illustrate the development of the consulting process over time in a couple's therapy.

First Consultation

The consultation was requested by Becky, an experienced family and marital therapist. Becky prepared the couple and contracted with them for the sequential consultation as previously explained. I came to this interview knowing only that this was a couple in their early 40s, with three young children. The husband, Amos, was an engineer and the wife, Edna, was a school teacher. They requested therapy because Amos had had an extramarital affair during the past year. They both came willingly and wanted to rehabilitate their relationship. They had five therapy sessions and the therapist felt that the therapy was going rather smoothly.

First Interview with the Couple

Responding to the evaluation questions about the therapy, both spouses indicated general feelings of satisfaction and hope. They reported getting closer to each other and communicating meaningfully for the first time. The husband, Amos, pointed out that this was the first time he had been able to talk about personal issues. They believed that Becky, professionally, had helped them through a difficult time. Both perceived her as perceptive, warm, and honest. They said they felt pleased and motivated to be in therapy with Becky.

The following are excerpts of the part of the session dealing with the potential problems that are needed to be considered in order to avoid impasse:

Consultant: Can you please tell me what is not useful or helpful in the therapy so far? or what might be missing for you?

Edna: (*sighs deeply*) Well, we didn't have many sessions... I know enough to say that I want to touch the whole issue of the affair more...We are here for that...because of it... (*crying*) I want to touch it more...We talked about it a lot, but not enough...To unload all that anger and need for revenge. That's it ... I think this is what I am missing.

Consultant: What about you, Amos? What is missing for you?

Amos: I think that, perhaps, we did not receive enough tools yet to deal with all this anger...I think we have to keep on touching everything. I think Becky should continue with what she did last time... going back to my own personal history and my own personal problems. It is important for me to learn to look at things differently.

Consultant: (*to husband*) What might turn out to be a problem for you in the therapy?

Amos: This issue of trust. If we don't get to trust each other...I don't know what might happen...We can't continue life this way.

Consultant: What may be the traps that someone—a therapist, or a friend—can easily fall into, with your family?

Edna: There is at least one trap for sure... My communication ability with people is very good. I express myself well. I am also a good actress. I can even cover up things and this is a trap that someone can fall into... Amos is not that way. It is difficult for him to make contact. That's why people tend to show more empathy and sympathy to me at the beginning (only) and that is a trap.

Amos: I think the largest trap for us is that all these years we made it look as if everything was O.K. and it wasn't. We are good in putting on masks. That is the biggest trap.

Consultant: Suppose this trap would come up in therapy, how would it be?

Amos: As we said we both have high motivation. So I don't think it will happen.

Edna: I disagree. I think it could happen, i.e., that we will get into a situation in therapy where everything will look as if it is O.K. but it isn't.

It is evident that despite the satisfaction and progress expressed by the clients at the beginning of the interview, several potential problems and traps were directly indicated in the answers. Edna did not feel she received enough space and recognition for her anger. Amos agreed that they need more tools to deal with that as well as with the issue of trust. Edna was vigilant to any potential threat of separation, cautioned about quitting, and implied that such an impulsive act could happen. They both cautioned that covering up and putting on masks was their specialty, particularly Edna's, and identified that as a potential trap for the therapist. The therapist needs to be wary of assuming that things are okay even if they look so. There was apparent discomfort around what they sensed as Becky's critical stance and emotional 'pull back' at times. They also both agreed that Edna will present more of a problem to the therapist, Becky, although they could not pinpoint the reasons. This may be a hint for a potential trap of triangulation.

First Interview with the Therapist

This interview immediately followed the consultant-family session. I am presenting verbatim the most relevant part of the interview without comment. My intention is to show the unfolding of the therapist's thinking, as well as the discovery of issues which could constitute traps in the future.

Therapist: They both said that they thought *she* would be more difficult for me. I think that if she would sense me a bit critical, she might fight me...feeling I am not receptive to her, or not sensitive to her. So, later on, when I demand of her to work hard, we may have a problem. I might fall into a trap of leaving her alone and not pushing her limits to avoid a struggle.

Consultant: How could you prevent the difficulties you just talked about?

Therapist: I think I have to mix my sharpness and my softness better. Sometimes I am either tough and sharp, or soft, warm, and understanding. When I have to confront her with something I could be both.

Consultant: If there were another professional in the session, what would he/she say?

Therapist: That I have a good rapport with them...that they trust me and are open with me. Also, that I don't allow myself to feel enough ...like perhaps I am hiding some feelings of hostility...I am saying this because of what the wife said about my empathy which she experienced as rising and falling...The professional observer might also say that I am too quick to leave the acute situation and feelings around the affair the husband had, and that I am too neutral or too distant from it.

Consultant: How could that influence what you do in this therapy?

Therapist: It makes me think that perhaps I am not helping this woman (*the wife*) enough with her depression over her husband's affair...perhaps I am thinking too professionally and not humanely enough.

Consultant: Which of the two would you like to be most, or least?

Therapist: I would not want to be the husband in the family because the wife is so fat. I identify with the difficulty that the husband must have with it, although he never said anything about it.

Consultant: What effect could that have on what you do in therapy?

Therapist: It could cause me to develop more of a readiness to protect him out of pity or empathy because I identify with this part...Perhaps understand him more easily...(*thinking*)... Unconsciously, perhaps even justify his affair.

Consultant: How could you prevent this from happening?

Therapist: I am glad I am seeing this. First of all, I will have to bring myself to a state of being indifferent to the question of who is right or wrong on the infidelity issue. It really is not relevant. I will have to be much more attentive and listen better to the emotional and behavioral reactions of each one of them. I also need to think about what it is for the wife to be fat....Perhaps she is missing some very important things which have to do with her feelings as a woman. I could be more empathic in my feelings.

Consultant: With whom do you think it will be most difficult for you—the husband or the wife?

Therapist: It is clear...I did not see it before...definitely the wife. She also reminds me of things that I have difficulty in accepting, like women who are too demanding or domineering...women who demand loyalty from now till eternity...

Consultant: Find 10 different ways to describe this woman.. it does not have to be "true"!

Therapist: (*thinking*)...Like the Queen in Alice in Wonderland, always giving instructions... like a scared child... like a director of plays... she is a teacher and she is always directing projects. A teacher who always knows better than the pupils... Dogmatic and domineering... Short-sighted, can't see ahead of her...Curious and intelligent. Can get excited over things in a positive way...despite her fatness I can actually see her as very sexy...like a nymph...flexible, smooth, and seductive. I can see her very warm and loving and giving of herself... I can see her walking in the nature, singing, very happy, and enjoying herself. It's nice.

Consultant: What could be the implications of these perspectives in the therapy?

Therapist: I think she feels very erased...I want to help her to soften up. She feels so hurt and vulnerable so she has to defend herself all the time—much strength, warmth, so that she could feel that she is O.K. even if she is not always accepted. I realize that it is my judgmental side that wants to call her to order...but I can perhaps ask her in therapy "which side of me do you need right now? the soft, supportive part or the pushing, challenging one?" She could choose...Both sides of me could be used well.

Consultant: If you could put a hidden camera at this family's home what would you be most and least curious to watch and why?

Therapist: I am most curious to see what happens between them when they are alone in the room and they have nothing special, no task to do...I am also curious to see them in a lovemaking situation. Recently they report having a lot of sex (this is the good thing that happened with the affair)...I am curious how it really is. I am least curious with how she is with the children, their relationships.

Consultant: How does this affect what you do or might do in therapy?

Therapist: It could lead me to take things for granted... For example: since we have been dealing with the crisis issue and they did not bring up any problem with children I assumed that their relationship with the children is fine without really having enough information...I probably would have regarded my lack of curiosity as evidence that they are O.K., and I would not have involved the children in the therapy...I really ought to think about it and check it out...

Consultant: Is there anything else you want to say about what you learned?

Therapist: I realize that I narrowed my view too much...I worked with this couple with a certain model that I use in Infidelity Crisis. I realize that working with this structured model helped me in avoiding the issues of my own counter-transference, my own difficulties, but they exist anyway. This interview made it very clear that these issues are present and active, even though they do not always get expressed directly in the therapy. Luckily, I have not hurt the therapy so far, although I can easily see how thy could create serious problems.

Second Consultation

The second consultation was requested by the therapist, Becky, six sessions later. She reported that the couple was beginning to come out of the initial crisis situation and getting into dealing with some of the major issues in their marriage. She thought that this destabilized the position that Edna has acquired as the victim in the crisis. They had begun to deal with the pattern in which Amos resorted to withdrawal, avoidance, denial, and lies in the face of conflict or pressure from Edna. Edna experienced these defenses as rejection and therefore either withdrew or became extremely angry.

Prior to the second consultation, the couple had a serious conflict. Edna discovered that the woman with whom Amos had the affair was working in the same department at his workplace. She demanded that Amos use his influence to fire the woman. Feeling guilty and pressured by Edna's anger and anxiety, Amos promised to talk with the Director of the company. He never did, which left Edna extremely angry. Edna refused to come to the next therapy session.

Amos informed Becky that Edna refused to come. Becky, without first checking with Edna, told him to come alone. In this session Becky worked with the husband on being more assertive with his wife about his feelings. Thus, she implicitly conveyed support of the husband in the face of the conflict with his wife. Becky left a message for Edna to phone. Edna did not call, and the couple cancelled the next session. When Becky eventually called, Edna said she was very angry. Edna agreed to have a consultation upon their return.

Second Interview with the Couple

In this interview, the couple was asked to talk mainly about what had happened since the last consultation, i.e., what they found helpful in therapy and what was not helpful enough; what were the positive things and what are the problems they expect if therapy continues; what might be the future traps in therapy; how they felt about the therapist, and how they think she felt about them.

Both spouses thought therapy was helpful in clarifying where exactly they were "stuck" and what brought them to dead ends. Edna said she could see how "stubborn" she had been and how difficult it was for her to accept someone's different needs. Amos was pleased that the therapist pushed and challenged him to define his feelings, although it was difficult for him. They both felt that the therapist cared for them and understood them well. However, they agreed that she understood Amos better than she understood Edna. They thought that they needed more help regarding their feelings surrounding the infidelity and the issue of mistrust.

Concerning future problems and traps in the therapy, Edna indicated that if she and Amos grew closer, Amos could become too dependent on her, which might be overwhelming. They both expressed concern that the therapist might be disappointed with them for not making enough progress and may press them too much. If this happened, they may want to stop therapy.

Second Interview with the Therapist

The following are some relevant excerpts from the interview:

Consultant: What difficulties can you predict now with this couple, in view of what was said and done?

Therapist: The wife may get more directly angry at me, because in her experience, the fact that I am supporting her husband in being more assertive may be perceived by her as if I am justifying his actions, even though cognitively she may understand what I am doing.

Consultant: How would this present a difficulty for you?

Therapist: Her anger is rather aggressive and even somewhat scary...it could actually cause me stomach aches, and I am not usually afraid of anger. I am concerned that I might respond by emotionally distancing from her...in a "super-professional" manner. That will not help her. She may feel rejected and become more angry, and that might cause an impasse situation.

Consultant: What alternatives do you have in dealing with this in the future?

Therapist: One way might be to talk about her anger, perhaps to share with her my internal struggle of having to choose between stomach pains or emotional distancing—that might be what others experience, too. I want neither, so we could talk about the feelings of rejection that are underneath the anger and how she might express her anger in a way that will help her gain what she really wants.

Consultant: More?

Therapist: I could also ask for the support of my colleagues to create more space between me and her anger, so that I could contain it better without getting stomach aches. I could then be on her side, helping her gain what she really needs with this anger. I still fell into the trap when their last crisis occurred. I assumed too much, by overly trusting the meaningful changes that I had in my relationship with her, and threatened her too much by supporting her husband without doing the same with her...

Consultant: More?

Therapist: I could envision her as a small, hurt child crying out of shame and neediness, as well as a soft women with all her anger melting when she is in the arms of someone who loves her and gives her a sense of security.

Consultant: Is there any new difficulty other than what was said in the past that you need to take into account?

Therapist: It could be that after the acute phase of their crisis is over they might lose interest in investing so much work in their relationship, and each may prefer to go back to the pseudo-comfort of living in different worlds, rather than to challenge their relationship and take it to new, unknown places.

Consultant: How could you prevent it?

Therapist: By being aware and watching for signs. I also need to be more conscious and tolerant of their individual pace as well as their joint pace. I need to look also for intervention that will create good experiences that will make progress more desirable.

The therapeutic system had begun to show problematic signs that could develop into an impasse situation.

The first consultation was helpful in pinpointing the potential traps. However, it was not enough to prevent all of them. The therapist began to develop a triangulated pattern because of her identification with the husband and her ambivalent emotional reaction with the wife. The wife, in turn, expressed her hidden mistrust and disappointment by not calling for the therapist's help at the time of difficulty. Both spouses were concerned with the therapist's perceived intolerance of their cautious, individual pace. Thus, there was an implicit threat of dropping therapy.

Despite all of these problems, the couple still gave the therapist credit for her professional competence. It was up to her to use the consultation to avoid further potential traps and to help the therapy come to a successful conclusion.

Third Consultation: Third Interview with the Therapist

The third consultation took place about 15 sessions later. Becky asked to be interviewed first, for logistical reasons.

Between the second and the third consultation Becky had shifted her perceptions quite a bit and integrated the new ideas, directions, and strategies discovered both during the consultations and since. The previous consultations forcefully made her acutely aware that she needed to attend more carefully to the transactional patterns that she was developing with this couple.

With help from peers, Becky acquired a deeper understanding of her emotional pattern with the couple. This indeed helped her to perform her role as she decided in the previous consultation, i.e., "to create more space between me and Edna's anger and contain this anger without stomach aches."

In therapy Becky gave Edna ample, sincere support while she was strengthening Amos's assertiveness, and helped her deal with her anger more fruitfully. Conscious of what the spouses said in previous consultations, Becky allowed enough space for the feelings around the affair and was considerate of each spouse's individual tempo. She was working with the couple on building new trust in their relationship, in accordance with their request. While the couple was working on the more difficult issues of their marriage, Becky was careful to supply them with enough new positive experiences to disarm the threat of separation that they had both expressed. This enabled them to continue therapy, rather than impulsively drop out (a trap Edna had predicted in the first consultation). She included the parents and the children (who were doing fine) for one session.

At the time of the third consultation Becky was working with the couple on fulfilling more of their individual potential with each other in a nonthreatening way. She thought the couple were doing very well and that they and she were having more fun in the sessions despite the hard work.

Therapist's Feedback

At the end of the third consultation, the therapist gave feedback about the consulting process.

Consultant: Is there any feedback you want to give me about this consultation?

Therapist: (*takes time to think over things*)...The consultation helped me focus on my own emotional and cognitive process in regard to this therapy, and in general....It also definitely intensified my feelings and interest and curiosity towards the family as a whole...I touched upon things that I am certain would have developed into problems, perhaps impasses, in the therapy...The fact that you, as a consultant, were not involved and kept "out" really helped me to express, even vent, some negative feelings without feeling threatened or judged. That was really cleansing for me. I felt I came back to this couple refreshed. In fact I was looking forward to it...I loved playing with my imagination and thinking creatively. This increased my warmth and liking for this couple... There were quite a few blind spots revealed. I was able to see the traps ahead that could lead to an impasse and I tried to avoid them. Until then I felt as if everything was going well. I was too narrow in my vision...The fact that this consultation was so uncritical, enabling, and stimulating was very helpful...It challenged me to move away from an analytical frame to a frame of playfulness...more creativity. I felt my mind was liberated...free to think in a richer way. I went back to this couple empowered with more options.

Third Interview with the Couple

The couple felt very good about the therapy and about Becky. They were happy with their progress.

Edna: The truth is that I never really thought we could make as many changes as we did. Even if I thought so, I don't think I really believed it. Becky taught us to really be each other's healers. I know now that our relationship is like a green tree branch. It could bend in the storm but it won't break. With all the difficulty, we also had fun, and that was a very important lesson for us to learn.

Both spouses felt that, for the first time, they could be without masks or pretenses, although they still had some way to go. They felt confident enough to follow Becky wherever she led them and learned to appreciate her challenges. They even pointed out that sometimes she was too considerate of their pace and assured her that they were much stronger. Although they could see the end of the therapy on the horizon, they wanted to keep the door open.

Couple's Feedback

Consultant: Could you please tell me what do you think, or feel about these consulting interviews?

Edna: It was fine for me. At first I was a bit apprehensive that another person would come in and intrude, but you did not intrude. I think it was helpful. Your questions about the traps were interesting because I could identify them as we went along. I appreciated the way Becky took our comments seriously. I think it helped in the therapy.

Amos: I agree with everything Edna said. I thought it was good to do. It was easier each time.

CONCLUSION

Family therapy consultation as a subdiscipline in its own right—an adjunct to therapy but separate from it—is still in its infancy. Therapeutic consultation often becomes a "fuzzy" process with difficulties in differentiating between supervision, therapy, and consultation.

The intention of this chapter was to offer a model of consultation with clear boundaries around it. This model is not intended to replace impasse-focused models, which have their own value; but rather to be an addition to them—one more useful tool in the hands of the therapist and in the service of family therapy.

Six major pillars are at the base of this consultation:

1. Predicting and preventing difficulties and impasses.
2. Maintaining the consultant's meta-position.
3. Preserving the therapist's position with the family.
4. Keeping a clear structure.
5. Enabling the therapist's own creativity and ability to generate alternatives.
6. Sequential meetings.

These six are interconnected. In order to avoid the pitfalls of consultation and preserve the therapist's position, the consultant must keep a meta-position. A clear structure is needed to enforce and protect the meta-position. Finally, sequential meetings are essential in order to predict and prevent difficulties as well as to evaluate the effect of consultation throughout therapy.

This model may be most useful for an experienced therapist who can work independently. It could also be used as an adjunct for supervision and training, even though these have many additional demands that cannot be met in this form of consultation. Other advantages worth noting are:

- SPMC need not be done by a senior or an expert therapist-consultant. It may be done by any experienced colleague. Colleagues are generally more available than any particular expert.
- The nontheoretical meta-position allows family therapy colleagues with different styles and orientations to consult with one another with greater respect for the differences.
- Since there is little intrusion on the therapeutic system, there is no problem of "giving the family back to the therapist." The family is never taken away.
- This model reduces the therapist's anxiety and competitiveness because the process of consultation is congruent with the assumption that there is no best way, but only alternative ways.
- Therapists are more likely to use this form of consultation because the ideas and insights are self-generated.
- Finally, this is a therapist-oriented consultation in the sense that the consultant is there to provide the opportunity for the colleague to discover his/her own way to do the best possible work.

REFERENCES

Minuchin, S. (1986). Foreword. In L. C. Wynne, S. H. McDaniel & T. T. Weber (Eds.), *Systems Consultation: A New Perspective for Family Therapy*. New York: Guilford.

Penn, P. & Sheinberg, M. (1986). Is there therapy after consultation?: A systemic map for family therapy consultation. In L. C. Wynne, S. H. McDaniel, & T. T. Weber (Eds.), *Systems Consultation: A New Perspective for Family Therapy*. New York: Guilford.

Whitaker, C. (1989). *Midnight Musings of a Family Therapist*. New York: W. W. Norton.

13

From Impotence to Activation: Conjoint Systemic Change in the Family and School

Robert N. Wendt and
Audrey E. Ellenwood

Historically, the two systems that have been acknowledged as primary in the social and emotional development of children are the family and the school. Of the two, the family has been recognized as the primary socializing influence for the child. In spite of this recognition, the focus of most home and school interventions has been child-centered and individual in orientation.

Both family and schools usually work independently of each other in attempting to deal with children's problems. The schools have long recognized the importance of family life to a student's academic, social, and behavioral functioning (Dockrell, 1964; Gurman, 1970; Pollaczek, 1964). Despite the recognition that problems are often due to family factors (Rutter, 1985), schools have tended to involve parents only to gain information and confirm diagnoses. Likewise, families referred to therapy because of children's difficulties in school rarely include school personnel in the sessions. Usually, school and family therapy interventions do not involve a systems perspective of the child's ecology.

Recently, the influence of family systems intervention and systems applications has been emphasized (Hannafin & Witt, 1983; Snapp &

Davidson,1982). In the field of School Psychology, there have been attempts to develop a more family-oriented and systems role (Anderson, 1983; Conoley, 1987; Green & Fine, 1980; Pfeiffer & Tittler, 1983; Wendt & Zake, 1984). Thus, the advent of systemic thinking in the schools requires different models of school consultation and intervention.

The need for schools to interface more directly with the family becomes critical for more effective resolution of childhood problems. The same can be said for the family, especially when family therapy is involved. In essence, both systems are primary resources for each other. For the family therapist, the school is a powerful institution that has the power and resources to impact the family at a number of different levels and this provides a resource for information and an impetus for change. For example, both teacher's and administrator's perceptions and evaluation of the child and the family can either reinforce the family's construction of reality or create an existential crisis about the adequacy, competence, and self-worth of parents and children.

One of the most difficult processes facing the therapist is to understand the "family myths" that provide an understructure for the family. Quite often, it is necessary to bring in people from the extended family or the community to assist with the therapeutic process in creating change. By expanding the session to include additional people, the therapist is able to diversify and creatively activate change in families, especially with rigid families. By including additional members in a session, the therapist can obtain an understanding of an individual's internal world and provide links between current behaviors being displayed and the unmet needs of the individual from the past (Andolfi, Angelo & de Nichilo, 1989).

One resource that is available to family therapists when dealing with the behaviors of a child is the school personnel who impact on the child on a daily basis. Bringing the school into the therapeutic process can also provide a resource for uncovering the family and school myths which often evolve conjointly regarding the child who is considered to be the symptomatic identified patient.

This chapter will focus on understanding the interactions between the family and school systems, various ways a therapist can utilize the school system to implement changes in a family, and how to use the family to implement changes in a rigid school system. Two case studies requiring a conjoint systemic change are presented. In both cases, the parents and the school felt impotent in dealing with the symptomatic child. By accessing the shared myths of the family and school, each system was activated to change.

CASE OF AMY—MYTH OF "NOT CARING"

Amy, age 13, had long, blond, straight hair that fell forward and hung down over her face and eyes as she stared toward the floor for most of the session. Her blue jeans had holes in both knees and her black rock "T" shirt epitomized her only goal in life, which was to become a guitarist in a rock band. The session was at a critical point as the therapist had directed her to look at the caring faces of her seventh grade teachers, three imposing nuns in their traditional habits, who were seated in a row across from her. After five minutes of agonizing silence she lifted her head slightly and one blue eye could be seen glancing up at the nuns.

Amy's behavior throughout most of the year was described by both her parents and teachers as being loud and disrespectful at school as well as at home. She was primarily an underachiever in school and, according to all present, she "just did not care." A plethora of explosive outbursts by Amy would accompany any slight and perceived injustice to herself and others. Despite both of her parents' efforts, the school was ready to block Amy's return for the next academic year. After several consecutive family sessions where the focus was around Amy's school problems, the therapist decided that a conjoint session with both key school personnel and the family would be beneficial.

The family had been in therapy for almost a year. They had been referred by Amy's school counselor because of Amy's behavior and perceived level of depression. However, it quickly became apparent to the therapist that Amy's difficulties were less pressing than her mother's level of depression and anger. Her mother was abused and neglected as a child and was currently emotionally cut off from her parents. Amy's mother, who was raised in a missionary boarding school in the Far East, indicated that she was physically and sexually abused by the teachers at the school. She also reported that her father was distant and abandoning in his behavior and tended to display an attitude of, "not caring toward her" as a child and an adult. She was adamant about not having him near the children. Interestingly, the initial problem as reported by the mother was intense hatred of her husband's parents. Ron, a teacher, seemed emotionally constricted as he continually balanced, checked, and controlled his wife's and daughter's anger. The younger daughter, Susan, aged 10, was described by both parents as the "good" child who was successful and a high achiever in school.

The therapist while acknowledging Amy's problem and anger, decided to work towards reintegrating the mother with her family of origin and helping her resolve her anger. This process was highly involved and extremely intense. It included a long emotional session with her family of origin that resulted in a reconnection with her parents. As Amy's mother began to resolve her own anger toward her parents, she became more open and flexible in regard to Amy's problems.

The school personnel and Amy's parents were both convinced that Amy, "did not care" and Amy was convinced that the school, "did not care about her." Amy believed that the nuns were overly strict to the point of being unreasonable and the school personnel felt that Amy was abusive with her language.

In the session that included the principal and two of Amy's seventh-grade teachers, the therapist talked to Amy about how maybe if she became cooperative toward the nuns, whom she perceived as caring only about religion, then she may become one of them. As a result, she would then have to give up boyfriends and sex. By playing with this fantasy, the move was made in the session to have the school see the pain of the family particularly as they struggled with the fear and guilt surrounding the development of sexually intimate relationships. By being a part of the session, school personnel were able to identify with how hard the family had been working to overcome their difficulties.

The school personnel also talked about their frustrations in dealing with Amy. However, they emphasized a tremendous desire to try anything to help her. Their level of caring was experienced by Amy in a way that she had not understood nor experienced prior to the session. By connecting through the symptom and the pain and embarrassment of the family, the therapist was able to initiate and intensify the caring process across both the family and the school system. The session was quite helpful as Amy's behavior began to improve; noticeably and during the next year at the same parochial school, she made the honor roll.

DUAL SYSTEMS IMPACTING CHILDREN

Historically, school systems have responded to the involvement of parents in a unidirectional versus a reciprocal approach. Typically the school approaches parents when problems occur but rarely invite the family to participate in the educational process. As a result parents and school personnel may tend to view each other as more conflictual than responsive (Paget, 1992). Often, parents are invited to become involved with their child's educational needs when a symptom occurs and schools begin to initiate demands and pressure for a "quick" fix or change. Frequently, the child will be having problems not only at school but also within the home environment. Parents often have not sought assistance because of feelings of guilt, blame, or inadequacy. It is only when the family has exhausted all of their internal resources or have received excessive demands or ultimatums from school personnel that they seek help from a therapist.

Selvini-Palazzoli, Cecchin, Prata and Boscolo (1978) believe that the family is a human group with a history and is a system with implicit rules that all members unconsciously obey and all members help define. Likewise, schools, as families, are comprised of uniquely configured and hierarchical subsystems, each with its own history of often implicit, rigid rules that all members who come in contact are expected to follow and obey. Children interact on a daily basis with the rules of the family as well as with those in the classroom, lunch, playground, school building, and larger school system. Each system operates in its own unique fashion based on the interrelationships among the various components (Plas, 1986). Of course, the family rules are the most powerful and influential with a child. However, the other subsystems within a child's culture (e.g., school) also have a considerable impact on the child's development (Wendt, 1992).

Behaviors exhibited by a child that concern others, such as being argumentative and refusing to do homework, can be understood by family therapists as the child's attempt to fit into both systems. The symptom represents at one level an inappropriate, harmful behavior that needs to be altered or eliminated in order for the child to be successful at school or in life. But more importantly, the symptom represents a message to the therapist, family, and school personnel that the system (family/school) is in some way dysfunctional. The behavior should not be looked upon by the therapist as a manifestation of an inner psychic disturbance, nor should it be interpreted in a narrow behavioral sense as something that a child is doing in anticipation of a reinforcement (Fine, 1992).

The symptom becomes a connecting point for the therapist upon which to unite all systems and create structural change. Although the symptom is often perceived by the family, school personnel, and therapist as "bad" and needing to be eliminated, the symptom provides for the therapist the starting point upon which to balance and connect the different systems.

The symptom becomes a window for the therapist (Fine, 1992), one that can be looked through to understand the child's place or role in the school and the family, how the child views or responds to the various roles, and the interrelationships within the system(s). By viewing the symptom as a message about a dysfunctional family or school system, a broader perspective in dealing with the complexities of the family will be developed for the therapist.

At times, family therapists need to become creative and move beyond the trigenerational levels within a family and draw upon outside resources such as available school personnel. Individuals available as resources for a family include principals, teachers, school psychologists, special education teachers, aides, social workers, speech/language therapists, counselors, bus drivers, and other school personnel. Therapists need to develop an ecological-systemic perspective that is child-based, teacher-based, and environment-based (Apter, 1982; Bronfenbrenner, 1979). Through interaction with various components of each subsystem in the family session, opportunities will be created for the development of multiple and mutually respectful relationships that can create strong family/school partnerships (Garbarino, 1983) and avenues for altering or eliminating the symptom will be developed.

DILEMMA OF THE THERAPIST

When a therapist is contacted by a family for assistance because of a child with behavioral, social, or academic concerns, the therapist is presented with a dilemma of having a child who exists in two different systems with different rules and problems while often having access to only one system, usually the family. The home is a powerful multi-generational emotional system with "vertical" pressure from previous generations. The school provides current or "horizontal" pressure on both the child and the parents.

For the child, the school becomes the place where a sense of competency develops and judgments about the level of competence are rendered. The school is the first external institution that makes decisions about who or what a child will become. If a child is perceived as being a failure in school, he or she is deemed by many to be a failure in life. For the parents, school becomes the institution whereby the behavioral, social, and academic success of their child speaks to their adequacy of parenting by society and by the other generations within their own family. Therefore the process of the child's entrance into school for many families can become a stressful event, especially for many parents who strongly believed that educational success is crucial for personal and economic success as an adult. Therefore, for many families, school-based symptoms are as important as the family symptoms.

The dilemma for the therapist is that the school can be as dysfunctional and rigid as the family, and, at times, even more so. In order for one to understand the rigidity of the school, it is helpful to analyze the school from the same perspective as one would analyze the family. The school is increasingly being viewed from a systemic and ecological perspective (Apter, 1982; Apontes, 1976; Fine, 1984; Fine & Holt, 1983; Mannino & Shore, 1984; Pfeiffer & Tittler, 1984; Plas, 1986; Swap, 1978; 1984). In addition there has been an increasing interest in the application of systems theory to the practice of psychology within the schools to deal with school-based behavior, social, and/or academic problems of children and adolescents (Anderson, 1983; Conoley, 1987; Lombard, 1979; Pfeiffer & Tittler, 1983, Wendt & Zake, 1984). Therefore, the therapist working through the family can most likely effect change at school when the school environment is healthy and the family has sufficient flexibility to change. However, if the school system is also crazy, overly intense, or rigid regarding the child, then changing the family alone may not improve the school situation. In the instance where systemic change is needed in both environments, the therapist either must collaborate with an outsider at the school, enter the school as an outside consultant, or bring the school into the family sessions.

THERAPIST AS A CONSULTANT TO THE SCHOOL

The therapist can make effective use of the inside professional, such as the school psychologist, counselor, principal, or teacher, either through direct contact via telephone or indirectly through the parent. What the therapist can bring to the school context through the use of the "insider" is a fresh view and optimism for change. The therapist, in continuing to work with the family, will develop new insights, understandings, and hope for the family. Through this continual contact with the "insider," communication based on this optimism for the child's symptom can be passed on to the school personnel.

Often, school personnel have given up on the child and may have labeled the child as "unmotivated," "lazy," or "uncaring." This is especially true of adolescents. Through linkage with an "insider" who is flexible, hopeful, and open to new insight, the therapist can create redefinitions of the problem that can activate change and produce less intense affect around the symptom. Through redefinition and having the "insider" work directly with the teachers and administrators, the therapist will not have to make concrete recommendations that could be viewed as criticism or unrealistic by school personnel; thus, potentially triggering increased rigidity when one is working with the child or family.

The "insider" in the school system can also serve as a resource person by providing feedback to the therapist regarding changes that are occurring in the child. When change occurs at school, the result will be less horizontal pressure on the child by the school, which in turn will allow the family to experience less pressure. This can allow the family to reduce its rigidity and free them to draw upon their own adaptive resources for creating change in the family.

By having the parents work with the school directly, increased communication is established and several things occur. The parents begin to recognize the problem and its impact on the school system. In most cases, as parents begin to become involved, their presence can create a context of pressure for the school to change. Likewise, the school will also increase the anxiety of the parents, enhancing the pressure and motivation for the family to change in the context of therapy. The anxiety that was once within the child has now been shifted and distributed between the school and family members.

THE THERAPIST IN THE SCHOOL

When a therapist senses that the rules and structures of the school system are too rigid and that the "insider" within the school may be unavailable or limited in his or her ability to implement change, an effective collaboration technique has been for the therapist to attend a conference meeting about a particular child. This process is particularly useful for a therapist as it provides an avenue through which the vertical structure of the school is represented across various disciplines in one setting. In instances where the therapist participates in the team process, he or she will be able to initiate and influence change at all levels represented throughout the system as well as outside agencies (e.g., children service boards) who are influential in the identified patient's life.

The manner that a therapist enters the school system can either increase or diffuse the anxiety of the system. Often, school personnel may be somewhat hesitant or mistrustful about the role of the therapist and may look upon his or her presence as being intrusive to their system (Wendt, 1992). Therefore, it is important that the therapist approach the meeting not as an "expert" to share with the faculty, school administrators, and other school personnel how they are failing or mishandling the child, but rather as a resource who can provide support to the teachers as they attempt to deal with the symptom of the child.

The therapist will need to employ a high level of communication skills in order to adopt the style of language and communication that is present among the educational staff. The therapist will need to listen to the verbal, nonverbal, symbolic, and metaphorical language that is reflective of the rules and pressure existing within the school. The therapist will need to employ techniques that will allow him or her to balance the ability to listen and support school personnel while at the same time acting as catalyst to change the interactional styles presently occurring in the system.

One fundamental, but very effective, technique has been for a therapist to redefine the symptom in order to help school and community agency personnel gain a new perspective on the child's behavior. Generally speaking, the greater the rigidity of the school, the more complex and broad-based the redefinitions. Redefinitions of the symptom can lead school personnel into being less rigid and more open to implementing new ideas when working with the child and/or family. However, the therapist needs to be cognizant that the pressure or anxiety within the family and school system can be reduced. If the anxiety level is reduced too much and the stress is removed from both systems prematurely without initiating change, then the symptom relief may be only temporary and will manifest itself either in the same or altered form within the child at a later time.

Connection is the main context through which effective collaboration takes place. A collaborative approach between the school personnel and the therapist can result in an atmosphere that will lead to the development of creative solutions and will shift rigid systems into change. The therapist brings to the school a working knowledge about the family and an understanding of the systemic context of the problem (Wendt, 1992). Through the application of redefinition, the therapist will be able to assist the school in developing alternative solutions.

Once the therapist has connected with school personnel, avenues for feedback and monitoring of the child's progress should be determined prior to the close of the conference. A mechanism or process for continued contact with the school needs to be established in order to cement the commitment and to collaboratively alter or reinforce the interventions.

SCHOOL PERSONNEL ENTERING THE FAMILY SESSION

A major resource to the therapist and the family is when the therapist brings the school into the session. The goal of the session is to evoke change in the family or the school, or conjoint change in both systems. When the goal is to change the family, the school can assist by intensifying the pressure on the parents that will relieve some of the pressure on the identified child. This is best served when the family is child-focused and feels the need to protect the child from the school and outside influences. The family's protective shield is activated to the extent that they believe that the child is unable to cope with stress.

In working with two systems simultaneously, the therapist more than ever needs to be highly active and involved in sometimes a dramatic and often a humorous and/or provocative fashion. At other times, the therapist may need to become the cool, distant expert who gives new insights that need to be employed.

By being flexible with oneself, the therapist can connect with all generations and both systems, thus penetrating the rigidity of the family and the school. By looking for and creating confusion, the therapist avoids the "truths" that keep everybody stuck. Through the confusion that is simultaneously developed in the school and family, the therapist can find and activate the functional and flexible part of the school system. This allows the therapist to activate the functional side of the parents, which in turn can allow for more functional behavior on the part of the child.

If, on the other hand, the goal is to change the school, the therapist needs to utilize the pressure and intensity of the family and the school in a slightly different manner. When change only in the family is the goal, it is most helpful to have persons closest to the child (e.g., teacher) in the session. When the goal is to change the school, it is essential that the hierarchical structure of the school be included in some manner. By having at least two or more individuals, including principals, supervisors, etc., the therapist can use the horizontal pressure from the family on the school and also activate the vertical pressure within the school. The creation of vertical pressure is accomplished by having the school personnel who are more objective and least emotionally invested in the child's problem see the need for the school to change. The therapist accomplishes this by connecting and bringing to the surface the pain and intensity of the family and having the school observe and connect with the emotional pain of the family.

When the school becomes a part of the emotional process, the therapist can then connect with the flexible part of the school and challenge the rigid part of the school system. If the intensity is great enough in the session, the school will respond to new insights and redefinitions of the child/family that are presented and begin to structure a different set of responses to the child. By sharing the family's pain with the school, the family, in turn, becomes less defensive and intense, and becomes willing to collaborate with the school on how to respond toward the problem of the child. A conjoint session between both systems can result in a renewed optimism, replacing the previous pessimistic stance of both the home and school. However, in some instances, the therapist may need to stimulate simultaneous conjoint change in both the school and family when both systems are dysfunctional.

CONJOINT FAMILY/SCHOOL CHANGE

When stimulating change in both the family and school, the therapist needs to have access to both hierarchies, as well as to the myths underlying each system. In trying to change systems, the therapist will be working with two different worlds that connect only through the symptom of the child. The therapist, especially one who is not trained in educational systems, may become overwhelmed if he or she attempts to understand all the component parts within each system. In most instances, the therapist will understand the family and how the family views the school, but may lack any information about the unique characteristics regarding the particular school, teacher, or classroom.

What is important is for the therapist to move beyond the content of both systems and be able to experience the school and the family through the symbolic language of the child and the metaphorical qualities of the symptom. This means that the child needs to be activated and become a central focus and leading participant in the session. The therapist in turn needs to allow these qualities that come from the child to activate his or her own internal symbolic and affective responses in order to become a conduit between child, parents, and school. Through this process, the therapist adapts to both the school and the family rather than requiring them to adapt to the expert professional.

CASE OF JAMES—MYTH OF EMOTIONAL FRAGILENESS

The family consisted of the parents, Mary and George, and two children, James and Julie. Mary was an artist and George a physician. Mary was very emotional and had a history of substance and sexual abuse originating from her father, an alcoholic physician. Mary was terrified that she would be labeled "crazy" and be hospitalized, which had happened about eight years previously.

Mary and George were seen conjointly for about a year until they decided they were incompatible, at which time they separated and divorced. The decision to divorce was painful, but mutual and quite amicable. George was highly rigid, serious, emotionally distant, with little affect or emotion displayed. Mary was more playful, artistic, and emotionally labile, and presented herself as physically and emotionally fragile. Her fragility was reinforced by uterine cancer that was discovered and treated during the therapy. After the divorce, Mary was seen individually for about two years during which time effective gains were made in assisting her to overcome her denial about the severe pathology in her family of origin, resolving her anger about the abuse and gaining confidence in her ability to withstand anxiety and pressure. While George remained single, Mary entered into a new relationship with a man who was a musician and was a stabilizing influence in her life.

As stated, there were two children, a boy, James, aged six, and a girl, Julie, two years of age when therapy originated. At various times over the duration of couple and individual work, the children would also be included in the sessions. One goal of the therapy was to keep the anxiety contained within the parents and to force them to deal with their conflicts rather than shift the symptoms to their children.

James' work in school during the first, second, and third grades was average to below average, depending upon the emotional stability of the home situation. While Mary was in her second year of individual treatment, she insisted that James was in serious trouble. She was concerned about his emotional strength, and his difficulty in adjusting socially in school. Psychological testing confirmed that James was bright, had good basic academic skills, and was relatively stable except for internalizing the anxiety of the parents. Since this data declared James "normal," we requested James' teacher to attend a therapy session. The teacher seemed very warm, flexible, and concerned about James. It also became apparent that the mother and father frequently called the teacher because they were concerned that the instability of the home left James upset, emotionally fragile, and unable to handle pressure.

The therapist, however, declared that James was normal and irresponsible, making it clear to everyone, including James, that he just did not want to do the work. Through redefinition of the problem as resistance and irresponsibility, the parents and teacher were challenged to begin to hold James accountable for completing his school work. The parents and the teacher successfully worked together to help James become more responsible. This allowed Mary the freedom to focus on her own issues and to keep the pressure contained within herself and the parental generations.

It has been almost four years since that session and Mary was contacted recently for an update. She is doing relatively well and James is now beginning ninth grade and is an honor roll student. Through redefinition and by dealing directly with the shared myth that James and Mary were both emotionally fragile and needed protection, there had been a major shift for James, Mary, and the family.

CONCLUSION

The school can be a valuable resource for the therapist to assist in dealing with the child who exhibits school-based symptoms. The school and family are both systems with a history and hierarchical structure. Both systems have myths about themselves and children that generate rules and roles to be adopted by teachers, parents, and children.

A family can be dysfunctional and the school flexible, while at other times the family may be healthy but are frantically adapting to a dysfunctional school system. In other cases, both the school and family are desperately in need of change as the child becomes increasingly symptomatic.

What is amazing is that each system rarely understands the power that each has in the interactive process. Both teachers and parents believe that they are impotent in effecting change within their respective systems, with each other, and within the child. Therapists can activate change for the child, family, and school through indirect consultation, which would make use of an "insider" to work with teachers, or the therapist can make a visit to the school and participate in a team meeting. In our experience, however, it is considerably more intense to bring the school to the family session.

By entering the conjoint session through the language and reality of the symptomatic child, the therapist is able to help both the family and the school connect with the pain and caring inherent in both systems. When this occurs, the hierarchical process in both systems can be activated to create more flexibility in dealing with the child.

In the conjoint therapy session, the underlying myths shared by the school and the family about life, family, education, or the child can also be readily uncovered. The intensity of the session moves both the family and school beyond the embarrassment about the feelings of impotence and allows each system to connect with the pain and caring that everybody has for each other. From impotence and pessimism, action and optimism can be developed. New realities about the symptom are created and the context for effective change is made possible.

REFERENCES

Anderson, C. (1983). An ecological developmental model for a family orientation in school psychology. *Journal of School Psychology*, 21, 179–189.

Andolfi, M., Angelo, C. & de Nichilo, M. (1989). *The Myth of Atlas; Families and Therapeutic Story.* New York: Brunner/Mazel.

Aponte, H. J. (1976). The family-school interview: An eco-structural approach. *Family Process*, 15, 303–311.

Apter, S. J. (1982). *Troubled Children: Troubled Systems*. New York: Pergamon Press.

Bronfenbrenner, U. (1979). *The Ecology of Human Development: Experiments by Nature and Design*. Cambridge, MA: Harvard University Press.

Conoley, J. C. (1987). Schools and families: Theoretical and practical bridges. *Professional School Psychology*, 2, 191–203.

Dockrell, W. B. (1964). Society, home and underachievement. *Psychology in the Schools*, 1(2), 173–178.

Fine, M. (1992). A systems-ecological perspective on home-school intervention. In M. Fine and C. Carlson (Eds.). *The Handbook of Family-School Intervention: A Systems Perspective*. Boston: Allyn and Bacon.

Fine, M. J. (1984). Integrating structural and strategic components in school-based consultation. *Techniques*, 1, 44–52.

Fine, M. J. & Holt, P. (1983). Intervening with school problems: A family systems perspective. *Psychology in the Schools*, 20, 59–66.

Garbarino, J. (1983). *Children and Families in the Social Environment*. New York: Aldine Publishing.

Green, K., & Fine, M. J. (1980). Family therapy: A case for training school psychologists. *Psychology in the Schools*, 17, 241–248.

Gurman, A. (1970). The role of the family in underachievement. *Journal of School Psychology*, 8(1), 48–53.

Hannafin, M. J., & Witt, J. C. (1983). System intervention and the school psychologist; maximizing interplay among roles and functions. *Professional Practice: Research and Practice*, 14(1), 128–136.

Lombard, T. J. (1979). Family-oriented emphasis for school psychologists: A needed orientation for training and practice. *Professional Psychology*, 10, 687–696.

Mannino, F. & Shore, M. (1984). An ecological perspective on family intervention. In N. O'Connor & B. Lubin (Eds.), *Ecological Approaches to Clinical and Community Psychology*. New York: Wiley.

Paget, K. D. (1992). Provocative family-school partnerships in early intervention. In M. Fine and C. Carlson (Eds.), *The Handbook of Family-School Intervention: A Systems Perspective*. Boston: Allyn and Bacon.

Pfeiffer, S. I. & Tittler, B. I. (1984). Utilizing the multidisciplinary team to facilitate a school-family systems orientation. *School Psychology Review*, 12, 168–173.

Plas, J. M. (1986). *Systems Psychology in the Schools*. New York: Pergamon.

Pollaczek, D. (1964). The school psychologist considers parent education. *Psychology in the Schools*, 1(3), 279–282.

Rutter, M. (1985). Family and school influences on behavior development. *Journal of Child Psychology and Psychiatry*, 26, 349–368.

Selvini-Palazzoli, M., Cecchin, G., & Prata, G., & Boscolo, L. (1978). *Paradox and Counter Paradox: A New Model in the Therapy of the Family in Schizophrenic Transaction*. New York: Aronson.

Snapp, M. & Davidson, J. L. (1982). Systems interventions for school psychologists: A case study approach. In C. R. Reynolds and T. B. Gutkins (Eds.), *The Handbook of School Psychology*. New York: Wiley.

Swap, S. M. (1978). The ecological model of emotional disturbance in children: A status report and proposed synthesis. *Behavior Disorders*, 3, 186–196.

Swap, S. M. (1984). Ecological approaches to working with families of disturbing children. In W. O'Connor & B. Ludbin (Eds.), *Ecological Approaches to Clinical and Community Psychology*. New York: Wiley.

Wendt, R. N. (1992). The use of systemic provocation in family therapy for school problems. In M. Fine and C. Carlson (Eds.), *The Handbook of Family-School Intervention: A Systems Perspective*. Boston: Allyn and Bacon.

Wendt, R. N. & Zake, J. (1984). Family systems therapy and school psychology: Implications for training and practice. *Psychology in the Schools*, 21, 204–210.

14

Peppa: An Indirect Consultation Concerning the Myth of Strength and Weakness

Lars Brok

You can't always get what you want, but if you try some time, you just might find, you get what you need.
ROLLING STONES

What is "Peppa"? According to the client, Mrs. Y., Peppa means "crazy little woman" or "ugly duckling." This nickname is an indicator of her role in her family of origin. After the consultation, it became clear that the dance around the "Peppa role" also resonated in the therapeutic system.

In this consultation, the consultant met with only one of the two therapists; he did not see the other therapist and the clients. The consultant used the position of the therapist as the focus of his consultation.

DIRECT VERSUS INDIRECT CONSULTATION

In a direct consultation, the consultant meets with the total therapeutic system, the therapists and the client system, and interviews them about the problems they experience in the family and in the therapy. The participation of the therapist varies according to the specific circumstances. The novel position of the consultant can create new realities for the family and open up new resources. This could help a therapist who was stuck in the therapeutic process by encouraging/modeling a different position in the therapeutic system. The consultant can influence the position of the therapist in the therapeutic system by interviewing him/her and the family members about their relations, fears, loyalties, hopes, despair, etc. Thus, the direct consultation helps expand the therapist's role in the therapeutic system by focusing on either the family system or the therapeutic system.

In an indirect consultation, the consultant meets only the therapist. Thus, perceptions and resources from the family are unavailable. The consultant may attempt to resolve their absence by requesting the therapist to provide information about the family's perceptions of their problems and the therapy. In my opinion, this leads to abstract storytelling and may result in the consultant giving the therapist advice about interventions that have worked in similar cases. The problem is that the consultant is limited to the fantasies and conceptualizations of a therapist locked in a therapeutic impasse rather than having first-hand perceptions of the entire therapeutic system.

In the following case, Maurizio Andolfi solved this problem in a different way: He focused on the relationship between the therapist and himself (the consultant). He looked for similarities or parallels between the way the therapist tried to involve him in the therapeutic system and the way the family involved the therapist in the family system. In the indirect consultation, he challenged the therapist's role by his choice of whether and how to participate as the consultant. Through his personal choices, Andolfi challenged the roles in many of the systems involved in the therapy: consultant and consultee, the cotherapists, the therapeutic system including the family and the cotherapists, the client system, and the intrapersonal system of the consultee.

PSYCHOSOMATIC COMPLAINTS AND MARITAL PROBLEMS

Mr. Y., an Italian man who had lived and worked in the Netherlands for seven years, reported to an outpatient clinic with a number of unfounded physical complaints. During the first visit, he said that his complaints could be linked to tensions in his job, problems in his youth, and difficulties with his marital relationship. The female therapist, Mariet, who handled the intake, explained that it was essential that Mrs. Y. be invited to describe her view of the problems.

Mr. Y. gladly agreed, but he thought his wife would be unwilling to come. He described her as very shy and unable to speak or understand Dutch since she had lived in the Netherlands for only a year. He had met his wife when visiting his native village on an Italian island. Despite a very short courtship (about six weeks), they decided to marry and live in the Netherlands. Shortly after her arrival, she became pregnant. At the time her husband sought help for his medical problem, the baby was eight weeks old.

Mariet and her team decided that she should include a male cotherapist, the author, who is able to understand and speak some Italian. It was hoped that a therapist/translator would relieve Mr. Y., who had some trouble in expressing himself in proper Dutch, from being the Dutch translator for his wife. Thus, from the beginning, the team chose an accommodating, safe approach to the therapy.

THE TEAM HYPOTHESIS

The team initially hypothesized that Mr. Y's physical symptomatology reflected the following interrelated problems:

1. Mr. Y.'s stagnancy at work. He felt very disappointed because he had not been promoted during the seven years of his employment. All of his former colleagues were promoted; consequently, he had lost contact with most of them.
2. The couples' developmental problems as partners and parents.
3. Cultural adaptation problems of Mr. Y. and especially Mrs. Y.
4. Mrs. Y.'s difficulty in emancipating from her family of origin.
5. Mr. Y.'s position in his family of origin. He said that his relationship with his father was the main reason for his emigration to the Netherlands. He still hoped to return to his island but, "of course this was impossible as long as my father was alive."

RELATIONS IN THE THERAPEUTIC SYSTEM: "STRONG MEN, PEPPA WOMEN"

Mr. Y. behaved competently by doing all the talking, while Mrs. Y. silently looked helpless. Questions in Italian to Mrs. Y. were usually answered, "Non lo so" (I don't know). On the other hand, Mr. Y. was very understanding and helpful. However, he constantly emphasized the weakness of his wife in words and attitude. For example, he de-

scribed his wife as very insecure and nervous and often paternally nodded behind her back when she stuttered or could not answer a question.

The Y.'s interactional pattern was mirrored in the therapeutic context. When Mariet, the female co-therapist, asked for information, neither Mr. nor Mrs. Y. responded directly to her. Both addressed (almost
provocatively) only me, the male therapist. I became increasingly talk-
ative as my colleague, Mariet, became more silent. Thus, we assumed
unequal positions of importance, which resulted in a division of roles
similar to those of the couple.

During a team conference, Mariet revealed that she felt more like a
burden than an asset in the therapeutic relationship. We attempted to
break this pattern by talking less and prescribing tasks (in between the
sessions) and role-plays (during the sessions) that focused on the daily
routine of the couple. For example, when the wife complained that she
felt as if her husband were not married to her, we asked her to role-play
one of these situations. She showed us how her husband walked about
10 meters in front of her during shopping trips and how she and the
little daughter had to hurry not to lose him. We asked the husband to
take care of the child next time they went shopping. The following
session we let them role-play how the shopping went. This approach
definitely brought about some changes in the way the couple related to
each other, but we still felt that the roles in the therapeutic system were
too stereotyped. Our roles as co-therapists seemed to parallel the complementary roles of the husband and wife: secure and all-knowing man
versus insecure, needy woman.

FAMILY RELATIONS: PARTNER AND PARENTAL ROLES

In many ways, Mr. and Mrs. Y. barely functioned as partners. Mrs. Y.
had dinner with her daughter before Mr. Y. returned from work. Mrs. Y.
slept in the couple's bedroom with her daughter while Mr. Y. slept in
the child's room. The couple justified this sleeping arrangement as being due to Mrs. Y.'s restlessness at night. There were minimal discussions about marital problems, yet they often quarreled about the
upbringing of the child. Mr. Y. thought his wife was too protective and
permissive while Mrs. Y. thought he was too tough. This disagreement
resulted in Mr. Y.'s complete withdrawal from the upbringing of the
child. Mrs. Y. complained, on occasion, about the huge marital distance: "We do not live as husband and wife." Nevertheless, it was very
hard for her to indicate what she expected or wanted from the marriage. Clearly, they were dissatisfied with the partner and parental roles.

FAMILY RELATIONS: FAMILIES OF ORIGIN

Mrs. Y. did not disclose much about her family. She was the fourth of six children in a family where her father was 30 years older than her mother. Her mother was only 14 years old when they were married. She described her father as an aggressive man who regularly threatened her mother with a pistol.

Mr. Y., on the other hand, elaborately described his family. He emphasized the physical and emotional abuse by his father, who regularly beat and rejected him during his youth. This, according to his mother, was due to his position as the eldest son. His father had to marry his mother because she became pregnant after they had a single sexual encounter. His father emphasized that he married her only because of the pressure from both families. In his village, the father was a respected and cheerful man, but at home he was unbearable. According to Mr. Y., his father and mother lived separate lives; they slept in different rooms and hardly spoke to one another.

Mr. Y. left home at age 15. Later, after unsuccessful attempts at reconciliation, conflicts with his father made Mr. Y. decide to go abroad. He still wanted to return to his native island, but worried about his relationship with his father. He described his mother as a very simple woman with whom he did not have a meaningful relationship. Despite father's abuse, rejection, and arguments, he had more respect for him than for his mother.

THE IMPASSE

As therapists, we concluded that we were stuck at this stage of the therapy. Indeed, we still thought that the couple had difficulties concerning the division of roles as partners and parents and that these problems were intensified by the cultural differences between their native village and their present environment. We believed that our interventions aimed at changing the rigid male-female complementarity had had some positive results, but we felt unhappy in the therapeutic system. First, the division of roles in the couple and co-therapy team still seemed too complementary. Second, and more important, we always had the idea that we missed some central point that seemed connected to the family of origin's influence in their marriage (or choice to be married). However, we were not able to reach Mrs. Y. around this issue. She hid behind her husband, who seemed to reinforce this, by saying that she could not understand us. Again, this led to the rigid complementarity between Mr. and Mrs. Y., as well as between Mariet and myself. We did not know how to resolve these problems.

Our need for an appropriate consultant was evident. We wanted a consultant who was sensitive to cultural and language problems. Since Maurizio Andolfi was scheduled to be at our institute, we decided to ask the couple to agree to a consultation session with him.

THE CONSULTATION

All members of the therapeutic system looked forward to the day that Andolfi, as a long-expected migratory bird, would be flying north. As we anticipated the consultation, two confusing events transpired.

On the day of Andolfi's arrival, one day before the consultation, Mariet said she did not dare take part in the consultation session. Since she seemed not to have a substantial reason for being absent from the consultation session, I tried to convince her to attend. I was unable to change her mind and we decided that I should go alone to the session, with the couple. "I understand that you are scared. I think I can manage alone, however difficult it may be," I said to Mariet.

During the evening before the consultation, I told Andolfi that Mariet, my co-therapist, would not come to the session. Immediately Andolfi responded: "Then it will be cancelled. No consultation without the co-therapist."

The next morning I discussed the problem with Mariet. Even though she believed the consultation was necessary, she still did not want to participate. Meanwhile, the couple arrived for the session and we informed them about the situation. At first, Mrs. Y. tried to encourage Mariet to participate in the consultation. When that did not succeed, Mrs. Y. laughed and confessed that she was relieved that it was cancelled. Mr. Y. regretted this course of events. The members of the therapeutic system decided that I should inform Andolfi that there would be no session. In addition, a new appointment was made to discuss the situation as well as the purposes, if any, of further sessions.

With this decision, I went to Andolfi, who with a hall full of conference participants, was waiting to see if there would be a live consultation. With each step closer to the hall, I realized more and more clearly that I had stirred up a hornets' nest. After hearing the state of events, Andolfi reconsidered the situation for a few moments. He said that although he could not give a consultation with respect to the therapy of the couple, he was willing to discuss the present position of me as therapist. He asked me if I was willing to do so in the presence of so many colleagues. Even though this proposal seemed to be instructive, I was in cold sweat. However, because of my confidence in Andolfi, I agreed to proceed.

So, Andolfi placed two chairs, close together, in front of the audience and asked me to sit beside him.

Andolfi: (*puts his hand gently on my shoulder*) Please, can you explain to me and the people in the hall, in short, why you are here alone?

Brok (*me, the therapist*): (Tells above-mentioned story.)

Andolfi: Your colleague-therapist did not want to come, I understand. Why did you not bring the couple alone?

Brok: (*amazed, looking at Andolfi who is smiling warmly*) Alone? What do you mean?

Andolfi: Exactly what I said.

Brok: (*a bit disturbed and not knowing what direction Andolfi is going*) But you yourself said that you did not want a session only with the couple and me, without my co-therapist.

Andolfi: Indeed, I did say so once.

Brok: (*angry about what Andolfi said but also disturbed by his trustful manner*) Well then...

Andolfi: (*with some humor in his voice, challenging the relaxed way I am trying to present myself in this difficult situation*) You have not at all tried to change my opinion.

Brok: (*tense, because I am realizing that Andolfi, although friendly in his behavior, does not want to make it easy for me*) I supposed you had a good reason for not wanting to.

Andolfi: (*laughing*) Absolutely, but you did not ask for that reason. Neither did you say anything about your motives to hold the session anyway.

Brok: (*hesitating and feeling more despair about the way I am overresponsible*) What... should I have done?

Andolfi: (*in a more serious tone, with his hand on mine*) You should not ask me. For example, you could have told me that I had to do the session because I was paid for it; however, you just agreed with my remark.

Brok: (*sweating, because Andolfi does not accept my shift from strong to weak, either. I wonder what that gentle bastard wants from me*) Oh really...

Andolfi: (*in a friendly but very serious tone now; still touching my hand very softly*) I just think that you do not dare to. You seem strong, now that you seem to be taking on all the responsibility of therapists and family, but, in fact, you behave like a scared little man.

(*The laughing, whispering and the sound of chairs moving reflect the audience's experience of the tension of this moment.*)

Brok: (*feeling tense too; in my mind are many pictures of personal and professional situations where I did not dare to ask people "to stay"*) mmm...

Andolfi: (*in a strict tone, but with a flavor of real concern*) You may be a psychiatrist, but you behave like a small boy.

We sat there in silence for some minutes. I felt a strong sense of relief. At that moment, I did not know how to explain exactly why I felt relieved. Later, I realized that Andolfi had opened up the possibility for me to be "weak and strong" at the same time.

Following this exchange Andolfi gathered information about how I handled my co-therapist's decision not to participate. I avoided a more intense conflict with Mariet by "understanding" her viewpoint; thus, I assumed more responsibility than I could handle and denied my limits. By doing this, I denied that I really needed her to solve the problem and that I felt abandoned by her. Since I acted so independently Mariet had got the impression that she was expendable. Indeed, Mariet provoked the behaviors that I typically use to handle abandonment. After considering the consultation for a while, I went to Mariet to discuss it with her.

THE POST CONSULTATION

Initially, there was a heated argument when I told Mariet that I felt abandoned by her. We had both decided that a consultation was necessary and then she had let me go alone, without any good reason. I told her about the session with Andolfi. Mariet then more fully expressed her motives for not attending the consultation with Andolfi. "I was afraid of having language problems; I had not thought for a moment that you would become angry or that the session would be cancelled when I did not come. I thought you could manage without me perfectly well," she said. She felt superfluous. Furthermore, choosing Andolfi, a distant "master" to her and a teacher/friend to me, further undermined her importance in the therapeutic system. This was the parallel process in the therapy sessions. She felt unnecessary and doubted that her ideas were valuable. Additionally, she believed the couple did not respect her. I told her that I also felt abandoned in the family sessions.

I noted that in particular, when tension developed with respect to Mrs. Y's position, Mariet retreated into not knowing and not understanding. I admitted that I complemented her withdrawal by my tendency to avoid conflict around separateness by assuming the role of all-knowing, all-understanding "grandfather." I realized that it had been a mistake to minimize our educational differences (a psychiatrist with extensive family therapy training and a social worker with less experience in family therapy). However, I no longer accepted that Mariet played a less valuable and dispensable role. She had a lot of experience in individual and group therapy with women and considerable experience in couples therapy. After an emotional discussion, we were able to see the following systems more clearly:

Therapist/Consultant Relationship

The therapists put Andolfi in the all-knowing role, appealing particularly to his knowledge of the culture and language of the couple. Andolfi broke the pattern by refusing to do a consultation without the presence of the co-therapist. First, he emphasized her importance for the solution of the problems in the therapeutic system. Second, by talking about my handicap—detouring conflict and assuming an overly responsible position—he provoked me to acknowledge and voice my competence and limits, and challenged my way of handling "being left alone."

Co-Therapy Relationship

Both therapists minimized differences in educational and personal background, possibly, because we feared disagreements about female/male role issues. When disagreements occurred, mostly provoked by the position Mrs.Y. took in the session, Mariet retreated into her role of "not-knowing." On the other hand, I played the part of the "knower," thus supporting my colleague in her "Peppa" role. My acceptance of her one down role prevented her from becoming a "partner." It is remarkable how this complementary pattern resembled the pattern of the couple. Similarly, the therapeutic impasse resulted in the "stronger" partner's solitary search for a consultant.

Couple/Therapists Relationship

All members of the therapeutic system generally minimized differences, or used them to create a complementary relationship which prevented the exchange of more intimate information, a real "meeting." The language problem is a metaphor for this issue. In this "pseudo-meeting," the therapists took responsibility for change and did not make Mr. and Mrs. Y. responsible for delivering vital (family-of-origin) information. The therapists dictated and the couple followed. Correspondingly, this rigid pattern facilitated little growth outside the sessions.

Husband/Wife Relationship

Mr. and Mrs. Y. had big differences in the way they wanted to form their relationship, but rarely discussed their differences. Each did not allow the other to understand his/her family of origin experiences and personal dreams. Instead, a rigid, complementary relationship developed in which Mr. Y. was the one who knows and Mrs. Y. was "the Peppa." The husband, almost painlessly, accepted the "weakness" of his wife, consequently excluding the possibility of partnership. When this solution of conflict avoidance no longer worked (after the birth of the child), the "stronger" one (husband) went to a therapist who could assume the position of the all-knowing one who had to solve the problem without productive conflict.

FOLLOW UP: MAXIMIZING CONSTRUCTIVE DIFFERENCES

We told the couple that the consultation with Andolfi had made clear that the knowledge of Mariet and Mrs. Y. had not been used enough in the therapy. Furthermore, we needed to know more about the position of each of them in their own family of origin. We proposed to temporarily split the therapeutic system: individual sessions with Mariet and Mrs. Y., and myself with Mr. Y. Conjoint sessions, however, could be arranged at the request of Mr. or Mrs. Y. In any case, there would be a conjoint evaluation session in six weeks. Mrs. and Mr. Y. agreed with the proposal.

The restructuring of the therapeutic system proved to have a strong impact on the different relationships. After several sessions, Mariet reported that the meetings with Mrs. Y. had become very meaningful. The language problem, paradoxically, actually helped them to clarify their communication. Several nonverbal means of communication, the genogram, drawings, pictures, and dictionary were used. The central theme of the meetings was Mrs.Y.'s experience in her family of origin. Her "Peppa" role kept her very dependent on her mother and sisters. The only time that she left the family, against her mother's will, was to take care of her ill father, who lived in another town. After his death, she returned home and was treated as "Peppa" again.

Her marriage was an endeavor to flee from home and from this role. Therefore, she was willing to live far from her home village. The individual sessions also focused on the differing gender roles of women in Holland and her homeland. The move to Holland enabled her to see much more progressive feminine roles.

Mrs. Y.'s individual therapy meetings set the stage for Mr. Y.'s first experience in taking care of his child alone. First, they came together to the institute; father and daughter then played or walked outside the building. Later, Mrs. Y. came alone and her husband stayed at home with their child.

In the individual sessions with Mr. Y., he initially emphasized his physical complaints. Later, he spoke about the problems at work: how he felt disappointed and discriminated against by his colleagues. He tried to improve his position by learning another profession (plumber, bricklayer), but educational reasons prevented him from following this course.

In the first two conjoint sessions, Mr. and Mrs. Y. behaved as they had prior to the consultation. Mariet, astonished by the behavior of Mrs. Y., concluded that the splitting of the therapeutic system was still necessary.

After five months, Mrs. Y. asked for a conjoint session to discuss a planned six-week visit to their native village. In this session, Mrs. and Mr. Y. presented themselves quite differently as they communicated with each other and with us on a much more "equal" level. Both reported that their relationship had changed a lot during the past few months (for example, they slept with each other while their child slept in her own room). Mrs. Y., however, feared that they would revert to their old roles during their vacation. Her husband would be with his friends and she would feel compelled to be with her family in the "Peppa" role again.

Although the session attempted to forge a strong marital boundary in the midst of their families of origin, the vacation was very difficult for them. Mr. and Mrs. Y. each lived with their own family and Mrs.Y felt particularly ashamed to have resumed her "Peppa" role. Following the vacation, the therapy worked through their estrangement and their need for a strong marital bond. After several months, the couple decided to return to their native island. They were confident that their marriage could withstand the pressure to conform to their old roles and the resulting separateness.

In the last session, Mrs. Y. declared that she felt quite different now than prior to the therapy. She said that prior to therapy she had felt unhappy every day and had regularly thought about suicide. Now she felt happy but realized that she had to do a lot of work to further improve her relationship with her husband and to maintain her strength in her family of origin. She did not feel like a "Peppa" anymore. Mr. Y. related that for the first time he really felt married. He felt that he could be more straightforward with his father and mother.

Mrs. Y. laughingly confessed that in the beginning of the therapy she had been afraid of me. This changed after the start of the individual sessions. She had learned to ask for help when necessary and to trust Mariet and later her husband. In realizing that asking for help did not mean that she would be a "Peppa," she was able to feel much less lonely.

Mrs.Y. asked me to thank Andolfi for the consultation. She felt the consultation had a good influence on the therapy, but, she said laughing, the real work had been done by Mariet and me.

The couple has been in Italy now for about one year. We have received letters from them saying that things are well.

CONCLUSION

In any consultation, it is extremely important to analyze the position of the therapist in the therapeutic system and the influence of his/her personal self in this position. In this case, the position of the therapist was the main issue. "Accidental" circumstances dictated that the consultant spoke just with me. The consultant uncovered and provoked the parallel between how I related to the consultant and how I related to my cotherapist. This information helped the cotherapists first and then all members of the therapeutic system to become more clear about expressing needs, resolving conflict, and respecting each other's competence. This diminished the need for both the Peppa and the overresponsible roles.

I am convinced that a consultation that does not focus on the position of the therapist(s) in the therapeutic system is just another therapy session. This oversight could result in "more of the same" (for example, a "competent" consultant and a "Peppa" therapist) and does not lead to a real shift in the therapeutic process.

PART IV

CONSULTATION AS PROFESSIONAL DEVELOPMENT

15

Consultation in the Training Moment

Joseph Simons, Peter D. Liggett, and Marsha Purvis

The timely use of consultation can greatly increase the effectiveness of a therapist. A consultant brings a *new perspective* to the therapeutic system so that it becomes possible for both the therapist and the clients to see possibilities for mobility within the therapeutic system that had not been seen before. Thus, clients and therapists discover new ways to relate to one another and to the presenting problem so that the system that has been "stuck" can transform itself into a state of greater flexibility and greater openness to change.

In addition, even very experienced therapists can often benefit from *observing the techniques* the consultant employs in his or her work with the clients, or with the relationship between the therapist and the clients. Furthermore, a consultation that is properly conducted invests the therapist with *greater flexibility*, which strengthens the therapist's position with his or her clients (both at the moment of consultation and later, after the consultant has left the system—in body, if not in spirit).

While these benefits of consultation are potentially useful for any therapist, they are a good deal more valuable for trainees.

Consultation may provide assistance that goes well beyond what other forms of training (such as ordinary supervision) can offer. Trainees are, after all, in the process of evolving and unfolding their ability to conceptualize therapeutic puzzles in ways that provide clients with more choices—that is to say, more flexibility. The infusion into the therapeutic system of new ways of looking at the problem is therefore especially valuable for an individual in a training process.

Consultation also gives a trainee the opportunity to closely observe the consultant working within the therapy process and provides the trainee with a model from which to derive his or her own interventions. While there is much to be said for the learning that can be obtained from instruction or suggestions provided by a supervisor to a trainee, it can often be more helpful (or at least helpful in a different way) for the trainee to directly observe the supervisor acting in a consultant role as he or she works with the trainee's clients.

The empowering quality of consultation may be not only the most helpful, but also the most gratifying result for the trainee. Strengthening the trainee's position, as therapist, arises from two primary consultation processes: the perceived alliance of the trainee with the consultant, and the repositioning of the trainee and the clients within the therapeutic system.

Our purpose in this chapter is to discuss and illustrate each of these three aspects of the benefits of consultation (*providing a new perspective, modeling of therapy techniques by the consultant, and empowering the therapist*) from a trainee's point of view. The examples of consultation presented here are drawn from experiences that have occurred within the context of a psychology predoctoral internship at an APA accredited university counseling center. We believe that this discussion can help to illustrate the value of consultation as a part of the training process, and therefore provide an impetus to the wider use of consultation in similar settings.

NEW PERSPECTIVES

Even the most experienced of therapists is likely to want fresh ways of looking at therapeutic impasses. However, trainees are a good deal more likely to feel as though they are merely treading therapeutic water or struggling with that "what-do-I-do-now" feeling. In instances such as these, being able to obtain a new perspective on a case is especially welcome.

On occasion, a single remark by a consultant who enters a therapy case with a "fresh eye" can shift the perceptions of every member of the therapeutic system. For example, during the beginning of a consultation[1] that involved a family, the intern who had been working as the primary therapist remarked to the consultant that a very large amount of competition existed between the "identified patient" and her sister.

[1]The consultant in each of these cases was Russell Haber, Ph.D.

The consultant, with apparent casualness, asked, "Competition to be good or to be bad?" There occurred a noticeable moment of gestalt in which every member of the client system, and the intern as well, suddenly became aware that the sibling rivalry was not simply a matter of competition, but rather represented a need that both siblings had for attention, at whatever cost.

However, it is often the case that a new perspective is obtained by the trainee and the clients as a result of more global interventions by the consultant. How this change in perspective can be brought about by a consultative experience can be illustrated by the following account of a consultation requested by a therapist trainee who was working with a married couple. In this case, an actual physical shifting of the clients provided an opportunity for the trainee to develop a new perspective and, therefore, new insights into her role in the therapy.

Tom and Sally were being seen in therapy because of conflicts in their relationship. The outward manifestations of the conflicts were Tom's combative nature and Sally's assumption of a helpless, nonassertive stance. Their therapist, a female psychology intern, felt that there was a "missing piece" in the therapy that she was unable to identify. In order for the consultant to identify unknown elements of the therapy, he proposed that the therapist interview each partner about the therapy while the other partner and the consultant observed from behind the one-way mirror. Thereafter, the consultant asked the couple to watch from the observation room as he and the therapist discussed the progress of the therapy. In this situation, the consultant focused on asking the therapist for her evaluation of the therapy and compared her evaluation to the responses the clients had made earlier to the question of how they thought the therapy was going.

Among other things, the consultant suggested that the clients' evaluation seemed more powerful than the therapist's evaluation. He said to the therapist that "the effect of the therapy is ... felt much more intensely in them, and it seems like in some ways that you really don't have a full appreciation of your importance to them, or the importance of the therapy to them."

As a result of the consultation, the therapist felt that she was able to broaden her perspective of the experience:

The consultant acted as a magnifier for the therapeutic process by interjecting new information and by highlighting segments of the therapeutic interaction. Through my restricted lens of focusing on "the problem," my view had become too narrow. I lacked the distance to see the whole system and the effects of the work which had taken place. I also lacked the experience to trust my own evaluation of "usefulness to the therapeutic system." The consultant's words of not having a "full appreciation of the importance of the therapy to them" were accurate. The consultation offered me a chance to have someone say that I could begin to trust my own work and process. Part of what I referred to as the "missing piece" was within me—it was the positive evaluation of my own work.

The consultation filled in the gap of the "missing piece" by offering a broader perspective in which to experiment with a shift in the roles or stance of the therapist for each client. More importantly, perhaps, it gave me the missing piece of permission to begin to view and trust my own work and process.

This illustrates the value a consultation can have for a therapist trainee. In this case, the therapist was presented with information about her value to the clients and to the process of therapy in a way that was infinitely more powerful than if the clients alone had given her the information—or if she had been told she was doing well by a supervisor outside the immediate context of the therapy process.

MODELING OF THERAPY TECHNIQUES BY THE CONSULTANT

The nature of consultation is such that the therapist trainee has the opportunity to not only observe a more experienced and accomplished therapist work with clients, but to observe him or her work with clients with whom the trainee has made an investment of professional time and energy. The modeling done by a consultant may be of relatively basic things such as what kinds of words are most helpful or what posture or tone of voice seems most beneficial. However, a consultant's modeling is more often of particular value to trainees in demonstrating more sophisticated interventions that provide the trainee with new ways of "being" with the clients. For instance, the consultant's natural inclination (because of the nature of his or her task) is to adopt a more "meta" level of conceptualization and intervention in the therapeutic system. Simply being able to observe this meta-processing as it occurs assists the trainee in developing new ways of thinking that can be integrated into his or her therapy later.

The modeling that occurs in a consultation provides an opportunity for the trainee to get a kind of "short course" or a brief, but very intense, exposure to the working style of an experienced therapist. The nature of consultation is such that there is the opportunity for the trainee to see some fairly unusual methods modeled. Consultants are, to a certain extent, freer to do more "outlandish" kinds of things and push against the accepted edges of conventional therapy, because they are expected to enter a system and—in a short period of time (i.e., one session)—do something dramatic to get the system "unstuck." This means that they model, for the novice therapist, new therapeutic possibilities that can be integrated into the trainee's repertoire of therapeutic interventions.

The case example we will use here does not involve any "unusual" methods, but it does provide an illustration of how consultation can model working with a larger system—and how an apparently "fragile" client can be handled in a less "careful" way.

Allison was a 21-year-old college student who had been seen on an individual basis for four sessions by a male psychology intern. She had come to therapy for help because of a drinking problem. Allison had been through a treatment program for alcoholism when she was 16; however, she was abstinent for only a few months following treatment. Her drinking had gradually become more serious until it reached the point where she experienced frequent blackouts. The event that precipitated her coming to therapy was a minor automobile accident which resulted in her being arrested for driving while intoxicated.

During the individual sessions, Allison invariably became tearful and expressed great remorse over her substance abuse as well as fear over the legal consequences she was likely to suffer as a result. However, she seemed incapable of moving beyond her tears, and the intern was beginning to feel frustrated with her extremely fragile emotional state, the generally helpless way she presented herself, and the resulting lack of movement in the therapy. Accordingly, he suggested to Allison that it might be profitable if her parents (who lived in a city about two hours away) could attend a session. Once these arrangements were made, the intern also requested a consultation from a staff member at the counseling center.

The consultation began with the intern explaining, in some detail, to the consultant the presenting problem and progress made (or not made) so far in the therapy. This process occupied about 10 minutes of the session while Allison and her parents listened silently. The consultant then turned to Allison and began to question her about her relationship with alcohol. In a relatively abrupt but clearly concerned fashion he asked her how long she expected to live; what the chances were that she would be able to abstain from drinking for the rest of her life; and, subsequently, what she felt were the chances that she would be able to abstain for the remainder of that day. This questioning produced (not unexpectedly) a tearful response from Allison.

The consultant then asked each parent in turn what they felt the tears were about. These questions served as an entry into an exploration of the roles of everyone in the family and of the family-of-origin influences that had helped to construct these roles. This exploration occupied the remainder of the session until the consultant "handed the family back" to the intern with some remarks about what he felt was occurring in the family system and some suggestions in regard to future directions for therapy.

The nearly exclusive focus on the family system (and away from the individual client) seemed to put Allison's "terrible" situation in perspective. It also seemed to help her to understand how the family system had contributed to her substance abuse and, more importantly, how it could help her in recovery.

For the intern, the consultation provided an opportunity to observe a master therapist, in a very brief period of time, enter and join with a family—and then shift the focus from the "identified patient" to the system as a whole. The intern remarked that "I not only developed an understanding of how to involve a larger system in a client's therapy, but I also observed that it was possible—in fact, really constructive—to be a lot less concerned about how 'fragile' my client was. After the consultation, I was able to be much more constructively confrontational with Allison."

As it happened, this family consultation had some very beneficial long-range effects for the progress of the therapy. Allison continued to be seen on a regular basis by the intern over the course of the next few months. Although the parents did not return for another formal family session, the intern was able to invoke the memory, as it were, of the consultation in order to help Allison understand and accept her addiction and learn how to enlist the aid of her family in continuing with her abstinence.

What was perhaps more significant was the way in which the consultation helped the intern develop the skills of working with other consultants. That is to say, the consultation experience was not simply a solution to a particular therapeutic conundrum, but also a modeled structure from which the intern was able to work with larger systems. For example, the intern was able to assist Allison in developing a peer-support system to effectively maintain her sobriety. More importantly, when Allison experienced a slip in her recovery program, the intern was able to bring both Allison's Alcoholics Anonymous sponsor and her mother into the therapy—to connect immediately with elements of the larger system within which Allison functioned and to provide a means by which she could quickly and safely get back on her program.

It is worth noting that the modeling in consultation quite naturally generalizes beyond the particular session or specific therapeutic problem to working with other consultants. It also provides the trainee with a model for what is involved in being in the consultant role. Having directly observed a master therapist functioning as a consultant, the trainee has a structure upon which to build his or her own role as a consultant in some future situation. Thus, the consultation provides the trainee with multidimensional modeling: how to solve specific problems within the therapeutic system, how to make better use of other consultants within the clients' systems, and how to provide consultation to other therapists.

STRENGTHENING THE TRAINEE'S POSITION

Even trainees who feel quite confident of their abilities as therapists generally welcome the opportunity to obtain greater flexibility—to become a stronger change agent—within the therapeutic system. It is also gratifying to trainees when consultations enhance the perceptions that their clients have of them as competent and professional. This strengthening is very likely even more welcome in those situations where a consultation is requested, since it is most often the case that the therapist trainee is feeling "stuck" or less effective than he or she would like to be.

One way in which a trainee obtains a stronger position within the therapeutic system is through his or her alliance with the consultant. The consultant is usually perceived of as an "expert" who has been called in to deal with a difficult or intractable therapy problem. There is sometimes an initial hesitation on the part of the trainee to ask for a consultation because of a fear of appearing to be incompetent. However, this feeling most often becomes completely reversed when the affirming, strengthening quality of an expertly conducted consultation becomes apparent.

The example above of the consultation done with Allison and her family is a good case in point. The first few minutes of the session were devoted to a discussion between the intern and the consultant about the course of therapy so far and how the intern felt about the work that had been accomplished. Throughout this portion of the session the consultant's tone was collegial and his questions were clearly nonjudgmental. At the end of the session the consultant returned the family to the care of the trainee. At this time he provided a brief evaluation of the family situation and made recommendations to the trainee for future directions for therapy.

Again, the consultant's tone suggested confidence in the trainee and his ability to deal with the therapy in a competent manner. The consultant's attitude was clearly that the difficulty the trainee had encountered was a system problem rather than the result of incompetence or even simple inexperience on the part of the trainee. As a result, the trainee felt as though his ability to deal with the client had been substantially enhanced—without any implications that his request for help was a signal that he had not handled the case well.

A more profound way of strengthening the position of the trainee occurs as the result of the consultant entering the therapeutic system at a meta-level and functioning in a way that brings about a repositioning of the trainee and the client(s) relative to one another. This is what occurred in the following example.

Lolly was a 52-year-old law student who was feeling overwhelmed by the combined responsibilities of school and family. As a mother she was feeling that her adult children needed her help and support—she was especially worried about a son who was "not doing anything with his life." As a wife she was concerned that her (second) husband was not as active physically as she would like. As a sibling she was angry with her brother and sister for not contributing more time and energy toward the care of their ill mother. And as a daughter, she was angry with her mother for needing her time and attention. In short, everyone seemed to need something from her—or to be deficient in a way that required her energy input.

Lolly was being seen by a male psychology intern at the counseling center at the University of South Carolina. After two sessions, the intern requested a consultation with a staff psychologist because he felt that the therapy had reached some sort of impasse—that he did not seem to be connecting with his client.

Even though this was technically an individual therapy, the consultant's entrance into the therapeutic system was very much like an entrance into an entire family system. This was partly because, in a very real sense, Lolly had brought her extended family into the therapy. It was also the case because Lolly had, in effect, made her therapist a family member.

The consultant's initial efforts to investigate and begin to stimulate a resolution of the impasse in this situation were to request that the therapist trainee talk about his position in the therapeutic system. This, in itself, created greater flexibility within the system simply because it gave both the trainee and the client permission to talk about something that had previously been covert.

The consultant next made use of Lolly's genogram and helped her decide where the trainee would best fit in. Lolly placed the trainee in her children's generation. Within the context of a discussion of the reasons for and appropriateness of this placement, it became clear that Lolly was feeling a reluctance to burden the trainee/son with problems he might not have experience with. That is to say, she was attempting to take care of her therapist in much the same way she was attempting to care for and manage everyone else in her family.

Having thus "uncovered" the relationship that existed between the trainee and his client, the consultant next had to create a way for the relationship to be able to transform itself into one that was more likely to produce therapeutic change. The consultant chose to use a little light-hearted humor, as illustrated by the following exchange:

"You know, your therapist is from California," the consultant observed. "Most of his family live in California. You could be his South Carolina mother if you want."

"Oh, I think I would like that," Lolly quickly responded.

"You could bake him some cookies or something," the consultant suggested.

The suggestion about baking cookies was humorous for both the trainee and the client. It was essentially a way to draw attention to the implications of the age differences (generational differences) of the trainee and the client. It appeared to help Lolly to see more clearly the difficulty she experienced in relationships that were interdependent in comparison to those where she was depended upon.

The trainee's experience of the consultant's intervention was that the humor and the discussion around it provided a way for both him and the client to develop more flexibility around their roles in therapy. This happened as a result of their increased understanding of their roles which the consultant's interventions provided, coupled with the "permission" they had been given to talk about their relationship. Furthermore, it seemed as though the consultant's suggestions about baking cookies was a way of exaggerating the relationship between the trainee and his client in a way that opened up possibilities for change:

It was as though the humor emphasized or drew attention to what we were doing in a way similar to what happens when an experientially oriented therapist suggests to a client that he or she exaggerate a physical movement in order to see more clearly—or understand more clearly—what it means. Suddenly it was okay for us to relate to one another in that way; after it was okay we knew we could go past that way of relating to something more productive.

CONCLUSION

What we have attempted to do in this chapter is to discuss the value of consultation from a trainee's point of view. The examples presented here have been intended to illustrate the special impact that a consultation can have on a trainee's development as a professional. We believe, in fact, that consultation is important enough to the process of professional development that it should not only be a part of clinical training, but also be included in the curriculum of students preparing for their internship experiences.

It is certainly true that ordinary supervision has the potential to provide a trainee with a more "meta" level of looking at his or her therapeutic process. However, consultation presents a meta-view of the process in a much more graphic and dramatic form. The message is unfurled before the trainee's eyes—in the room with the clients and in the moment of therapy. The inherent drama and immediacy of consultation is what makes it such a memorable and effective training method.

The lessons we carry with us the longest after our formal training has come to an end are most likely to be the ones that involved us most in a dramatically experiential way. Consultation is a training device that has the greatest potential for that.

16

Increasing Mastery: The Effects of the Workshop Consultation on the Consultee

Mary Hotvedt

In America we have the long-standing tradition of the road show, a traveling cavalcade for entertainment, religion, sales, and education. For the last two hundred years, Chatauqua speakers, opera singers, and circuit riders have brought culture to the hinterlands, connecting the more rural areas with the East Coast cities and with Europe, if even for a brief time. As America has become more sophisticated, so have the road shows. Now they are tailored for specific professional audiences. There is still a freshness and immediacy, even in this age of electronic communication, to seeing an artist or expert with a gathering of the community.

Perhaps more than any other field, psychotherapy makes use of the road show for continuing education. An integral part of the visit of a well-known expert psychotherapist, particularly a family therapist, is the live case consultation. In this format, the master therapist works with a family from the community, usually brought by another therapist who has been seeing them. The object is for the audience to view the process and art of the expert, to see principle made into practice, and to enhance their own clinical skills. Since therapy is such a highly variant, interactive, and relatively private activity, observation of the process is an essential part of training and continuing development.

This chapter will focus on the reactions and interpretations of five therapists in Tucson, Arizona, and the relevance of an expert consultation to their work. Each of them presented a case for live demonstration as part of three different two-day workshops held in that city. The workshops took place in 1986, 1988, and 1991. The consultant was Maurizio Andolfi, M.D. The presenting therapists were interviewed within three months to two years following each workshop.

In his book, *The Theory and Practice of Mental Health Consultation*, Caplan (1970) defines consultation as a combination of *"help* plus *education"* (p. 23). Consultation, in his model, differs from supervision or teaching in that there is a symmetrical, rather than hierarchical, relationship between consultant and consultee. "...[T]he consultee is continually free to come and go and to accept or reject" (p. 23). Likewise, consultation differs from therapy for the consultee because it also lacks the hierarchy of the doctor-patient relationship.

> This does not mean that the consultant is unaware of the emotional reactions of the consultee, and that he (sic) is blind to distortions of perception or of professional behavior resulting from them. In certain types of consultation...he is particularly sensitive to these issues; but he deals with them nonverbally and by the way in which he chooses to discuss relevant aspects of the client's case, never by uncovering the consultee's private problems or by interpreting the connections between these and the professional difficulty (Caplan, 1970, p. 25).

Caplan (1970) makes a further distinction between case-centered and consultee-centered consultation, the former being an emphasis on the client's situation and the latter on the role of the therapist, either with that case or in parallel instances. To some degree, this distinction is blurred in the live consultation with a family and a therapist in the middle of a workshop. The live consultation becomes an amalgam of both; the consultant often explains, in didactic sessions surrounding the actual family session, his/her theories and ideology not only about families and mental health but also about the position and movement of the therapist. Throughout the demonstrations and following discussion, there is shift and interplay between these two facets of therapeutic thinking. The consultee, focused initially on the presented case, may not see broader implications for his/her professional self until later—even months later. This is appropriate if the consultant has maintained the symmetrical relationship with the consultee and only obliquely addressed the personal issues that may influence the therapy (as discussed above).

The consultant, Maurizio Andolfi, has put great emphasis on the nature of the involvement of the therapist in constructing and moving the therapeutic system. The therapist, in his model, is seen as creating, dissolving, and reconnecting various therapeutic alliances with individual family members throughout the course of the therapy. This use of self, shift of role, and relatively active stance allow the therapist to "act...as a catalyst in the search for new relational connections which can give different meaning to the family reality as a whole" (Andolfi & Angelo, 1988, p. 246).

Andolfi, in his international practicum, has developed a form of consultee-centered work called the "handicap intervention" (Haber, 1990). Attendees at the month-long practicum are experienced therapists working together away from their usual contexts. Each participant is encouraged to present to the group a view of his/her own most common impasse in therapy. Andolfi and the practicum group may accept the impasse or help each therapist redefine it. A role play is devised by the group to implode the "handicap" and to help the therapist develop new insight and behavior around the issue. The work is intense but, as in Caplan's model, highly respectful of the personal life or problems of the therapist. Haber notes, in the only in-print description of the handicap intervention:

> Although Andolfi employed the term "professional handicap" to depict a characterological limitation of one's professional work, it is not intended to be pejorative of the trainee. Rather, this work encourages and appreciates those who are willing to reflect on how their personhood contributes to and distracts from the therapeutic process. (Haber, 1990, p. 375)

Andolfi does not seek to recreate the handicap intervention session in the live case consultation. To the contrary, he has held that this method was most appropriate in the international practicum, which allowed for freer self-exposure. Nonetheless, Andolfi, as a systemic and experiential therapist, has been highly concerned with the position and experience of the therapist in the family and therapeutic systems (Andolfi & Angelo, 1988). Most of the consultees interviewed for this chapter expressed how the consultation gave them insight into themselves as therapists, in a manner similar to the handicap intervention.

THE CONSULTEES AND THEIR CASES

Usually, problematic cases and issues are addressed within the bond of trust between the consultee and a more experienced supervisor, colleague, or training group. The workshop format is a much higher-risk setting for seeking consultation. For the local therapist, there is the exposure in front of an audience of peers. For the family he/she brings, in addition to the audience exposure, there is the lack of continuity in the therapeutic setting. For both, there is the promise and the peril of the expert's consultation. The motivations of the consultees and the process by which they were selected will be discussed, along with a brief profile of each therapist and a description of the family and their presenting issues.

Dr. Schuller and the Angry Boy's Family

Dr. Schuller is a psychiatrist, now specializing in therapy with children and adolescents. At the time of consultation, he was in his residency, finishing a rotation at a private psychiatric hospital. Dr. Schuller, prior to his psychiatric training, was an experienced family practice physician.

I was asked by one of the organizers to bring a family at which point I got in free. It was my first year in practice ...they were looking for a case (from the sponsoring hospital) and it just happened that I was working with this child at the time. I thought it would be interesting to see how someone else approached this problem.

The family he presented consisted of a 13-year-old boy, his mother, and his father. The "identified patient" was hospitalized for a conduct disorder. There had been mainly individual therapy, between Dr. Schuller and the boy, with one or two family meetings in a three-week period.

The 13-year-old was brought into the hospital for acting-out behavior. He would have temper tantrums, fits of rage. He would suddenly run from the house. Then there was one episode that I recall where he and his family were going through Winter Haven and he didn't want to be going and he just became angry and started yelling and screaming and it ended up getting to a point where his father had to sit on him to prevent him from running away. That was sort of the last straw for the family and they decided to bring him back. When he was on the ward he would be very pleasant and cooperative until he didn't get something that he wanted and his behavior would rapidly escalate to the point where they had to put him in seclusion, hold him down. He was threatening to leave the hospital. He grabbed a telephone from one of the staff people and tried to hit him with the telephone.

Ms. James and the "Green" Family

Ms. James is a Master's level counselor now in private practice. She has worked in public agencies and Employee Assistance Programs. At the time of the consult, she was in the early stages of a private practice.

Her case involved a woman in a live-in relationship (the I.P.), her boyfriend, and her two children, a daughter (13) and a son (10). The mother was suffering a great deal of anxiety, mostly around the safety and whereabouts of her children, since relocating from the midwest. She was widowed. Her husband, the children's father, had died in a car crash in Ohio.

Most of the sessions Ms. James had before the consultation were with the mother only.

Andolfi came in March or April. I had seen the woman five or six times and met her boyfriend once or twice and met her children probably once or twice. She came to me on her own, originally because she was having anxiety attacks. She had recently moved here from a small town and was seeing a male psychiatrist that she was very unhappy with. She needed medication and she needed therapy but she didn't want to go back to him, and so she was really nervous about coming to me because it was changing therapists and because she was nervous anyway. Her most severe presenting problem was what she described as heart palpitations that would start in her throat when she got scared and she couldn't breathe, and then real fear would set in and she thought she was going to die. So as a result, she hardly left the house, she felt alienated in this town, she felt like she was alienating her family who were sick of her problems.

Dr. Barnett and the "Two Worlds" Family

Dr. Barnett is a marriage and family therapist in private practice. An experienced clinician and teacher at the time of the consult, Dr. Barnett had just retired from the university. He was focusing on his practice and the family therapy institute of which he was a co-founder.

The family Dr. Barnett brought for consultation was a mother, father, and adult son. The son (the I.P.) was the center of an ongoing debate between the parents. The father saw the son's behavior, in and out of the home, as the result of maternal overindulgence. The mother thought her son was mentally ill and in need of help.

Dr. Barnett remembered, "Our training institute cosponsored the event with the hospital, so we felt responsible to provide a family." He had seen Dr. Andolfi work before.

There were other siblings, but the case specifically was a man and woman in their 50s, a mother and father that is, and a son who was in his early 20s. The man, the father, was from Europe originally. He immigrated here and was quickly drafted into the United States Army as a welcome to American citizenship. It was while he was in the service that he met his wife. The woman was very much his junior, I forget exactly but I think she was 15, and he was 21. He wooed her and married her. She was from a French Canadian family. The family migrated from Canada to the United States and so they both had some old country emphasis.

The presenting problem was that they were fighting a lot and the subject of their fighting was that she would not let go of her son whom she had classified, with some therapist agreeing, as mentally ill. He had been, she said, clinically diagnosed as manic-depressive and his argument, the father's argument, was that the kid was irresponsible and had never learned how to work, would not hold a job, and was on his mother's apron strings, so to speak, and so he wanted the kid to grow up and get out on his own. The mother said the kid is sick, he can't go out on his own until he is well, and they argued interminably on this.

Dr. Ibanez and the Family that Lost Men

Dr. Ibanez is a psychologist and experienced marriage and family therapist. She has now, as at the time of the consultation, a private practice.

Her case involved a divorced woman and her adolescent daughter (16). Another child, a son (19), was living on his own. Most sessions had been with mother and/or daughter. The son had attended one session. He was not present for the consult.

This mother and daughter had experienced a great deal of pain through separations. The first husband, father of the children, had left when they were young. The second husband had brought his two children into the marriage. When he left, the mother of his two children took custody and broke all contact. So the family was immediately cut in half. It was very bad for both the mother and daughter because they were close to the stepchildren. The daughter began to act out with delinquent behavior.

The daughter had just come out of a year's residential treatment in a group home here for girls, and she was doing much better. I was the follow-up treatment for this girl with her mother. The mother and daughter were sliding back into old patterns of high conflict. The first month or so when she was out, everything seemed pretty fine, and then the daughter wouldn't come home, and the mother would assume that she was out drinking and doing everything she used to do, so the conflict level was really growing between them.

Dr. Halverson and the Navaho's Family

Dr. Halverson is a marriage and family therapist. At the time of the consult, as now, she was in private practice.

I chose to present a case because I organized the workshop. I had attended the month-long practicum with Andolfi in Rome the previous year. I wanted to present a "risky" case, one where I had good joining but was stuck.

The family consisted of an older man (59), his wife (39), and their two sons, ages 21 and 16. Both the parents had chronic pain and limited mobility. Only the younger son was living at home, and he was the identified problem. The older son, following in his father's footsteps, was in the military. The younger son had been depressed, had suicidal thoughts, and was not doing well in school. He was having severe headaches.

I had seen the family together, the parents alone, and the son alone. The son hardly talked in sessions with his parents. His anger and frustration at school, parents, brother, and himself came out only in solo sessions. All three of them came for the consultation with Andolfi.

LIVE, ON STAGE

The format of the case demonstrations was similar in all cases. Dr. Andolfi and the consultee met first, in front of the audience, to discuss the therapy to date. This was usually brief, no more than 20 minutes. Dr. Andolfi's questions usually centered on the therapists' self-perception of their own familial roles within the clients' family, rather than on the expected clinical picture of the case. He also asked how the therapist had decided on presenting this particular family and the help the therapist needed.

> *Dr. Halverson*: I was surprised when Andolfi asked me what sort of relative I was to the Navaho's family. I think I tried to avoid choosing, defining myself. I said I was the mother's sister. He asked me, 'Which one? Older or younger?' I felt a little pinned down.
>
> Later, the next session with the family, this made a certain sense with me. As the mother's sister, I had less power and influence even than she, in this struggle between father and son. But I was also less likely to upset this father who had written off and been written off by his own mother.

This initial approach is consistent with Andolfi's "handicap" model. He is initially most interested in the material of the I.P. or the issues that the family provokes in the therapist that lead to the consultation. "As a relational being, the therapist becomes a part of the family set and assumes and/or receives a position in the family genogram..." (Haber, 1990). Unlike the handicap sessions, done in the international training experience, the consultee is initially presenting a problematic case, not necessarily a perceived professional impasse. However, in the course of the session, some of the therapists began to see ways in which they might have been limiting themselves.

> *Dr. Schuller*: I was really involved with this angry boy. I saw him as coming from the other end of the spectrum of dealing with his feelings than I was. I keep my feelings in and he acts out, so there was a part of me that was really attracted to this young man who could be so passionate and angry with his feelings...It looked like he was doing the same thing to the father. I wasn't aware of that until the case consult.

Sometimes the clients expressed surprise, in their next visit with the therapist, that the therapist was so silent after turning the case over to the expert. The ability to sit rather quietly during the consultation session, coupled with the opening questions, allowed the therapists interviewed to see their cases with new eyes:

> *Ms. James*: What struck me was how he was able to, instead of focusing on the woman in the "Green" Family, which is what I

had been doing, focus on everyone but her. He didn't ignore her, but he focused on the homesickness of the children.

Dr. Barnett: I felt more like he was doing the work and I was watching. I was on the edge, and I could watch him climb inside and pull out different things from these folks.

Dr. Schuller was articulate as to the self-awareness he experienced in the consultations with the Angry Boy's Family:

I didn't have time to feel anxious and so it all worked out well. What stood out for me was that I felt threatened by Andolfi. I felt he was describing the father as a weak, wilted person....He referred to me as soft (in the pre-session consultation) and he referred to the father as being soft. ...It was a real mixed feeling. I didn't like it. Here was this Italian, macho kind of guy telling me that I was a pushover. I didn't fall apart. I figured I had some things to learn from the experience and I think I value the softer side of my personality....My fantasy was that the father experienced a lot of the same feelings that I did...He was viewed as being weak and emasculated and that came across in how soft his voice was. I thought that Andolfi needed to bring that up and show him that he needed to be stronger.

He also learned a lesson that he has carried into his current clinical work:

The other thing that struck me was the contrast between Andolfi's attitude toward involving the family and the hospital's, which was to isolate the boy from the family and deal with him as if he had the problem. I felt this aggravated things and I remember feeling almost ashamed of the hospital for having done this, because I saw how quickly Andolfi got to the core issues by having everyone together. In whatever time you spend on stage, he had a much clearer picture of what was going on and how to resolve the problems than we ever did working alone with the child. You know, seeing that outweighed some of the insecurities that I may have had about being too soft.

In the handicap session, Andolfi frequently works with "the parts of the story that seem to be missing, such as the trainee's position in various triads within the therapeutic system or the trainee's family of origin" (Haber, 1990). Likewise, in the consultation sessions, Andolfi often focused on what or who was missing from the session. This incorporation of other elements, those not seen, allowed the therapists to see an expansion of the system and the family story.

Dr. Halverson: Andolfi seemed to become fascinated by the disappearance of the father's mother. The father is half-Native American and half-French Basque. His mother, after his father's death, returned to France and refused to visit her grandchildren. Years would go by between letters. The father was nonchalant about his mother's emotional and physical distance. The father identified with his father's tribe, but not with his mother's side.

At first I thought Andolfi was being almost romantically drawn to this strange piece in the family story. But then I began to think, maybe this tells something about how this father keeps his own son from being close. Maybe this tells something about how he keeps me from getting too close to what troubles him also.

Healing for the family centered on the incorporating of those absent people:

Dr. Ibanez: He had the girl practice, right there, calling the estranged brother and trying to convince him to come in. She actually went out and made the phone call, and he wasn't there. I thought that was really potent....He really empowered the daughter...in having her make that phone call.

In another consultation, Andolfi's absent figure was a place, not a person; he focused on the homesick feelings of the children in the "Green" Family.

Ms. James: He said there wasn't enough room in the family to breathe, and that they missed the green of Ohio, that they needed to create more greenery for themselves.

Place was also an important metaphor for joining with the "Two Worlds" family. Andolfi built on the homesickness of the man, a gardener, for the beauty of his native land, and for the difficulty the husband and the wife, French-Canadian, had in understanding each other's background.

Dr. Barnett: He (Andolfi) could understand what it was like to be new to this country, how confusing it was; what her ancestry must mean to the wife; and how the kid must have felt. My big hope was that he would enlarge the system and, with metaphor, get them unstuck.

The therapists were asked in interview to describe the subsequent therapy with the families they had brought, and the effect of the consultation for their work. In four out of the five cases, therapy ended very quickly after the consultation. This was interesting, given that only one family, the "Two Worlds" family, expressed dissatisfaction with the consultation. In Dr. Schuller's case, the end of his rotation brought about termination, but the case of the Angry Boy's family was referred on to another family therapist. The other two families, Dr. Halverson's and Dr. Ibanez's, came for only a few more sessions and felt satisfied, according to the therapists, with the therapy and the consultation. Ms. James worked with the "Green" Family a long while, and brought in a cotherapist later when she felt stuck again.

What about the impasses that the therapists themselves felt with their cases? What was their perception of the effect of the consultation for their own work?

Dr. Barnett: The consultation with the "Two Worlds" Family gave me a 'left-hand boost'. I felt a little less guilty or inept as a therapist. There was a kind of consolation. I think the most important thing I learned was to not oppose the presenting analysis or the two presenting analyses of the clients. It made me aware that I want to watch out and sidestep standoffs and go on from there. I think it would have been stressful to continue with the family. Part of the stress would have been the amount of philosophical differences between the hospital's and Andolfi's approaches. I had also felt I got a lot of positive feedback and support from others in the audience, and that helped me not to worry about being too soft or mushy.

Dr. Ibanez: I learned, out of doing the consult with the Family That Lost Men, the whole potency of pulling in more people and not letting the family shut me out. Although I have the attitude that I can pretty well tackle most people, I never had tried to get the brother back into the sessions. I realized there were certain things I'd let go of that I didn't have to let go. So I have a kind of new energy to go forward.

Dr. Halverson: After the consult with the Navaho's Family, I changed my position. I got much more involved with the father and the invisible French grandmother. The father was not comfortable at all with it, but the mother and son seemed cheered by my attempt. The boy became far more active and independent. I know he had setbacks, but he made it to living on his own. I learned to be less afraid of the real emotional power in the family. I had never seen how the power lay with the parts that were invisible.

Ms. James: The consult with the "Green" Family had a lot of impact for me. First, he encouraged me to continue building the connection with the boyfriend, that it was all right to use my personal style to do this.

Second, his work with metaphors really appealed to me. I was an English major, and I automatically did some of that: He took it one step beyond and made it more fun.

Some time after this interview, Ms. James followed through with a letter describing how she had returned to creative writing, her first interest, in addition to continuing her work as a therapist.

Andolfi kept using the metaphor "green" because these people had just moved to the desert from the midwest, and they were homesick. His metaphor described me, too. I was very "green" for them. "The Case of the Green Therapist." Instead of just writing about it, now I could focus on the mistakes. It wouldn't be so negative either. There is humor in the story. The family did not end up in ruin. They actually ended up back in Ohio. I can finally drop the grandiose idea that my therapy was harmful for them.

SUMMARY

There are, of course, differences among the therapists in their response to the consultations. There are, however, common themes as well.

All the therapists saw, through indirect method, both their professional strength and their "handicap" in the consultations. Consistent with the respect afforded the consultee in Caplan's (1970) model, Andolfi never directly challenged the therapist's interpretation, nor, consistent with his own model (1988), that of the families'.

Yet each therapist, in interview, presented a new viewpoint on his/her own skills—a "handicapable" position, similar to the outcome of a handicap session (Haber, 1990). Dr. Barnett, for example, learned he need not challenge the competing analyses the parents had over their son's mental health. Dr. Schuller felt his "softness" paralleled the father's response to the acting-out son; he felt threatened and also reassured about the value of his own approach. Ms. James learned to accept her "greenness" and be comfortable with her own creativity as a therapist. It was difficult not to continue the interviews, to go back and find out more about how the consultation is viewed, farther and farther out from the event. What did become clear, however, was that the impact for the therapists was less specific to the cases (their original focus) and more generalized to their own options as therapists.

REFERENCES

Andolfi, M. & Angelo, C. Toward constructing the therapeutic system. *Journal of Marital and Family Therapy*, 1988, 14, No. 3, 237–247.

Caplan, G. *The Theory and Practice of Mental Health Consultation*. New York: Basic Books, 1970.

Haber, R. From handicap to handy capable: Training systemic therapists in use of self. *Family Process*, 1990, No. 29, 375–384.

17

The Body as the Expert: Gender Perspective in Consultation with "Young" Therapists

Marcella de Nichilo

Transgenerational sculpting is a form of therapeutic art that centers on the body as the expert in highlighting those bonds that oppress and those that support growth in affective relationships (de Nichilo, 1992a). By affective relationships I mean commitments that are based on verbal and nonverbal communications that are inspired by tender feelings, modulated by empathic attitudes of mutual support, and acknowledged appreciation of differences.

Consultation provides an opportunity to influence such affective relationships. Here, inner needs, omissions, and unexpressed feelings are orchestrated in a chorus that includes the therapist, the various members of the family, the observing group, and the consultant. As a consultant, I encourage the participants to use their bodies both as a transactional message and as a transitional object; a resource for healing. What has been perceived as missing in the intra- and intergenerational patterns of communication can emerge in trigenerational sculpting. The person who sculpts will be asked to focus on a critical moment of the life cycle in which she or he felt more *oppressed* (if she is a female) or more *constrained* (if he is a male) by the belief system of the extended family.

When a system is dysfunctional, time is frozen in a dimension falsely considered as fixed and unchangeable. It is therefore crucial to see how the ideal self-image, the consensual role-image, or the repudiated[1] image activates fears of inadequacy and rage, which, in time, have become circular and self-reinforcing.

During my years of providing clinical training, I've found that very often therapists who are beginning their profession may be caught, despite their academic curriculum, in resistances or projective mechanisms similar to those of the family in treatment. This happens more frequently when therapists have some fixed functions that originate with their family of origin in common with a particular client or family. Under such conditions, both therapist and clients may be mirroring the impasse and feel caught in a trap. Feelings of impotence evoked in those situations reveal that neither the therapist nor the clients have yet overcome "unfinished business" with their families of origin.

Self-reliance is validated and promoted when the body is recognized as the protagonist in mirroring the unspoken story or the hidden culture of a family saga (Anzieu, 1985). The skin, being the widest organ of the body, can be acknowledged as the expert in decoding signals and highlighting ways out of the unbearable status quo. The sensory receptors, via the nervous system, inform the organism about how to accommodate the stimuli of the outside world (Montagu, 1971).

The skin, therefore, is a more primitive and direct life-force than reason, which is governed by societal norms and sanctions that regulate the behavior of males and females. Sexist assumptions and expectations, misogynist practices, and a debased or grandiose sense of self establish a dichotomy between the sexes to avoid complexity and to cover up inequality (Hare-Mustin & Mareck, 1990).

THE BODY IN INDIRECT CONSULTATION

In indirect consultation of therapeutic impasses, the body of the therapist provides an entrance into the rigidity of the family. My goal is to activate awareness of and competence in the process of transformation through sculpting as a metaphor of the internal world. Often, the sculpture elicits feelings from the past that can offer new choices about how to act on those feelings in the present. In this artistic as well as cathartic representation, the inside world built up by the sculptor as the architect becomes manifest first through the eloquent voice of the body,

---

[1]Vision of self that is first accepted and then denied.

then through verbalization and feedback. The work includes all the people who participate in the sculpture, in addition to the consultant and the observing group. I also use a helper, whose gender is opposite to that of the sculptor, to visualize the parts of the self that are "traditionally" negated and need instead to be amplified. For instance, assertiveness is expected in a male while caring is presumed to more adequately fit a female (Gianini-Bellotti, 1975). These conformist beliefs need to be confronted and evaluated in the therapeutic system as in the social domain.

When senses and perceptions are not well integrated, a large portion of language and information that come from the skin will be ignored or denied by means of distorted learning. Being a female family therapist, I consider the body to be a healthy language, which is a counterpart and balance to what the masculinization of our culture has repressed and mortified in both men and women through rationalization and blaming (de Nichilo, 1988).

STAGES OF INDIRECT CONSULTATION

The following are three basic stages of indirect consultation:

1. Presentation of the case when the family is not in session.
2. Sculpture of the deadlock s/he experiences in the senses in connection with some critical moments of her/his life that are similar to the impasse presented by the family in treatment.
3. After sculpting, the therapist focuses on the transformation process that s/he has gone through in order to help the family to overcome the difficulty in the session.

In the verbalization process that follows the sculpture, the consultee is asked to externalize either her/his sense of the void or of emotional rejuvenation that results from the analogic process. The achievements will be focused in three major areas:

1. The dysfunctional myths or rituals that have been perceived or assumed as the norm in both subsystems: the therapist's and the clients';
2. The stereotypes that have been preserved in the behavior or ideology in both subsystems;
3. The variations on a common theme or script that can be integrated on a clinical meta-level.

INDIRECT CONSULTATION WITH EMMA: SCULPTING AS A TRANSFORMATION PROCESS

Emma asked if I could help her in indirect consultation. She was stuck with a family she had seen three times. She felt ineffective and lacking authority. Her major difficulty, she said, was with one of her clients, Aunt Silvia, with whom she identified too much. Aunt Silvia was overprotective with her nephews. In session, Silvia called herself "the pump" of the family. Emma similarly felt overprotective of her brother, Paolino, who by now was 29 years old, and his family.

Although Emma identified mostly with Silvia, she was also aware of her problem with authority (Ault-Riché, 1988), which dated back to when she was a teenager. Her impasse was rooted in her family of origin and in her relationship with her own father.

Emma expressed the desire to use sculpting in consultation as a clarifying technique to uncover the hidden culture of her family of origin as well as her own ambivalence with the client family. Her goal was to be more alert and skillful both on the personal and professional level. I considered her a talented and sensitive therapist. I expressed my commitment by saying: "I'll do my best to help you *to add* what is needed to feel more at ease with your own self and with the family in treatment. I think *we* will learn a lot in the process." In front of the observing group and the one-way mirror, I asked her to show her impasse with the client family through using her own body as the metaphor for her definition of the therapeutic system.

Emma sculpted herself as "a piston." The piston is a mechanism that moves back and forth by the pressure of a fluid so as to transmit reciprocating motion. Her mouth, her arms, and her legs became the piston. Later, she explained how she felt exhausted by playing the piston as if her role as therapist was that of moving up and down, repeating the same moves without moving forward. In particular, Emma said she was frustrated at not being able to elicit "nodal points" (Andolfi, Angelo & de Nichilo, 1989) and introduce new information in the family perceptual schema.

I asked her where she liked to start working. She said: "With my own family."

Emma's Family

Emma is a single therapist, 33 years of age. She was born in a small town in Calabria (Southern Italy) from a rather poor family. From the genogram, it appeared that her mother, Maria, was the only female child in a family of three boys. Both her grandparents were sharecroppers and worked night and day to provide food for their children. The whole family was bound by mutual care and affection. From the representation Emma gave of her extended family, it appeared the family lacked clear boundaries.

When her mother was a child, the whole neighborhood was very cohesive. Since her grandparents worked in the fields from dawn to dusk, Emma's mother and her brothers had grown up either in the streets playing with their peer group under the eyes of friendly neighbors or helping their parents take care of the crops.

Emma's mother, Maria, was the second born. When Maria was 17, she had started working as a part-time maid for well-to-do people who lived in the neighboring town. She was beautiful, cheerful and caring for everybody. She loved to sing. Courage was her main quality.

When she was 19, she became pregnant with Emma. Emma's father, Pietro, was a rich man, the son of Maria's employers. He was 15 years older than Maria, married, with two children. Pietro had never legitimized Emma, although he had provided for her education and met her once a month at the house of a close friend.

Four years after Emma's birth, Maria had another relationship with a man from out of town. Their relationship did not last. From this relationship, Paolino, Emma's brother was born. Maria, in spite of her difficult life as a single woman, never contemplated the possibility of having an abortion. She always said she couldn't say no to a new creature she had conceived. She always told Emma that the only man she had been deeply in love with was Pietro. Her extended family had helped Maria in taking care of her two children, whom they loved dearly. Pietro provided for Emma's education by sending her to the best schools and University.

I asked her to show nonverbally a critical moment of her own life-cycle when she felt most oppressed as a female by the belief system of her family of origin. She could use the members of the observing group as pieces of clay. The group said they were willing to collaborate and learn from her as she could learn from them.

I asked Emma to choose, one by one, members from the group who could represent significant members of her family of origin, according to the principle of assimilation. I also asked her to locate each of them according to:

1. space-distance;
2. posture;
3. affective quality;
4. eye contact.

I also invited a male helper to work with Emma and myself as a vicarious figure who would replace Emma in the sculpting after she had taken her place inside her trigenerational family presentation.

After thinking for a few minutes, Emma said she was 13 years old. Her mother had died a year before. It was Sunday. She represented herself sitting at the table. Her father was standing behind her and pouring "rosolio"—a sweet liqueur he had made with his own hands—to please her. Their host was sitting at the head of the table.

Through her body she expressed stiffness and uneasiness, being torn in a conflict between the need to perform the ritual of meeting her father once a month on Sundays and her desire to be with her little brother, Paolino, who was then nine. After her mother's death, she had protected Paolino as if she were an "old" aunt, even though she herself was a teenager.

In the sculpture, Paolino was inviting her to play and calling her at a close distance, smiling. Further away, facing herself, Emma located the empty chair of her dead mother, Maria. Maria was surrounded by her brothers, parents, and neighbors who waved at her in a tribal celebration where touching, laughing, singing, and crying were validated.

Emma showed herself oppressed and paralyzed at the impersonal banquet table as if she were half-dead. Her arm and hand were compelled in the automation of picking up the food she hated. She was incapable of overtly saying no to her father or otherwise displeasing him. She could not look her father directly in his eyes.

When the male helper replaced Emma in the sculpture, the scene changed. He accidentally spilled the father's liqueur on the table, cutting the ritual and later verbalizing anger towards the father. He unleashed the anger that Emma had buried inside herself, afraid of desecrating her mother's romantic love for her father, or her own obligation towards him as a provider.

The internal world of Emma, which had come out from the condensation and visualization process of sculpting as a therapeutic technique, focused on perceptual change. Sculpting was followed by feedback and comments by the members of the observing group.

Emma verbalized her feelings, saying her sight was veiled while she was sitting at the table. Her neck was stiff and her legs felt as heavy as iron under her boarding-school uniform. She felt the "impending mandate" that she could not disobey her mother's expectation to be good, while she was hiding contempt and rage for her "coward" father.

Through the expressiveness of the body, Emma had become aware of her extended family's dysfunctional myths and rituals:

1. Her mother's overidealized image of her father;
2. Her family's consensual image or stereotype: "You need to be good and submissive";
3. The negated part of self: anger for lack of recognition.

The male helper had visualized Emma's alter ego or the buried feelings she had covered up for years. She felt a strong desire to face her father and talk to him without feeling submissive. Parallel to this need was Emma's awareness to stop worrying about her brother, Paolino, who by now was 29, married, and the father of a rather hyperactive eight-year-old son. As the observing group pointed out, Emma, since she was born, seemed to have assumed the role of the old aunt[2], who sacrificed her vital needs as a female and instead overprotected her mother, brother and natural father.

Through the analogic process of sculpting, Emma had become aware of some dysfunctional myths and rituals belonging to her extended family. However, she was also able to praise the affectional and caretaking attitude of her extended family as a viable, exquisite human quality.

THE CASE AFTER INDIRECT CONSULTATION

The subsequent session of the case began in a dramatic fashion because Silvia (sister of Mario, her brother, and aunt of his two teenage boys, Adriano and Fabrizio) has just found out that her two nephews have been taking drugs for a year. Luisa, the mother of the boys, left Mario and the children when they were very young. Mario and Luisa had never married. Silvia has helped the grandmother (her mother) parent the boys. She felt like a mother to these boys and treated them like her own children, although she had her own family and grown-up kids. She was angry with her brother because he has been an absent and largely neglectful father except for giving them money that actually served to support their drug usage.

In the session following the consultation, the therapist, Emma, was able to assert her authority by requesting that the family deal with painful issues and by separating enmeshed units with competence and caring. She used her own personal story and body as tools for change. Her clear view of her overinvolvement with her brother, Paolino, intensified her power of resonance in expressing personal feelings. Her con-

---

[2]In the Italian tradition, the aunt who is unmarried and without children frequently dedicates her life to taking care of everybody else in the family at the expense of her own needs.

frontation with her personal past counterbalanced her fears of impending doom and failure in the client family.

After listening to Silvia's futile attempts to help the family by blaming her brother and by trying to create a protective environment for the boys, Emma asserted her catalytic position in the therapy session by standing, looking directly at the boys, and announcing:

Therapist: Mother heroin seems to be your foster mother. But you have a biological mother. Where is she?
Brother: She seems to be living in Milan. I have written her many times, but there is never an answer.
Therapist: Who wants to try again? Who wants to take the risk?

Silvia moves in her chair. She is ready to help. Emma stops her with a motion of her hand. She brings a toy scale to her, puts an arm around Silvia's shoulder, and while looking straight into Silvia's eyes, she says:

Therapist: See, here is a scale. We must work together to make it even. Too much is too much. You are an excellent mother in your family. But you can not take a space that is not your own. You are Aunt Silvia, not Adriano's and Fabrizio's mother. You can help them as a loving aunt. But, if you take a place that is not your own, you are no longer a human being, Silvia. You are a useless "pump".

I have felt like you in my own family. I felt as if I was a piston, pressing up and down all the time. It's an unpleasant feeling that does not really help. Let's share the feeling. We can sit together and wait. It's difficult for me too. Yet we can take our portion of risk. (*Looking to the other family members*) Who can take care of the unbalanced scale?

After the indirect consultation with me, Emma has been able to enhance authority, separating unmeshed units with competence and caring, using her own personal story and body as tools for change. She has been able to show how teaching and learning are a reciprocal process where *we* become essential. The common denominator lies in the desire to help each other in a more affectionate way: reliance on each other's potential and need to rest facing turmoil in a more effective way (de Nichilo, 1988).

Emma knows she has been sharing common themes with her client family: refusal, fear of abandonment, overprotection. Yet she knows by now, as Lévi-Strauss points out (Lévi-Strauss, 1981), that myths and homeostatic events never repeat themselves as they were. There are variations on the theme such as straying from the "good path," mutinies and secrets that may become pathways for change when used properly.

By pointing out "the missing spots" of the pattern that connects, the therapist, as a woman, has been able to highlight "common denominators" between her personal experience and the client family. This exposition of self strengthens responsibilities and differentiates Emma in her relationship to the client family (Jordan, Kaplan, Baker-Miller, Stiven & Surrey, 1991). In the therapeutic system, Emma feels empowered and connected as she discovered more of her own voice.

Therapist: How was Luisa's family?
Mario: I don't know. She never introduced me. (*Silence*)

Adriano's eyes pause on Daddy. Mario's face is flushing. His eyes are fixed on the scale. Fabrizio is looking at the floor in silence.

Therapist: Let's imagine somebody writes a letter to Mommy. What will be in it?
Mario: I would like to ask her why she left me.
Therapist: How was Luisa's family?
Mario: I don't know. She never introduced me. (*Silence*) Maybe Luisa has not been able to be a mother because she has never been a daughter. She was frightened by her parents. They never understood her. Both of us were very young then.
Therapist: (*to the boys*): What would you say to her?
Adriano: Maybe we are to blame...
Fabrizio: I would like to know how she lives.
Therapist: (*to Mario*): If you can take a second risk, you may feel more rewarded than when you give money to your kids. Now you can give them a different gift. You can tell them the story of your love for Luisa and Luisa's love for you.
Mario: Yes, we have loved each other a lot.

Emma moves towards the window and opens it. Sun from the outside comes into the therapy room. Emma sits back close to Silvia.

Therapist: It's warm outside. Maybe Grandmother can rest.
Silvia: I don't know if Mario and the kids can rest. I'm worried.
Therapist: Just a moment, Silvia. Instead of worrying, we can listen to them. They will tell us.
Mario: The season is good. I can go to the park with the boys.

Fabrizio: I would like to go to a quiet park. Remember when we used to go to the lake at Villa Borghese?

Mario: You were little then.

Adriano: We can sit on the grass.

Mario: I can bring pen and paper. What can you bring?

Adriano: We can bring ourselves.

Mario: We can share stories, we can write words.

Fabrizio: And if she doesn't answer?

Mario: Writing together is more important. Together as in the old times. When I wore pants and you wore diapers.

Therapist: If you like, you can bring a copy of this letter to me. We can read it together. Another copy will be mailed to Luisa. Mario you keep the original.

CONCLUSION

The metaphor of the piston and the use of the body are bridges that challenge sterile, gender stereotypes. The therapist's body is a vehicle to uncover knowledge of the self and of our clients. The emotional and physiological experiencing of this knowledge in the consultative sculpture provides a new language for the therapist to consider when in clinical sessions. Furthermore, the therapist learns that the body and the self can be our own personal consultant in our clinical sessions. The body becomes the *mirror* and the *lighthouse* that sheds light on new roads.

ACKNOWLEDGMENTS

I am indebted to Virginia Satir (1967), "the Mother of family therapy," who expressed her firm belief in the body as a resource for healing. My article (1993) restropectively acknowledges her evolutionary significance to our field. I also would like to acknowledge Peggy Papp, Olga Silverstein, and Elizabeth Carter (1973), whose article and demonstrations have inspired my use of sculpting in clinical practice. I (de Nichilo, 1989) have extended the work of these creative women by including families-of-origin sculpting in supervision, consultation, and training.

I want to thank Emma, the therapist, for the trust she has in me and for the work we have been able to do and elaborate together. I also greatly appreciate the comments and contributions of Elizabeth Ridgely in the preparation of this chapter.

REFERENCES

Andolfi, M., Angelo, C. & de Nichilo, M. (1989). *The Myth of Atlas: Families and the Therapeutic Story.* New York: Brunner/Mazel.

Anzieu, D. (1985). *Le moi-peau.* Paris: Bordas.

Ault-Riché, M. (1988). Teaching an integrated model of family therapy: Women as students, women as supervisors. In L. Braverman (Ed.), *A Guide to Feminist Family Therapy.* New York: Harrington Park Press.

de Nichilo, M. (1988). Crisi di coppia tra pseudomutualità e emancipazione (Couples in crisis between pseudomutuality and emancipation). In M. Andolfi & C. Saccu (Eds.), *La coppia in crisi.* Roma: Instituto di Terapia Familiare.

de Nichilo, M. (1989). La vita abiurata: Studio sulla rinuncia femminile attraverso la scultura dei miti e dei riti familiari (Abdications of female well-being: A study on transgenerational myths and rituals). In *Atti della I Conferenza Internazionale sul disagio psichico della donna.* Roma: Consiglio Nazionale delle Recerche.

de Nichilo, M. (1992a). Il ruolo della donna terapista: Prospettive di cambiamento nel sistema terapeutico familiare (The role of the woman therapist: Perspective of change in the family therapy system). In M. Andolfi & C. Saccu (Eds.), *La famiglia tra patolgia e sviluppo.* Roma: Istituto di Terapia Familiare.

de Nichilo, M. (1992b). L'approccio evolutivo di Virginia Satir alla famiglia: una retrospettiva (The growth-approach of Virginia Satir to the family: a retrospective). *Psicologia, Psicosomatica, e Psicodiagnostica della Donna,* 1, 36–41.

de Nichilo, M. (1993). L'approccio evolutivo di Virginia Satir: Una retrospettiva. *Terapia Familiare.*

Gianini-Bellotti, E. (1975). *Dalla parte delle bambine.* Roma: Feltrinelli.

Hare-Mustin, R. & Mareck, J. (1990). *Making a Difference: Psychology and the Construction of Gender.* New Haven: Yale University Press.

Jordan, J.V., Kaplan, A.G., Baker-Miller, J., Stiven, P.I., & Surrey, J. (1991). *Women's Growth in Connection.* New York: The Guilford Press.

Lévi-Strauss, C. (1981). *Introduction to a Science of Mythology* series. New York: Harper and Row.

Montagu, A. (1971). *Touching: The Human Significance of the Skin.* New York: Columbia University Press.

Papp, P., Silverstein, O., & Carter, E.A. (1973). Family sculpting in preventive work with "well families." *Family Process,* 12, 197–212.

Satir, V. (1967). *Conjoint Family Therapy.* Palo Alto: Science and Behavior Books.

Name Index

Subject Index

Abuse: child, 48; physical, 221; sexual, 221, 229; substance, 132–141, 229

Addictions, 132–141

Adolescent(s): accessibility of, 78–79; judgments of, 84; separation, 118

Algorithms, 94, 95

Alienation, 35, 36

Alliances: with children, 77; cross-system, 167; formation of, 9; therapeutic, 57, 103; therapist, 15, 16

Ambivalence, 35, 78, 104

Anxiety, 16, 84, 90, 91, 92, 97, 166, 168, 226, 227; changing focus of, 102; containing, 230; group, 98; in impasses, 15; separation, 83; uneven, 102, 103

Authority: acceptance of, 41; figures, 67; given to consultant, 49; personal, 25

Autonomy, 114, 125

Avoidance, 141, 164, 175, 212

Behavior: antisocial, 80; complementary, 15, 16; dependent, 12; destructive, 77; dysfunctional, 119; group, 97; modified, 13; motivation for, 18; outside family context, 120; pathologic, 77; patterns, 94, 95; regressive, 77; school-based, 225; social, 119; stereotypes in, 276; symmetrical, 15; symptomatic, 75; of therapist, 182

Bisociation, 190

Boundaries, 167, 175, 217; around therapeutic experience, 68; confusion with, 82; rigid, 38, 168; system, 133

Case examples: action metaphor, 100–101; addiction treatment, 134–135, 139–140; anorexia, 54–64; chronic pain, 165–166; consultation as training, 253–254, 255–257, 258–260; cross-cultural consultation, 35–36; cultural translation, 43–45, 48–50; family group psychosis, 96–98; family of origin, 90–93, 97–99; family-school process, 221–222; friends as consultants, 122–130; mind-body disorders, 165–166; school/family collaboration, 229–231; Sequential Preventive Meta-Consultation, 207–218; sources of symptoms, 54–64

Change: activation of, 225; capacity for, 13; conjoint school/family, 229; desire for, 15; efforts to, 67; hope for, 56; pathways for, 23; permission for, 110; pressure for, 103; process of, 11, 64; reaction to, 75; resistance to, 82; structural, 223; systemic, 219–231; therapeutic, 27, 110

Children: as alarm signals, 74; alliances with, 77; assumption of parental functions, 80; competence of, 77, 79; as consultants,